WENG'S CHOP #10
2017 HOLIDAY SPOOKTA...

EDITORIALIZING	2
Cover Review: **PHENOMENA**	5
ARTICLES AND FEATURES	13
Fantastical Movie Timeline	15
Greek VHS Mayhem 9	29
Horrorant 4 Festival	43
Steve's Video Store: Thanksgivingsploitation	52
INTERVIEWS	59
Gabby Schulz a.k.a. Ken Dahl	61
Mark Savage	75
Rex Sikes	82
Jimmy ScreamerClauz	91
Ted V. Mikels	105
Cortlandt Hull	108
REVIEWS	115
Shaitan Made Me Do It	162
The *Violent Shit* Collection	171

VOLUME 5 · ISSUE 2
NUMBER 10.5 · DECEMBER 2017

Brian Harris – Publisher, Editor, Grand Poo-bah
Tony Strauss – Editor, Proofing, Layouts & Design
Tim Paxton – Editor, Additional Design

Cover Art by Joe Deagnon (joedeagnon.com)

EDITORIALIZING...

They've Got Cars Big as Bars, They've Got Rivers of Gold…

Welcome to the 2017 *Weng's Chop* Holiday Spooktacular! I hope the holidays are treating you well and that your stress levels are as low as this hectic time of year allows!

Sitting here writing this just a couple of days before Christmas, I can't help but be immensely thankful. While 2017 has been a pretty crazy and difficult year for us all here at WK Books, we've made it through relatively unscathed, thanks in large part to the passion, drive and friendship that brought us together in the first place to make our little publishing house a reality.

For me, personally, one of the greatest medicines for life's trials, tribulations and annoyances lies in the rewards brought by the creation of something that shares my love of cinema with my fellow humans, and for five years now since the start of *Weng's Chop*, that medicine has been a powerful and welcome one. It takes an indescribable amount of time and work to put one single issue together, which can be exhausting when crammed-in with having a day job and dealing with day-to-day life, but the reward brought by not only holding that finished issue in my hand, but also hearing back from those who share the same passions and joys as myself, is far beyond measure.

Which brings me to *you*, Dear Reader. Regardless of whatever love and passion that drives us to create our publications, whether it be *Weng's Chop* or *Monster!* Digest or any of our other WK Books releases, it would all be pointless effort without the love and passion that you share with us. It's one thing to publish a book that you're proud of…but it's on a whole other level to hear back from so many of the people that read and enjoy it. Without you, we would literally cease to exist, regardless of all the time and effort that goes into each of our releases. We owe the ability to continue our labors of love entirely to *you*. And we thank you for your continued support and encouragement. Words cannot describe how much you mean to us, so I would like to dedicate this issue, our fourth Holiday Spooktacular digest, to you, our beloved readers. We hope you'll enjoy this horror-centric holiday issue as much as we've enjoyed bringing it to you.

Before closing, I would be remiss if I didn't mention some of our recent WK Books releases that are out there for the grabbing. As you may already know, back in August we released our second film book, *Australian Gothic* by Daniel Best, which is a fascinating historical study of the Australian 1929-1931 stage tour of *Dracula*. In November, we released our very first comic book, *The Land of Many Monsters*, which is a gorgeous collection of fantastical tales of monsters and creepers from frequent *Monster!* and *Weng's Chop* contributor Denis St. John. And last, but far from least, just a few days ago we *finally* unleashed the long-awaited deluxe two-volume color edition of Troy Howarth's *Real Depravities: The Films of Klaus Kinski*, which is, if I may say, a beautiful thing to behold. If you haven't already checked these releases out, I urge you to do so, because they're probably up the alley of anyone reading this or any other WK Books publication.

We have much in store for you next year, as well, including but not limited to a new book from Troy Howarth on the films of Paul Naschy, our first book on Indian cinema from resident expert Tim Paxton, the much-anticipated release of our massive *Monster! International* revival, plus a few other planned goodies we're keeping under our hats for the nonce.

So as I bid you a very fond *adieu*, I would like to wish you happy holidays from everyone here at WK Books, and invite you to join us in setting our sights on a bright and shiny 2018. We love you great big giant bunches. *~Tony Strauss*

Dunkle Träume von Licht

HAPPY HOLIDAYS, READERS! Hopefully you've all had a haunting Halloween, a food-filled Thanksgiving, and a Christmas overflowing with joy!

As I sit here, eating squid salad, sipping rum barrel-aged Dunkelweizen, watching **HOW THE GRINCH STOLE CHRISTMAS** (2000), I'm reminded of just how lucky I am to be a part of something as unique as WK Books. We've been at it for years, gathering together some of the best and brightest cinephiles in the scene, still just as criminally underrated today but still kicking ass. 2018 is going to be the year we return to form, as if it was our first year in print. More books, more mags, music, movies and more! (Maybe movies… maybe. Let's not rule anything out.)

On the personal tip, I'll be repackaging and republishing my old *Gimp* volumes. I'm also working on my return to *filmBRAWL*, which will likely see the light of day by the second or third quarter. I'm excited about getting back in to the ring.

We hope you enjoy our 2017 Spooktacular, and we've got *Weng's Chop* #11 coming at ya sooner than you think! *WE'RE THE NUMBER ONE MEGAZINE FOR A REASON!* **~Brian Harris**

Cut and Print!

This is it, folks—another of the amazing *Weng's Chop* Holiday Spooktaculars—those lovely mid-issue mini-marvels which are the boiled-down essence of what Brian, Tony, and I love to bring to you in print. In print. PRINT. No digital cop-outs. We have a paper product for you to hold in yer mitts to read on the toilet, out at the bar, at home curled on the couch, or whatever. The weight of the book, the smell of the paper, flipping the pages back and forth…then placing the tome tenderly back on the bookshelf for later perusal.

Art by Alejandro Collucci

Now, imagine a life without power. You know, electricity. Say, a massive solar flare pops out of the sun one Sunday morning and in seven minutes strikes the Earth and totally fries the entire planet's electrical grid. The scientific term is a Carrington Event (it happened in 1859; granted, a very minor time for electrical devices worldwide to get fried), and a big enough one will destroy everything electrical. No kidding. There will be nothing you can do. No power means no nothing nohow.

No digital media.

No ebooks.

No light…except if you have an oil lamp or a bundle of candles. Or you like to read out on your front porch or in the park or a café in the daytime. With a copy of *Weng's Chop* or *Monster!* in your mitts. **~Tim Paxton**

SO…MANY…MONSTERS!

"This collection is wall-to-wall dueling dinosaurs, mad monsters & gorgeous girls (and plenty of monster-girls), from the unexpected drought relief one venerable ol' creature finds in a hot tub party to the ferocity of the duel-beyond-death debut of Furiosa Frankenstein. It's a cover-to-cover fear-and-fun feast!"
-Stephen R. Bissette

Get the new monster-rific comic from Denis St. John and WK Books!
Available now at Amazon.com

YOU BETTER 'SQUATCH OUT!

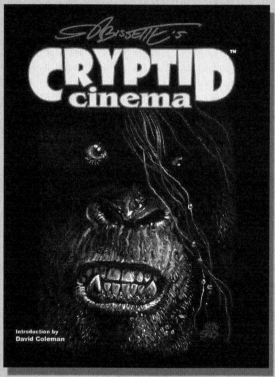

From filmland's fear & fun-filled real & "reel" history, *Swamp Thing* artist & *Constantine* co-creator Steve Bissette spotlights select "Are They Real?" cryptids like the Yeti & Sasquatch, "They Can't Be Real!" critters from **THE KILLER SHREWS** to **THE GLASS-HEAD** to **CREATURE**, TV series from *One Step Beyond* to *Stranger Things*, and a menagerie of eccentric creators & creations from H.P. Lovecraft, Ron Ormond, and Janos Prohaska to Kevin Smith and the Duffer Brothers!

ENTER, IF YOU DARE, THE REALM OF CRYPTID CINEMA™...
the Movie-land of Sasquatch, Bigfoot, Bayou Beasts, Backwood Bogeymen and Bloodwater Brutes!

Available Now at Amazon.com

SEE! The Elusive Bigfoot, Its Kith & Kin, in Their First Film & TV Appearances!

SEE! Women Mate with Sasquatch of the Northwest & the Gator-Man of Louisiana!

SEE! Mad Science Turn Men into Walrus-Weirdos & Walking Catfish Man-Monsters!

SEE! Beyond the Yeti, Sasquatch & Bumble— the Alien Terror in the Midnight Sun!

SEE! What Strange Things Came Before Swamp Thing & Stranger Things!

SEE! Occult-Spawned Monsters & the Weird Whateley Brothers!

SEE! Sleepy LaBeef Beat a Man to Death With His Own Arm!

Cover Review:

SOMETHING LIKE A PHENOMENA
or: OF SCHOOLGIRLS AND FLIES (AND A MONKEY)

by Brian Harris

<u>DISCLAIMER:</u> The views and opinions expressed in this article are solely those of the author. These views and opinions do not necessarily represent those of *Weng's Chop* Magazine, WK Books or its affiliates. So suck it.

As I'm sure many of you have noticed, the world around us is becoming more and more polarized by the day. Positions on everything from politics and religion to art and science invariably lead to animated, often heated battles. They can even lead to offline fisticuffs. These days you're either assailant or the assailed; there's rarely a digression from either side of an issue. It's slug it out until the original debate/discussion has been lost, and the side with the wickedest burn wins the day, regardless of their position's validity.

It's unfortunate, but this state of things most definitely applies to the cinephile scene as well. You can't stumble into a film discussion group without tripping over knock-down-drag-out fights over things such as remakes, overrating/underrating, evil critics, transfer quality, cut/uncut prints, slipcovers, who has the best releases and, of course, the battle over whose choice for best director is indeed the best. You know what I'm talking about, "VHS is better than…", "Who would win in a fight, Pinhead or Freddy?", or "Who made better films, John Carpenter or Wes Craven?" Yeah, that last one is always a minefield guaranteed to trigger a few culties. The argument that never seems to get old also happens to be one of my favorites, "Argento vs. Fulci". You know the drill: Argento fans proclaim themselves intellectual cineastes devoted to truly mature, artistic horror, while condescendingly insinuating that Fulci fans are nothing but empty-headed, gore-loving juveniles. On the flipside, Fulci fans set themselves up as a near-extinct community of self-appointed "true" horror fans tasked with protecting their beloved genre from the snotty, patronizing horror elitists that seek to dismantle everything bloody and brutal. As one might expect, there's rarely a clear victor. Comparing the two is like comparing Kurosawa and Miike.

In a "normal" horror film, you'd think that something like a scalpel-wielding monkey might show up during the thrilling climax...but Argento's batshit insane **PHENOMENA** is no "normal" horror film. Nope...**PHENOMENA** is just getting started!

Now, before my last comment is misconstrued, I'm not saying at all that Argento was or is on par with Kurosawa; I'm simply trying to illustrate the fact that both filmmakers were working on very different levels at the height of their fame. Both brought distinctive styles and unique visions to the genre, and contributed tremendously. But, if I may be so bold, everybody knows Deodato and Mattei owned both of them. Let the ad hominem fly, crybabies! I kid.

Seriously, reality isn't kind to the folks falling on the "Fulci was better" side of this debate. From a purely technical, aesthetic perspective, Argento was the superior director. End of story. Does that mean Fulci was the lesser filmmaker? That depends entirely on what you enjoy and what you're looking for in cinema, doesn't it?

As history has shown us, though, being a great director doesn't mean diddly to the fans when the final product doesn't pan out. In the case of Argento, when you've been doing it for as long as he has, you're bound to win some (**THE BIRD WITH THE CRYSTAL PLUMAGE** [*L'uccello dalle piume di cristallo*, 1970], **DEEP RED** [*Profondo rosso*, 1975], **SUSPIRIA** [1977]) and lose some (**MOTHER OF TEARS** [*La terza madre*, 2007], **GIALLO** [2009], **DRACULA 3D** [2012]). Oh boy, has he lost some.

That leads me to Argento's **PHENOMENA** (1985)[1], a film so strange and off-putting, yet surprisingly endearing, that it's both a win *and* a loss. Is it an Italian *giallo*, American slasher or a supernatural horror? Can it be all of the above? Sure it can, and it does it all with a deadly serious determination. Co-writers Argento and Franco Ferrini even trot out some classic Poe for good measure. Buckle up.

PHENOMENA, screened theatrically, aired on television and released on home video in the States as **CREEPERS** during the '80s, seems to have been the first Argento production many non-horror people became familiar with. That's...a bit sad. Despite the dreary critical response, and its occasional doodiness, the film has continued to grow in popularity over the years with fans, just as **HALLOWEEN III: SEASON OF THE WITCH** (1982) did. Sort of. This is nowhere near as "playing guitar while nude in the streets"-crazy, but still fun.

The film opens with fresh-faced teenager Vera, played by Argento's lesser-known daughter Fiore (**DEMONS** [*Dèmoni*, 1985]), missing her bus ride. Unable to flag it down, she strikes out in search of the nearest phone, leading her to a nearby home. Instead of finding help, her presence drives a chained-up occupant berserk. Having broken free of the chains (and obviously homicidal), the unseen assailant chokes, stabs and chases the wounded Vera

---
[1] Also released in the US video market in a heavily-truncated 82-minute version under the name **CREEPERS**.

You know that if you're hanging out with Donald Pleasance phoning-it-in from a wheelchair, you're definitely in safe hands...

from the house. She meets her end in a waterfall observation station, when more vicious stabbing causes a sheet of cascading glass to sever her head. Already off to a good start, right?

Months later, with a police investigation in full swing, we meet Inspector Geiger (Patrick Bauchau, A VIEW TO A KILL [1985]) and his assistant Kurt (Argento protégé Michele Soavi, director of the amazing CEMETERY MAN [*Dellamorte Dellamore*, 1994], among many others) consulting an expert entomologist on cadaveric fauna, Professor John McGregor (Donald Pleasance, HALLOWEEN [1978]). During the meeting, the duo are introduced to his "nurse," a scalpel-wielding red herring…er, helper monkey named Inga. After relieving Inga of her razor-sharp toy, McGregor informs them that the stages of insect activity evident on the decaying decapitated head he was given places the murder a little over eight months prior. The Inspector suspects it's likely a missing Danish girl, our Vera. Now McGregor's worst fear is realized: his beloved secretary Rita (or was that Greta?) was most certainly a victim of the maniac.

"*After finding this, what's the use of hiding from the facts. There's a killer, a vicious killer…a girl killer.*" Yargh.

Elsewhere, Frau Brückner (Argento's ex Daria Nicolodi, DELIRIUM [*Le foto di Gioia*, 1987]) is sent to pick-up and welcome Jennifer Corvino

Yup...uh...totally safe hands...

Weng's Chop

(Jennifer Connelly, **DARK CITY** [1998]), the newest admission to the Richard Wagner International School for Girls, in Switzerland. Brückner learns that Jennifer is full of surprises: her father is super-hot celebrity actor Paul Corvino, away in the Philippines shooting a new film, and an incident in the car with a rogue bee reveals her close affinity with insects...apparently, one which does *not* lead her to burn them all with holy fire. As you can guess, it doesn't take long before Jennifer is wrapped-up in the killer's escapades. A recurrence of sleepwalking leads her directly to a murder-in-progress! Attempting to escape, but still stuck in a cheesy reverse-negative dream world, she wanders into town and directly into the path of an oncoming vehicle, where she's promptly clipped.

The two local gents are all too happy to help this dazed and confused young schoolgirl into their car, but the still out-of-it Jennifer hurdles herself from the car and tumbles down an embankment. Not into chicks that fight back, the two bail, leaving her to snap out of it on her own. Upon becoming fully aware of her surroundings, she's surprised by Inga, McGregor's nurse monkey, lurking in the brush. The primate promptly takes her by the hand and leads her away to John McGregor's. There, he checks for a concussion and finds her connection with his insects fascinating. One of his beetles takes a liking to her. McGregor gets creepy, and one begins to wonder if he hasn't as well. It's an awkward sequence.

The next day, Jennifer is brought to the hospital for observation by Frau Brückner and the headmistress (Dalila Di Lazzaro, **PAGANINI** [1989]) of the Richard Wagner International School for Girls. They're concerned that the sleepwalking may be a symptom of early schizophrenia, or perhaps an indication of epilepsy. Determined to prove them wrong, Jennifer defiantly settles in and begins seeing flashing images of the previous night's ordeal, making the EEG recordings go wild. Satisfied that they're all stunned, she storms out of the room. That probably did her no favors.

Later that night, instead of watching Jennifer closely to make sure she doesn't sleepwalk again, her roomie Sophie (Federica Mastroianni) heads out to meet up with a guy. Unable to stay long, the guy leaves a disgruntled Sophie alone in the dark. Seizing the opportunity, the killer makes his move, setting off Jennifer's nighttime psychic "Spidey sense", sending her into another bout of sleepwalking. This time, before she can leave the dorm room, she wills herself awake just in time to hear Sophie's blood-curdling scream. Intent on investigating, she's heads outside where she meets—hold for, it now—a lightning bug. The glowing insect leads her to a thorn bush where a glove has been discarded. She retrieves it and heads back inside, where she notices maggots crawling all over it. Upon closer inspection, one of the wriggly buggers "shows" her images of her friend, dead. Her startled scream awakens the dorm and draws the police, but the headmistress directs them to dismiss her story as the ravings of a lunatic.

The following day Jennifer heads back to visit with McGregor, where she gives him the glove to identify the larva. When McGregor points out the heightened

Above: Trade magazine ad for the (heavily-edited) US home video release of **PHENOMENA** under the name **CREEPERS**.
Opposite page: Three Italian half-seet posters for the film

agitation of his caged insects in her presence, Jennifer gives him the details of the lightning bug and "maggot vision". Probably to shut him up. Instead he begins to postulate that she may be tapping into an ESP connection shared by the insects. *This can only make her more popular.*

Back at school, she finds her classmates and the headmistress in her room, reading private letters she'd written to her father. Her attempt to stand up for herself is only met by further derision, as the girls surround her, mocking her with buzzing sounds. Pushed to her limits, her psychic power reaches out, calling to a massive swarm of flies, which blankets the school. The bullying abruptly ends, Jennifer slumps to the floor unconscious and the flies dissipate. When she comes to, she hears the school nurse and headmistress discussing her

a flesh-sniffing fly in a cage. Reasonable, perfectly reasonable.

Jennifer is about to venture into a nightmare world of darkness and depraved insanity. The fly totally bails.

PHENOMENA is…not good. That's not to say it's bad, but certainly the opposite of good would be bad, so I guess I'm talking out of my ass. It's bad. I genuinely enjoy it, though, and I'm betting many of you out there do, too. If you've never taken the opportunity to check this film, or its ugly mutant twin **CREEPERS**, you're missing out on a mildly entertaining head-scratcher worth checking out at least once.

transfer to a mental hospital. Unwilling to settle in for a stay at the booby hatch, she removes her IV and slips out. Back, once again, at John's place, he shares with her the identification of the larvae on the glove. Turns out it's the larvae of The Great Sarcophagus, a fly that deposits hatched larvae—not eggs—on human remains. This means whoever dropped the glove was in close proximity with rotting flesh. That could only be the killer, and John has devised a perfectly logical way to locate the killer's lair: *send a 14 year-old psychic girl out with*

So what exactly makes it "work"? Honestly, it's the absolutely bonkers fairytale-esque story, combined with gruesome bits of maggot-covered gore, Argento's usual heap o' style (though not as much as usual), the occasional tracks by Goblin, and the angelic face of a young soon-to-be starlet, Jennifer Connelly. All of these things are also, unfortunately, what make the film so uneven and flat-out strange.

The story, a supernatural slasher, blatantly borrows from 1984's **FIRESTARTER** and a few of the *Fri-*

Jennifer Connelly follows a lightening bug to an important clue (top)...but, as we all know, following trails of clues almost always leads to falling into a creepy cesspool of maggots and corpses, as demonstrated in the lobby card above.

...In fact, maggots play a pretty important role in this film. Neato!

day The 13th films. That's not much of a news flash when it comes to Italian horror cinema, though; the Italians made an art of ripping Hollywood off. Combining certain elements of those productions—while also clumsily weaving in Poe's "The Murders in the Rue Morgue" as the red herring/foreshadowing—Argento and Ferrini's kitchen-sink approach definitely keeps you guessing. But not tense, "edge of your seat" kind of guessing, nothing like that. A riveting thriller this is not. It's more like, "Where in the hell is all of this going?"

To distance viewers even further from what they're already being asked to swallow, Argento shovels on this insanely inappropriate (read: shitty) soundtrack. It does the production no favors as it not only ruins a few sequences, but also dates the hell out of the entire thing. I know there's a ton of horror fans out there that love Iron Maiden, Motorhead and Andi Sex Gang, but to me it just sounds awful, like '80s ear puke.

Not to be outdone by a bonkers story and crap rock soundtrack, the acting is sure to melt away any hope people may have of this film being one of Argento's underrated gems. It's not just an exercise in bad dialogue; the acting simply isn't up to snuff, which makes bad dialogue worse. I think the performance that really disappointed me the most was Pleasence's—it was creepy and his character was flat and unlikable. I doubt it was intentional. It feels more like he was phoning it in for a paycheck. A brief glance at his mid-'80s filmog confirms this, at least to me.

So, yeah, I know I'm not doing this film any favors here, but I'm being honest. It's among Argento's worst. There's nothing worse than an unrealistic fanboy. That said, I have a soft spot for its strange premise and dreamlike quality...I just dig it. The communication with bugs thing is fun, I always cheer Connolly and the flies on during the school bullying sequence, and the "killer on the loose" just adds a little seasoning to this shit taco. It all feels very Del Toro...if he made duds. Hell, one might even mistake this for a Fulci film with as much gore as there is here! *MIGHT.*

Japanese poster

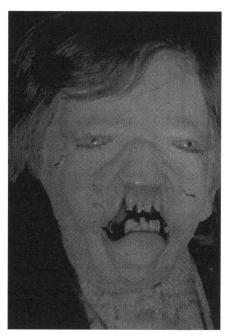

Bet you didn't see the maggot-faced monster midget coming, did ya? Told you this film was batshit insane.

ing Derek Botelho and David Del Valle, **DARIO ARGENTO'S WORLD OF HORROR** (*Il mondo dell'orrore di Dario Argento*, 1985) documentary, an interview with Andi Sex Gang and a few trailers. It's a pretty impressive package for folks that really enjoy this film.

Now, this is where most writers will swear this release is the "best this film will ever look," but that's not the case. For those seeking the very best version of this film possible—Criterion-esque, word on the e-street is—Arrow Films is releasing a 4K version in January '18 and by all accounts, that's the one to purchase. You'll need to be region-free, of course. If you're not, or you're just a Synapse loyalist who's more than satisfied with 1080p, I'd recommend grabbing the standard now. The colors are vivid and the sound is killer, even on stock entertainment speakers.

What can I say, I'm a sucker for **PHENOMENA**. It has a bit of everything necessary for a good (and bananas) cult film. The only thing it's missing is a bunch of tatted hipsters, guffawing through their handlebar moustaches, throwing back their Misfits scarves so they can get a rousing golf-clap going. It needs weirdos dressing in black wigs with short, silky shorts or bald caps and wheelchairs. Somebody rent a midget...and bring your pet monkey!

I already own the original Anchor Bay release of this on DVD, but a few months ago I grabbed the steelbook and standard editions from Synapse Films. You cannot go wrong with the quality they deliver for the price they ask. The films look fantastic, certainly better than I've ever seen them, but the real plus is the three different versions of this film included in both editions, including **CREEPERS** in 1080p!

Both editions carry the same extras, with the exception of a CD soundtrack release which is exclusive to the steelbook (limited to 3,000). The extras include the 116-minute "Integral Cut," the 110-minute international cut and the slightly incoherent 82-minute **CREEPERS** version. You also get an audio commentary for the international cut, featur-

1985, ITALY. D: DARIO ARGENTO
AVAILABLE FROM SYNAPSE FILMS [A/1] AND ARROW VIDEO [B/2]

Dario Argento (barely visible on the other side of the woman in white pants) directs Connelly in this behind-the-scenes still from **PHENOMENA**

ARTICLES + FEATURES

The Fantastical Movie Timeline
Part 1:
Where Film Mythology Becomes History

by
Adam Carl
Parker-Edmondston

Imagine if the films we know and love actually happened for real and were not cinematic creations. If these events had been documented for future generations to see, what would that timeline look like? A universe where movies character exists for real and have their history on one continuous timeline would be a fascinating thing to behold.

Well thanks to a combination of Wikipedia, the Internet and my own film knowledge you can now experience what this reality would be like right here. It is a time filled with contradictions and anomalies. How is it possible for Earth to be invaded so many times by aliens and get destroyed on numerous occasions at the same time? Seems anything is possible in this new timeline, The Fantastical Movie Timeline, where all film events go together in one handy reference guide. I have tried to make this all seem as if it is actually been narrated somewhere as definitive factual information to make the timeline feel more like an historical entry.

So get ready to delve into this filmic past as we go from the very start of the human race right through to its very end—which, as you will see in future editions, happens constantly!

Billy the Kid, Socrates and time-travellers Bill and Ted in London, *circa* 1901

65 million years ago
The Earth passes through the tail of a comet, seemingly killing off all of the dinosaur population. (**NIGHT OF THE COMET** [1984])

4 million years BC
Monolith is seen by Cro-Magnon man.[1] This introduction triggers some kind of mental evolution and causes the first weapon to be created. (**2001: A SPACE ODYSSEY** [1968])

The dawn of history
Discovery of an Iron staff by an exiled tribesman, Ironmaster, leads to a battle for ownership of the new material by the tribes of the era. (**IRONMASTER** [*La guerra del ferro: Ironmaster*, 1983])

1123
Godefroy, Count of Appremont and Papincourt, saves the life of King Louis VI and accidentally kills a Duke, ruining his chances of marrying Frénégonde, the Duke's daughter. Magic is used to try reversing the event, and due to this magical interference the duo manage to arrive ahead of their designated timeframe and are witnessed emerging in 1993. (**LES VISITEURS** [1993])

1209
A small group of Mongolians are terrified when they are visited by strange individuals in a large, flashing object. (**BILL AND TED'S EXCELLENT ADVENTURE** [1988])

1386
Goza the flesh-eater is created when he is cursed by his fellow Brotherhood members Blozor, Lonezor, and Azog. He is believed to be immortal, but only if he keeps eating human flesh, otherwise his body starts to decompose. These rumours seem to have merit when he is seen in 1986. (**GOREMET, ZOMBIE CHEF FROM HELL** [1986])

1429
Bright flashes are seen from within Joan of Arc's room. (**BILL AND TED'S EXCELLENT ADVENTURE** [1988])

1805
Napoleon seems to vanish in the flashing stream of a flying object. Reports like this are seen throughout the timeline and would seem to be the work of the pair known as Bill S. Preston, Esq. and Ted "Theodore" Logan—possibly to do with their upcoming history test. See 1988 for more details. (**BILL AND TED'S EXCELLENT ADVENTURE** [1988])

1810
Beethoven and his piano are kidnapped by two strangely garbed assailants. (**BILL AND TED'S EXCELLENT ADVENTURE** [1988])

1863
One of Americans greatest presidents, Abraham Lincoln, is visited by Bill S. Preston, Esq. and Ted "Theodore" Logan. (**BILL AND TED'S EXCELLENT ADVENTURE** [1988])

1879
Billy the Kid vanishes in what locals at the time called a large, metal box. (**BILL AND TED'S EXCELLENT ADVENTURE** [1988])

1901
Sigmund Freud falls afoul of the metal flying box. (**BILL AND TED'S EXCELLENT ADVENTURE** [1988])

---
1 See image on previous page. *-Ed.*

The demonic car later to be known as "Christine" rolls off the assembly line in 1957

1917
Jim Ferguson arrives in the past after falling through a time vortex and meets his time twin Biggles. The two will continue to meet throughout 1917. (**BIGGLES: ADVENTURES IN TIME** [1986])

1957
The creation of the supernatural car, Christine. Two people die while the car is on the assembly line. It is assumed to be destroyed, but is actually left forgotten in a back yard. (**CHRISTINE** [1983])

That same year, student Mary Lou Mahoney is accidentally killed on prom night when a prank sets her on fire as she is about to be crowned prom queen. Though this seems like a shut case, this action will have grave consequences in the near future. (**HELLO MARY LOU: PROM NIGHT II** [1987])

1959
Alien life form appears. A fraternity member is infected by an alien parasite which gives the infected host zombie-like properties. He is put into deep freeze, but is awoken decades later. (**NIGHT OF THE CREEPS** [1986])

1966
Inventor Doctor Who with policeman Tom Campbell, niece Louise and granddaughter Susan set off to the year 2150 in his TARDIS, a time-travelling machine. (**DALEKS' INVASION EARTH 2150 A.D.** [1966])

1967
One of England's most famous spies, the International Man of Mystery Austin Powers, fights his arch-nemesis Dr. Evil, who escapes and cryogenically freezes himself, to awaken at a time when he will be able to rule. Austin also volunteers himself to be frozen also, to be ready for Dr. Evil's return. This is the first example of many time-travelling adventures with Mr. Powers. (**AUSTIN POWERS: INTERNATIONAL MAN OF MYSTERY** [1997])

1969
Dr. Evil goes back in time and extracts Austin Powers' mojo from his frozen body with the use of a time machine. Austin returns to 1969 himself via a different time machine to get it back and with the help of Felicity Shagwell. They must stop Dr. Evil, who is once again holding the world for ransom with his clone, Mini Me. (**AUSTIN POWERS: THE SPY WHO SHAGGED ME** [1999])

Austin Powers and Felicity Shagwell in 1969, attempting to stop another fiendish Dr. Evil plot

In 1984, the Earth passes through the tail of a strange comet, turning most of the survivors into murderous zombies

1975

Austin Powers arrives in the past to stop Goldmember and to try rescuing his father. He fails and returns to 2002, whence Goldmember has escaped also. (**AUSTIN POWERS IN GOLDMEMBER** [2002]).

That same year, an oil crisis causes the rise of a single unified party, the Bipartisan Party, ruled over by United Provinces of America, which in turn is run by dictator Mr. President. (**DEATH RACE 2000** [1975])

1978

The media-dubbed "killer car" Christine is rediscovered by Arnold "Arnie" Cunningham, who repairs it. Reports from his friends suggest that he becomes slowly overtaken by the demonic forces within it. Arnie's life starts to be put in jeopardy when the car seemingly becomes jealous of his newfound popularity with women. The car, with help from Arnie's friends, is destroyed, but because of its ability to seemingly recover from massive damage it is unclear whether this is really the end for Christine. (**CHRISTINE** [1983])

1980

The Bipartisan Party creates the Annual Transcontinental Road Race, a three-day death race across America, where vehicular manslaughter accumulates points in the contest. (**DEATH RACE 2000** [1975])

That same year, Captain Frank Chapman's spaceship Luna 1 gets dragged to an asteroid. He discovers he has shrunk down to the size of the asteroid's small inhabitants, who are under attack from Solerites. (**THE PHANTOM PLANET** [1961])

1984

The Earth passes through the tail of a comet. Though most of the population come out to see the event, some do not witness it. Reports suggest the survivors are left in a world where most people are dead and others have been turned into violent zombie-like creatures. (**NIGHT OF THE COMET** [1984])

1985

Psychic criminal Martin Whistler and police trooper Jack Deth arrive from 2247. Jack must destroy Whistler in the past, having already destroyed his body in the present. Jack, like Austin Powers, has numerous adventures throughout the timeline, though Deth encounters and exterminates the zombie-like creations of Whistler, formerly-human creatures known as Trancers. (**TRANCERS** [1984])

That same year, there is excitement on the streets of Hill Valley, California as a flying car is seen parking outside the abode of one Marty McFly. It soon disappears again. It transpires that Marty and scientist

Jack Deth in 1985, in pursuit of psychic super-criminal Martin Whistler, who can turn people into zombie-like killers known as "trancers"

Dr. Emmett Brown are frequent time-travellers. (**BACK TO THE FUTURE PART II** [1989])

A few people have recalled a 1985 different from the recorded timeline here. The time they describe shows a depleted Hill Valley run by Biff Tannen, where his greed has turned the place into a disgusting hangout for undesirables. This is an interesting side note to the timeline, but is unconfirmed because this did not happen in this timeline. Could it be an alternative reality? (**BACK TO THE FUTURE PART II** [1989])

The 1987 high school prom goes badly for student Vicki Carpenter

1986

Goza, the immortal flesh eater, has set up a restaurant and now uses it as a front to continue his flesh-eating escapades. The Brotherhood try and stop him, but it is the arrival of the cult's High Priestess which finally turns the tide on Goza ending his 600-year murdering spree. (**GOREMET, ZOMBIE CHEF FROM HELL** [1986])

Also that year, Chris Romero and his friend J.C accidently release the alien visitor from 1959 when they steal a corpse for a fraternity pledge. The corpse's head cracks open releasing swarms of the slug-like creatures. It is up to Chris and company to contain what they have accidently unleashed—which they do, but not before a large percentage of Corman University are infected. (**NIGHT OF THE CREEPS** [1986])

Elsewhere, American Jim Ferguson is transported to 1917 and meets Biggles. He is sent back to his own time shortly after. Both Biggles and his time twin Jim will have numerous trips in time between 1986 and 1917. (**BIGGLES: ADVENTURES IN TIME** [1986])

Also in 1986, a hot tub and a combination of liquids causes a time travel trip where a group of friends (Adam Yates, Nick Webber-Agnew, Lou Dorchen and nephew Jacob) find themselves transported into their younger, teenage bodies (aside from Jacob, who had not been born at that time). They plan to change the future by making sure their younger selves tie up all the loose ends they left behind, regardless of how this affects the time-stream. This changing of history starts to affect Jacob, who is in danger of never being born. It is difficult to say how these events changed the modern day, but it seems the friend's lives have been reported as being a lot more satisfying now this trip has taken place. (**HOT TUB TIME MACHINE** [2010])

1987

High school student Vicki Carpenter finds Mary Lou Mahoney's old prom dress in a trunk and somehow unleashes Mary Lou's spirit. Both Buddy and Billy, former lovers of Marylou now grown up, are targeted. Vicki's body gets taken over by Mary Lou's spirit and it is up to Billy to try and stop a repeat of the events that happened 30 years ago. Mary Lou has a habit of returning from the dead on more than one occasion. (**HELLO MARY LOU: PROM NIGHT II** [1987])

1988

A time-traveller named Rufus uses a time machine in the shape of a phone box to travel back in time to meet the founders of his society, Bill S. Preston, Esq. and Ted "Theodore" Logan, and help them pass their history test, putting them towards a future which will see them become the biggest band on the planet and deliverers of world peace. (**BILL AND TED'S EXCELLENT ADVENTURE** [1988])

In New Zealand, a group of villagers from the 14th century arrive via a ladder they found in a cave while looking for gold. (**THE NAVIGATOR: A MEDIEVAL ODYSSEY** [1988])

A natural disaster and a rise of 400 percent in crime means Manhattan is turned into a massive prison for lifer prisoners. (**ESCAPE FROM NEW YORK** [1981])

Chaos ensues in San Dimas, California when reports of numerous people dressed in historical garb run amuck. Napoleon is seen on a water slide, shots are fired in one of California's many malls by someone dressed as a cowboy, and a gentlemen dressed as a Mongolian warrior smashes up a sports shop. Luckily, police are on hand to arrest the mischief-makers. (**BILL AND TED'S EXCELLENT ADVENTURE** [1988])

1990

The Bronx has been declared a no man's land. Numerous gangs rule there, and the gang known as The Riders find themselves the target of the other gangs when they rescue Anne, the young heiress of the Manhattan Corporation, who has escaped into the wastelands to avoid her corrupt father's company.

A group of 14th century villagers arrive in 1988 New Zeland, allegedly via a ladder they found in a cave

(**1990: THE BRONX WARRIORS** [*1990: I guerrieri del Bronx*, 1982])

Also that year, two seemingly indestructible human shaped aliens start battling on Earth. They both claim to be peacemakers (law enforcement) chasing a criminal and cause havoc while they are here. (**PEACEMAKER** [1990])

1991

Formula One racing driver Alex Furlong is killed while racing. Later on it is revealed that he was taken by Bonejackers, mercenaries from the year 2009. (**FREEJACK** [1992])

Also that year, Jack Deth, now living in the past with his wife Lena, teams up with his dead wife

The Bronx, *circa* 1990, has been declared a no man's land, and is ruled over by warring gangs of ruthless bikers

Godefroy de Papincourt and Jacquouille la Fripouille arrive in 1993 from 12th century France

Alice (who has been sent back to 1991, before she died) to stop E.D. Wardo and his Trancer farm. (**TRANCERS 2** [1991])

1993

Godefroy and Jacquouille arrive from 1123 to 1993. During a series of mishaps in the modern day, Godefroy meets various incarnations of characters from his 1123 life and also manages to go back to his home time and stop the killing of the duke, completing his time-travelling circle. (**LES VISITEURS** [1993])

1997

The President's plane is hijacked by terrorists. He escapes, but his escape pod lands in Manhattan, the prison city. The Duke of New York, who is the ruler there at this time, takes him hostage. The government employs the services of ex-US Special Forces agent Snake Plissken to retrieve the President in exchange for removing the trace of crimes Snake had recently tried to commit himself. Snake manages to rescue the President, but destroys a valuable cassette tape while leaving. This action will once again put him on the most wanted list. (**ESCAPE FROM NEW YORK** [1981])

That same year, Dr. Evil returns and, even though his henchmen have turned his company into a hugely profitable business, goes about blackmailing the world for more money. He also has a son, created from his semen when he was in cryogenic sleep. Austin Powers is also awakened and works with the British Military defence team to thwart Dr. Evil's plans. (**AUSTIN POWERS: INTERNATIONAL MAN OF MYSTERY** [1997])

1998

Society has crumbled and sin is rampant in the derelict streets after a plague has killed off 100 million people. One remaining piece of evidence from this era shows us a crippled teenager's revenge plot on a group of thugs (who destroyed his mobility and his family life) by using a remote-controlled drone and his computer to kill off his assailants. (**WIRED TO KILL** [a.k.a. **BOOBY TRAP**, 1986])

1999

The Monolith is discovered on the Moon. (**2001: A SPACE ODYSSEY** [1968])

In 1997, Snake Plissken is employed by the government to rescue the President, who is being held hostage by the Duke of New York

The Transcontinental Road Race celebrates its 20th anniversary in the year 2000

Also that year, Dr. Evil goes back in time to take away Austin Powers' mojo, leaving him powerless and impotent. Austin goes back in time to retrieve it. While in the past Dr. Evil plans to hold the world hostage again, this time with a giant laser. He is thwarted by 1969 American agent Felicity Shagwell and they both return to 1999. (**AUSTIN POWERS: THE SPY WHO SHAGGED ME** [1999])

Elsewhere, The Doctor (a Gallifrian time traveller who can resurrect himself when wounded into a different human-shaped form) arrives in San Francisco's Chinatown with the remains of another time traveller, The Master. These remains cause his TARDIS to break down. He is shot soon after, but regenerates into a new face. His nemesis The Master also manages to return. They inevitably face off against each other. (**DOCTOR WHO** [1996])

2000

The Death Race celebrates its 20th anniversary, but sabotage means the drivers have a wild card to contend with. Frankenstein, a driver in the race survives the rebellious attempts on his life. Mr. President declares war on France after the Death Race. Frankenstein manages to fulfil his desire by killing the President. He becomes President and marries Annie, a resistance group member who was also his navigator in the final race. (**DEATH RACE 2000** [1975])

Also that year, an earthquake hits Los Angeles and floods out most of California. (**ESCAPE FROM L.A.** [1996])

2001-2100 and beyond

Humanity wages war on intelligent machines of their own making. Humanity loses and are turned into batteries to power the very same machines they fought. While this happens humankind is kept in a virtual reality set in 1999. Sometime after this, at an undisclosed time a few people have broken through and are aware they are in said simulation. Morpheus is one such person and recruits Neo into the fold believing him to be "The One", the person to end humanity's plight. After a series of events, including one of the machines own agents deciding to rule the Matrix and humanity, Neo sacrifices himself to reset the Matrix and a truce between humanity and the machines is forged. (*The Matrix Trilogy* [1999-2003])

2001

The monolith's origin is discovered and this takes humanity into a new evolutionary stage. An onboard computer called Hal becomes self-aware and decides to eliminate his human crew mem-

Neo, often referred to as "The One", fights against the man-created machines who overthrew and enslaved humanity in the 21st century

bers. Crewman Bowman goes through a star gate and through this journey becomes a new evolutionary being, the Star Child. (**2001: A SPACE ODYSSEY** [1968])

2002

Goldmember uses Dr. Evil's time machine to kidnap Austin Powers' spy father, Nigel Powers. Dr. Evil escapes prison, and flees into the present. Austin and co. (including Dr. Evil, Mini Me and Foxxy Cleopatra) stop Goldmember from dropping an asteroid on the planet. (**AUSTIN POWERS IN GOLDMEMBER** [2002])

Formula One racer Alex Furlong is brought from 1992 into 2009, "bonejacked" to use as a physical host for the ultra-rich in their quest for immortality

2005

Strange events occur on Earth. The dolphin population suddenly seem to vanish, then giant ships are seen in the sky. Overheard during the panic is the name of the ships' owners, called the Vogons, who seem to believe Earth is ready for destruction to make way for a bypass. This seems to happen, but shortly after the planet Earth is back again as if nothing had happened. Did this event occur at all? Does the planet Earth regenerate, or is the Earth a construct which will keep getting rebuilt by benefactors unknown to us? The answers so far remain unknown. (**THE HITCHHIKER'S GUIDE TO THE GALAXY** [2005])

2009

Robotic machines have taken over Earth and forced the citizens to live underground due to their modification of the atmosphere. This is due in part to a failed attack on a terraforming machine, which dumps toxic gasses into the atmosphere. (**TRANSMORPHERS: FALL OF MAN** [2009])

Also in 2009, Formula One racer Alex Furlong is brought from 1992 to 2009. This future is ruled by mega-corporations, and environmental and ecological disasters have made society crumble into decay, making drug use rampant. Alex is to become a host for the rich, who have achieved immortality by jumping into bonejacked bodies (people from the past taken just before they die). Furlong escapes (becoming a freejacker, the term used for people who have escaped the transformation process) and has to avoid his former captors, who are desperate to retrieve his body for their boss to jump into. Eventually captured, he is put within the transformation equipment, but due to interference from his friends the transfer goes array. Furlong has managed to stay in his body, fooling the corporation into thinking the transfer worked, (**FREEJACK** [1992])

2010

During a drunken night in a hot tub a group of three friends and one of the guys' son are transported to 1986. The group of hot tub time travellers return, minus one member, to a (supposed alternative) fu-

Four friends from 2010 mysteriously travel back to 1986 by means of unknown hot-tub technology

In the post-apocalyptic Oregon of 2013, a mysterious stranger delivers an old bag of mail he found

himself with his family. Soon after, a group of people try to murder him. He stumbles onto a plot involving the illegal use of clones. (**THE 6ᵀᴴ DAY** [2000])

JAWS 19 is released. Flying boards, self-lacing shoes, video conferring and '80s-themed restaurants are some of the many novelties of this era. (**BACK TO THE FUTURE 2** [1989])

The Norsefire party gains power in UK, while viral attacks cause numerous deaths and anti-fascist riots erupt. (**V FOR VENDETTA** [2006])

Overpopulation in the UK causes martial law to be put in place. Most services are now privatized and London is now a home for the numerous gangs that live there. (**SHANK** [2010])

ture where they are wealthy and happy. (**HOT TUB TIME MACHINE** [2010])

2013

Cuervo Jones, a member of the revolutionary group Shining Path, seduces and brainwashes the President's daughter Utopia to give him access to the President's Sword of Damocles project, a series of satellites which will destroy all the planet's electrics. Utopia joins Cuervo in L.A. as he plans to blackmail America. Snake Plissken, now on the verge of being exiled to L.A., is given a job by the President to retrieve the stolen remote control. He has ten hours to do this, otherwise the virus the President injected into him for his compliance will kill him. (**ESCAPE FROM L.A.** [1996])

Elsewhere, in a post-apocalyptic Oregon, one man is seen reviving the job of a postman, which was a well-known profession before the apocalypse. This strange occurrence inspires people to join him in his seemingly odd idea to post the mail he has found. (**THE POSTMAN** [1997])

2015

Cloning is commonplace, though human cloning is illegal but still possible. Adam Gibson comes home one day to find an exact replica of

Also in 2015, a new ice age is created when scientists try to counteract global warming through climate engineering. This kills almost all life on Earth, aside from the people aboard the *Snowpiercer*, a huge train powered by a perpetual motion engine. (**SNOWPIERCER** [2013])

2016

First confirmed appearance of a giant lizard creature and giant robotic warrior in Seoul. On initial viewing the lizard-like creature seems hostile, but turns on the robotic destroyer, who is actually the real threat. The lizard disappears, while the robotic creature turns vicious and destroys parts of Seoul, only to be removed by a seemingly invisible force. (**COLOSSAL** [2016])

Following the 2015 ice age, all that remains of humanity lives aboard the perpetual-motion train, *Snowpiercer*

2019

A group of Replicants, genetically engineered humans with short life spans used for dangerous labour, flee to Earth, where they are forbidden, in search of their own freedom. Former Replicant hunter (or Blade Runner) Rick Deckard is brought out of retirement to hunt the illegal interuders (**BLADE RUNNER** [1982])

Also that year, Chance O'Brien, the last remaining kickboxer in a game now ruled over by cyborgs is blackmailed by Tung, whose group specializes in cyber-enhanced fighters. With the safety of his trainer and finances held in Tung's vice grip, he is forced to fight for them and must defeat their toughest cyborg, Xao. (**HEATSEEKER** [1995])

2024

The world is now a wasteland after a nuclear war decimates the planet. Vic and his telepathic dog Blood search these wastelands for food as well as physical companionship for Vic. It is on one of these travels they meet Quilla June Holmes and her underground utopia home ruled by The Committee. Vic is to be a breeder there. Quilla escapes with Vic, only to be murdered by him when he feeds her to his dying dog. (**A BOY AND HIS DOG** [1975])

2031

The *Snowpiercer* still travels its lonely route along the barren ice land that is now Earth. The train has numerous social compartments within it. The Elites inhabit the front and everyone else, called the scum by the rich, lives in the tail. (**SNOWPIERCER** [2013])

In 2019, former Blade Runner Rick Deckard is brought out of retirement to "retire" four renegade replicants

2035

The organization known as Unicom rules over the remains of society after an economic collapse has left the world in peril. The ozone layer has gone, causing skin blistering for many of the planet's residents, and food and water are scarce. Unicom has banned robots and computers, but do use their own synthetic humans to kill off any resistance fighters against their cause. When a Unicom delivery worker witnesses this, it sets him on a course that

A young man named Vic and his telepathic dog, Blood, travel the nuclear wastelands of 2024 in search of food, shelter, and female company

With war having been outlawed after World War III, pilots in 2039 known as robot jox use giant mech-bots to pummel-out disputes between territories

will change the future for the better. (**CRASH AND BURN** [1990])

2039

50 years after World War III and the nuclear holocaust, war has been outlawed. To settle disputes, territories have their own giant robots piloted by humans (known as jox) to fight for them. Russia makes a power play on the US and starts to use illegal means to win. It is up to Achilles, the American jox, to save the day. (**ROBOT JOX** [1989])

2044

Solar storms have turned Earth's surface into a radioactive desert. The population is now reduced by 99.7 percent. The Roc Company build Automata, robots that build defences from the radioactive material and which also look after humanity's survival.

Sometime after this event an insurance investigator for the company finds examples of Automata that have been modified. His investigation enlightens him when he comes across a group of Automata that are changing from their core programming. (**AUTOMATA** [2014])

2073

An attempt to send a robot probe to the past (1973) fails and instead sends scientist Nicholas Sinclair somewhere else. Thoughts are that he went into an alternative dimension where mankind fights against killer machines. (**A.P.E.X.** [1994])

2084

On a remote mining planet called Ordessa, the underground resistance movement have been fighting the mine's management to try to improve living conditions for the workers and stop them being beaten by the mine's robotic military police. (**STARSHIP** [1984])

2101

The unlikely duo of salvage operator Wolff and teenage girl Niki begin their trip to "The Zone", where they meet cyborg Overdog who rules that area. (**SPACEHUNTER: ADVENTURES IN THE FORBIDDEN ZONE** [1983])

In 2102, salvage operator Wolff travels to the plague-ridden planet Terra XI to rescue three captured women and collect a 3,000 mega-credits reward. He joins forces with a teenage Scav named Niki, and the pair (pictured left) run afoul of an evil mutant named Overdog (right).

British time-traveller/inventor/adventurer Doctor Who travels to the year 2150 to find the Earth devastated and ruled over by the Daleks, a race of cyborgs determined to exterminate any and all races they find to be inferior to themselves

2150

British inventor Doctor Who travels to 2150, but sees a desolated environment caused by his old enemies, the alien race called the Daleks. He helps to lead a revolution which ends up with the Daleks being cast into the Earth's core. (**DALEKS' INVASION EARTH 2150 A.D.** [1966])

2247

Police trooper Jack Deth attempts to apprehend Martin Whistler, who uses his psychic powers to "trance" people into doing his bidding. Using drug-induced time travel, Whistler escapes with Jack Deth in tow. (**TRANCERS** [1985])

That same year, Jack Deth returned back from 1991 by his wife Alice to save Angel City from a possible Trancer-related war. (**TRANCERS 3** [1992])

2247 or 2253

E.D. Wardo, brother of the deceased psychic Martin Whistler, travels back in time to start a Trancer farm. Alice, a from-the-past iteration of Jack's dead wife, is saved and also returns back in time on this date. (**TRANCERS 2** [1991])

2309

Humanity is finally ready to face off against the robotic invaders from outer space after years of living underground. The elite team set up a plan to capture a Transmorpher. It works, but the unit has a tracking mechanism in it. The team attempts to destroy the main tower, which seems to be the source of the robots' powers. This proves to be a correct assumption and they shut down their robotic overlords. (**TRANSMORPHERS** [2007])

In 2309, humans face off against the Transmorphers, the invading robotic race which drove them underground years earlier

2312

The planet Sol 3 (formerly known as Earth) is sold off to Kress, who plans to use Sol 3's population as his personal slaves. (**STAR ODYSSEY** [1979])

2688

Society now lives in a musically utopian state, thanks to the teachings of the two Great Ones. Rufus a member of this utopia is tasked with travelling back to 1988 to a time when the Great Ones, Bill S. Preston, Esq. and Ted "Theodore" Logan, were just high school students. They have a history test which would separate the duo. This would have dire consequences for the future that Rufus knows. (**BILL AND TED'S EXCELLENT ADVENTURE** [1988])

Rising levels of radiation aren't the only concern for survivors in post-apocalyptic 2889

2889

Another nuclear war has destroyed most of the Earth's populace. (**IN THE YEAR 2889** [1967])

3008

Galaxina, an android servant, is taken aboard the Intergalactic space cruiser *Infinity*. The *Infinity* gets orders to go to the prison planet Altair One to retrieve a stolen gemstone called The Blue Star. As the journey takes 11 years to complete, the crew go into cryogenic sleep, leaving Galaxina in charge. She uses this time to reprogram herself, making herself more human. With Galaxina's help the crew retrieve the gem and Sgt. Thor, a member of the team, falls in love with Galaxina. On the return flight home, one of the locked-up prisoners, a rock eater, eats the gem stone. (**GALAXINA** [1980])

21,000 years in the future

Humanity lives on various planets in the galaxy, all ruled by different hieratical families. Due to the banning of A.I., humanity has now decided to expand its mind more. This is all because of the use of "The Spice", a substance which expands the mind and also extends the lifespan of its users. It is only found on one planet, Arrakis. When infighting between the families ensues and a hostile elimination occurs, it sets one member of the family on a journey that will change the course of humanity forever. (**DUNE** [1984])

For now, this is where the timeline has to end; otherwise we would be stuck here in this alternative reality for all time. But hopefully we will return when new historical entries arrive. As you can see, it is an interesting trek through the sands of cinematic time. What I love about doing this timeline and looking at all the events that transpire is seeing how they relate to each other. The contradictions, for me, make it all the more fun, and I hope it was fun for you, too.

Galaxina, an android servant, reprograms herself and becomes an intergalactic heroine in the year 3008

GREEK VHS MAYHEM & SCREEN GERMS[1]

by Christos Mouroukis

I rarely remember my dreams, but there is a recurring one that I see so often that it is impossible to forget. I see a supposed store in Thessaloniki that sells random things, among them some rare VHS titles, but each time I visit it I cannot buy any of them because they are so damned expensive. Although such a store never existed in the particular area my dream is set in, I have seen a similar (but a bit dodgier and less clean) version of that store (an antique-dealing one, really) in the same city, but the tapes it held were nothing special. Life blurred with dreams in that same city for me also many years ago, when I and my friend George discovered a video store (called "Star Wars", no less) in a nearby village. It had an incredible amount of rare tapes, yet it wouldn't sell any of them to us. I tried to find it many years later, in order to try my luck again, but it wasn't there, and I couldn't find any record of it anywhere; it is as if it simply vanished, or as if it wasn't there in the first place—yet we both know that it was.

But, sometimes I look at my collection and I am amazed by what was released on tape back in the day in Greece. From demonic films (bear in mind that the Greek state always had strong ties with the Greek Christian Orthodox Church, and books have been banned many times) to rape stuff (pretty much all "rape and revenge" films made it into these shores)[2], and from extreme gore (cannibal films etc.) to strong pornography (sometimes with unbelievable subjects) and whatnot. And the vast majority of these things were unleashed uncut because after the fall of the Junta in 1973, censorship was abolished. Recently I started developing affection for pulp books as well (as you might notice reading this column) and these amaze me as well, thanks to their "anything goes" approach to taboo subjects (you can literally find anything you can imagine in porn paperbacks from the 1970s), and it was then that I realized that videotapes in the 1980s were the pulp books of cinema. And is there anything better than pulp fiction?

---

1 Contrary to what this title is suggesting, I consider none of the films reviewed in this article to be "germs", but I liked the wordplay on the name of major studio Screen Gems too much to not use it. In another wordplay that would mock Studio Canal, I wanted to name an article Studio Anal, but I don't think that this would have made it past the editors.

2 The 1970s were the unfortunate decade of rape cinema, in which every other film (be it exploitation, porn, or plain mainstream) contained at least one rape scene. But have any of you noticed how many of these rapes took place in train carriages? It makes for an interesting observation.

Some other times I look at my collection's big VHS boxes and I admire their artistry (it took me a few years to realize the reason behind my obsession), but also their size (let's face it, size matters), and the fact that they are a physical item. I have nothing against people who lean more towards V.O.D. (I do that myself for most of the new releases), but a file on your computer or your cloud is just a file, whilst a tape makes you feel that you actually hold and own the damn movie, and there can be nothing more beautiful than that when it comes to fandom.

I am a struggling writer. Not in the sense that I'm struggling each month to pay my rent, because I don't, as I am absolutely certain that the rent will not get paid and I will get evicted. I am struggling in the sense that I often watch the most meaningless films about which I struggle to come up with a few words in order to review them. The present column is a different story altogether, as it is the most passionate writing project that I have ever committed myself to.

It was in August 2016 that I finally managed to fly from Alexandroupolis to Athens with a huge suitcase full of the aforementioned videotapes that George had for me. I will review these two dozen films in future installments of this column, but I will ignore **SLUMBER PARTY MASSACRE II** (1987), **CANNIBALS** (1977), **REPTILICUS** (1961), and **THE TERROR WITHIN** (1989), because I had seen all these previously.

In September 2016, most importantly (at least in the context of this column), I was randomly browsing a flea market when I came across something that from distance looked like a porn video tape, yet when I approached closely I found out that it was an 8mm reel (film length 41.7 meters, as per the cover) of the *Swedish Erotica* series' "Film #148 through #155". Unfortunately, I don't have an 8mm projector to screen it, so I am not exactly sure what I purchased, as there were literally hundreds of these things produced and distributed, yet I am very excited to possess such a rare cultural artifact. If you happen to know the name of the loop that hides under the box art that I scanned, please write to *Weng's Chop* and let me know.

In October 2016, and also at the same flea-market (not to be confused with the one in which I scored the dozens of tapes that I regularly review here), I came across a huge bunch of old cinema books (some old film buff must have ran out of cash, be-

cause only desperate people sell at such humiliating prices) and I scored three for five Euros, namely Peter Cowie's *Screen Series: Sweden 1* (1970), Ann Lloyd and David Robinson's *Movies of the Fifties* (1982) and *Movies of the Sixties* (1983). I learned so much from these books about many wonderful films.

In November 2016, during one of my most recent forays to the flea-market, I scored the vintage Greek editions of the following pulp books: *Inside Linda Lovelace* (1976), Emmanuelle Arsan's *Emmanuelle, la lecon d'homme* (1974), and Sam Benson's *Sucettes a la Nice* (1982) and *Le Flambeur demi-sel* (1982). These things come cheap and they entertain me.

In December 2016 I visited the nearby flea-market once again, and I scored a vintage edition of a book by C. Povillet (a date is not given, but it looks like it was produced in the 1970s, making it a curious item, considering that Greece was under the Junta rule from 1967 to 1974, and such things were prohibited); the Greek title is Λεσβιακοί Έρωτες, which roughly translates as *Lesbian Loves*, but the original French is not given. It is a faux-medical book that is trying to explain how unnatural lesbianism is, but it mostly comes across as a conservative religious nut-job's rant (its non-stop quoting of The Old Testament is particularly hilarious). On a more interesting note, I also discovered two stashes of 8mm films. The first stash was just regular films (cartoons, comedies, and such), and the other one was porn (mostly installments from the *Sexorama* series). At 15 Euros a pop it was impossible for me to buy any of them, but I am glad that I now know that back in the day 8mm pornography actually reached Greece—who knew?

But I struck gold in the flea-market in February 2017. I don't normally talk about magazines here, but this one in particular is amazing, and might be of interest to the pop culture archaeologists that frequent this column. I scored the Volume 4, Number 6 (December, 1961) issue of *Real Life Guide* magazine. The outrageous blurbs on its front cover alone were enough to convince me that I had to own this treasure and I was sold, but the advertisement on the back cover that was urging the readers to order Alan Hull's Walton *Aphrodisiacs: from Legend to Prescription* book was classic exploitation as well (it also helps that the supposed author looks like Gerard Damiano). And the contents of this 132-page monster, you ask? Man, oh, man! These include "How to Make a Sexual Cripple" (Part Two), "Nipping Sexual Problems in the Bud" (about sex change, and it comes complete with a creepy ending reminiscent of the evil kid films of the 1970s), "Women Who Ask for Rape" (a lengthy article on women that hate men so much that they incite their rape by them, in order to see them prosecuted), "Pornography and Sex Crimes" (a very intelligent take on censorship), "Test Tube Children" (about planned parenthood), "Acceptance for Homosexuals" (a surprisingly open-minded article), "Fallacies about Abortion" (which seems terrifying, now that choice is so widely spread), "Pioneers of Sex Education" (a history lane tour), "The Child's Sex Play" (this could have gotten really creepy, but apparently it does not), "Fear of Pregnancy" (yes, apparently it exists), "What's New in Childbirth" (this actually gets quite weird), and "Strange Marital Practices" (it has a "mondo" quality about it that makes it outstanding). There are two regular columns, as well, one in which similar books are reviewed and another in which the readers' questions are answered. And all that rounded by advertisements for books such as *The Art and Science of Love* and *American Handbook of Sex and Marriage*.

The same day I also acquired my first British porn paperback, called *Men Ensnared* (no author or date is offered, but it looks very 1970s or maybe 1980s; the publisher is Swish Publications Ltd.), which is—you guessed it—about men wearing ladies' clothes. It is illustrated with gorgeous drawings, but the text can't hold a candle to its U.S. counterparts.

In March 2017 I scored the Maitresse Series' *A Lady's Maid* (no author name is provided, but the book was handled by New York's Star Distributors, LTD.), which is from 1980 and as it is to be expected by this stage the pornographers have left behind all attempts at a plot, pretty much the same way the adult films were going. This book is full of lengthy descriptions of sexual acts, with very little story in between to connect the dots (this trend makes this title and the others like it quite boring as a result).[3] One thing about it that stands out is that the author uses multiple exclamation marks rather than one whenever he/she feels like it (essentially making the whole thing appear to be rather amateur—not that I was expecting Nobel-level writing from such fare). What excited me the most though were the ads in the book's last few pages; these were mostly for other pulp porn paperbacks (some of these titles are too outrageous to even include here), but my favorite part was a two-page spread on "Your favorite XXX full-length movies are now on video tapes! Vivid sound and color!" Color me sold.[4]

But enough with the pulp books; you're here for the tapes, and here are the ones I watched in December 2016, and March-April 2017, using my trusted Panasonic NV-FG 620.

SON OF A BITCH
(a.k.a. *Un uomo americano*)
1979, Italy. D: Nino Marino

Bob (Luca Barbareschi) is selling hot dogs in the streets of New York. He is not a son of a bitch, but he keeps on wearing a t-shirt that insists so (hence the title). One day he returns home with a cake for some sort of celebration or anniversary, but his girlfriend Lina (Lynette Johnson) is nowhere to be found, and it soon becomes apparent that she left him, as poor Bob found a goodbye note. A neighbour finds Bob and together they drink the champagne the latter had bought for his now-ex. This neighbour is not above some gossiping and is also quick to inform Bob that he saw Lina leaving with one Miguel (Joaquim de Almeida). Bob and his friend figure out that Miguel and Lina must have gone to Hollywood because they are artists. Bob

---

[3] On an interesting side note, a surprising reference to **TIME AFTER TIME** (1979) is made.

[4] I also scored a Greek pulp porn paperback from the legendary Adam publishing house, entitled Νοσοκόμες Λεσβίες Βιτσιόζες. The original title is not given, but the Greek roughly translates as "Nurses Lesbians Perverts" (which we would be better off arranging as "Pervert Lesbian Nurses"). The name of the author is Carol Frankel and the date of publication is 1989. There is not too much story to speak of, as a group of nurses is abducted by their superior (for not following orders, no less) and are given at the mercy of a group of doctors that just happen to be sadistic rapists. From then on the entire book is just a series of sexual combinations accompanied by excessive use of foul language. It should be added that next to it I noticed a vintage **BLACULA** (1972) poster (of all things) which I ignored simply because I don't collect posters. I now regret that decision.
Later that same month I got a hold of the much more interesting *Pick-Up Chicks*, written by one Hank Walpole (I assume it is a pseudonym) and published in 1977 by New York's Carlyte Communications Inc. and The Bee Line Collection of theirs. It is about the titular group of female hitch-hikers that go on a raping spree. Oh well!

grabs a pistol and decided to drive his way to L.A. in order to kill them both.

The film then of course becomes a road movie, and Bob comes across a series of incidents that are supposed to be funny, as this appears to want to be a comedy, yet the jokes all fail miserably and this is a very unfunny film indeed (it resembles a very bad 1970s Lloyd Kaufman sex comedy, albeit without too much sex). These vignettes include a nymphomaniac junkie (she provides much-needed nudity, albeit very brief). They also include a desperate woman in her mid-40s that is after Bob, and when Bob leaves her behind she masturbates with a gun and shoots herself between her legs (and thanks to a very awkward zoom-in to that particularly area it becomes apparent that she died). We are also introduced to a Native American on a bike who doesn't seem to mind the endless racist comments that are targeting him. For a comedy, this is a very mean-spirited film that aside from being racist is also quite misogynist in its assumptions, too.

This Stefano Film production (the production company behind my favourite **EROTIC NIGHTS OF THE LIVING DEAD** [1980] and the distribution company behind **THE TRUE STORY OF THE NUN OF MONZA** [*La vera storia della monaca di Monza*, 1980]) was directed by Nino Marino (who co-wrote **THE THRONE OF FIRE** [*Il trono di fuoco*, 1983]). If only the box cover wasn't so awful.

DEVIL OF ISLAND
19??, ? D: ?

This Cyprus-set spy film is as confusing as these things can get plot-wise.[5] It is about Naci, Costa, Jimmy (who goes by various names, including Ali Baba—I am *not* making this up), Nana, Leyla, and some other characters (mostly gorgeous women and men with awful moustaches[6], which make me think that this was made in the 1970s) that are involved with some secret services and drug-smuggling business. But this is all I know about it, as I am not really sure which film exactly is this. There is no **DEVIL OF ISLAND** (sic) on IMDb (not to be confused with Nico Mastorakis' **ISLAND OF DEATH** [1976] which is also known as **DEVILS IN MYKONOS**) or any other such websites, and the Greek tape that I own was released by the fairly obscure label All World Video Production, under the title **ΤΟ ΝΗΣΙ ΤΩΝ ΚΑΤΑΣΚΟΠΩΝ**, which translates as *The Island of Spies*, about which I could find no information online or in print (at least not in my 400+ cinema books collection).

5 You how they go: subplots get spawned left, right, and centre, and plot-twists appear and disappear one after the other.

6 Several of said men look like redneck versions of Tom Savini.

Greek VHS covers for **SON OF A BITCH** (top) and **DEVIL OF ISLAND** (above)

The credits in the beginning did not help too much either, as most of them are obscured and include both Greek and Turkish names, none of them familiar to me (none of the performers on screen are familiar to me, either). Considering that this was filmed in Cyprus, it makes me think that it could be a co-production between the Greek side of Cyprus and the Turkish one, or a co-production with which even Greece was involved, because legendary Athenian studios Finos Films is mentioned in the credits (although again, obscured, and I couldn't tell what their role in the production was), but Iason Triantafilidis' *Tenies gia Filima* book, which is the authority on the history of this particular studio, does not make mention of any film resembling even remotely the one under review. What's more, the credits in the beginning are spliced with the first scene, essentially creating a mix-tape that doesn't seem very original, and could well have been bootlegged and messed about, as at some point three people are credited as "ass directors" (whatever that means)![7] And the credits in the end simply bear the word "ΤΕΛΟΣ",

which is Greek for "end" (the credits in the beginning were in English) before we see (only for a split second) unrelated credits that were obviously taken from another movie, as an old ship is in the background, reminiscent of pirate epics. The box cover art that I scanned for you mentions one Artemis Tsarmi (who may well be adult film actress Artemis Tsani, if this is indeed a typo on the part of the distributors, as it was so often the case with such low-profile fare) and two Turkish names that I could not cross-reference (possibly due to how ignorant of Turkish cinema I am). The presentation, though, is in widescreen, and the dubbing seems to have employed British performers. There is not too much to see here other than an oriental dance and a fairly cool shootout in the end in which a few cars and a small plane are involved, and it even includes the occasional welcome explosion, but the man-to-man fights look ridiculous at the moments when the speed was obviously messed with in post production. At some point I also noticed a Charlie Chaplin poster, although I'm not sure from which film that was.

Okay, the above were all the clues that I could gather and after endless hours of research, and I still don't know what the film I watched was, but because I know that this column and this magazine are frequented by serious geeks (writers and readers alike), my hopes have not died, and I still believe that someone out there might enlighten us further.

IN AND OUT OF AFRICA
1987, USA. D: Fred J. Lincoln

I have found out that a common defense amongst porn connoisseurs for their favorite films is their complaint that sexual content goes unrated or X-rated (therefore supposedly losing potential audience), whilst violence goes R-rated or even PG-13. This at first may sound unfair, and I am always against harsh ratings, but one thing the advocates of porn forget to mention is that these adult films show actual, *real* sex, whilst the violent movies show staged violence. Sex movies show actual penetration and exchange of bodily fluids, whilst violent films don't use actual bullets in the shootout scenes or actual punches (well, for most of the time, anyway). My point is that although we, the audience of dirty films,

---

7 It most likely is a short for assistant directors, yet the choice doesn't make too much sense.

Greek VHS release of **MONDO SENZA VELI**

must put our films in context and view them by their own merits. One adult film that can be absolutely enjoyed for what it is is the one under review.

This adult movie's focus is interracial sex, in particular white men doing black girls, but we get a bit of the other way around as well. It is set in Africa (amidst a safari) and the box cover on the back even claims that it is "A movie shot in its natural environment" implying that it was actually shot in Africa, but this doesn't seem to hold a candle to the truth, as this is a Penguin Productions film (which was an outlet mostly known for cheapo stuff such as **THE RETURN OF JOHNNY WADD** [1986]), and all exterior shots look so generic that they could have been accomplished in any forest (any forest in the US, in particular). Still, director Fred J. Lincoln (here credited as F.J. Lincoln) attempts to actually make a real film out of the seemingly meagre budget, and that can be read only positively. What can be read negatively though are the desperate attempts at comedy that don't work at all (the most ridiculous one has a native speaking as if she was from some New York ghetto). Although this could well be because most of these jokes are referencing jungle movies and I am absolutely ignorant of those, as I have never been a fan of Tarzan or Jungle Jim.

One welcome element is the presence of the classically beautiful Nina Hartley, who has a very sexy scene with F.M. Bradley. The other pairings find Angel Kelly coupling with Francois, Jeannie Pepper with Jerry Butler, Nina Hartley with Sahara, and two threesomes: Angel Kelly, Jerry Butler, and Peter Jacobs make up the first, and Patricia Lockhart, Sahara, and Jerry Butler make the last.

The running time given on the tape's sticker states that it is 90 minutes long but this is wrong, as the accurate length is 72 minutes, which is the same that is correctly stated at the Internet Adult Film Database. [8] The same website also states the year of release as 1987 and I will stick to that, rather than the 1986 that the often misleading Internet Movie Database has. Also on IMDb this particular title has only 7 ratings as of this writing, resulting in a score of 6.0 which tells us that the few people that have seen this actually liked it.[9]

MONDO SENZA VELI
1985, Italy. D: Bitto Albertini

Back in the early 2000s and during one foray into the wild and into a "mom and pop" video store, in Komotini in particular, I was browsing the documentaries section and picking up the usual Mondo

---
8   http://www.iafd.com/title.rme/title=In+And+Out+Of+Africa/year=1987/in-and-out-of-africa.htm

9   http://www.imdb.com/title/tt0183250/?ref_=fn_al_tt_1

titles that I love so much, when the owner asked me if I knew how hard this stuff was. I of course knew what I was getting myself into, having grown up with **FACES OF DEATH** (1978), but what surprised me was how this random person in the middle of nowhere knew what a shockumentary was. Fast-forward to the film under review, that on its back cover states that the movie will "leave speechless even the most demanding viewer". The conclusion is really simple: there was a huge audience for these sick films back in the 1980s, many moons before Live Leak and other such websites, or the ill-named "torture porn" era that the slashers went through during their recent extreme years.

It is a little bit difficult to cross-reference which particular movie the one under review really is, as the Greek title is ΣΚΛΗΡΟ ΚΑΙ ΑΛΗΘΙΝΟ 2, released by distributors Rex Films Home Video as a sequel to ΣΚΛΗΡΟ ΚΑΙ ΑΛΗΘΙΝΟ which was of course the Greek title for Bitto Albertini's[10] **MONDO FLASH** (*Nudo e crudele*, 1984) which many people have seen, mostly under its alternative title **NAKED AND CRUEL**, from which the Greek title comes, as a liberal translation, and both titles come from the original Italian title which is *Nudo e Crudele*. The present film's English title given on the cover is *Mondo Flash No2*, but such a title does not exist in any online database that I checked or in any reference book. The "*No2*" part seems particularly Greek too, as many home video distributors in Greece used to stick such numbering to titles, rather than "Part 2" or "Vol. 2" etc. However, there is a sequel to *Nudo e Crudele* in IMDb, aptly named **NUDO E CRUDELE 2** (1985) which nobody seems to have seen (as of this writing it doesn't even have the five votes that are required by users in order for the website to perform its rating). Adding further confusion to the mystery, the title card in the film under review is **MONDO SENZA VELI** (1985), which also has an entry in IMDb (albeit again, with less than five ratings, making it obvious that nobody has seen it). Both appear to have been directed by Bitto Albertini, and since both were released in 1985, maybe they are one and the same film? I may love Mondo films to death (see what I did here?) but I beg for someone with more knowledge than yours truly to come up with further info and clarify this mess. Why, you ask? The film that I own and watched is a blast and more should people should see it. It is as disgustingly racist as all these films are, but it also goes the extra mile and it becomes outright misanthropic! So, I'm going to give you as much information about the scenes that it is featuring (some of them might have been lifted by other films too) and I'll be hoping for the best. Also, the print that I own comes with complete credits, but I don't know if they would be of too

---
10   Who is of course better known for writing and directing **BLACK EMANUELLE** (1975) featuring Laura Gemser.

much help as neither of the films under suspicion are fully referenced anywhere. The back cover makes a point to let us know that the music (which is particularly exciting, reminding the best works of Riz Ortolani from the 1960s and 1970s) is the work of Nico Fidenco, who of course has also composed Joe D'Amato's outrageous **EMANUELLE AND THE LAST CANNIBALS** (*Emanuelle e gli ultimi cannibali*, 1977). So, let's start, shall we?

There is a scene here in which an old lady ceremoniously pierces her cheeks, whilst another man hangs from hooks (a long time before this became a staple in the BDSM community, but how would I know *that*?). There is also the usual sequence in which an animal handler is supposedly risking his life by petting crocodiles, but the beasts are obviously (and sadly) sedated. The crocodiles don't seem too sedated, though, when we see them getting fed with some poor ducks that try to escape death, to no avail. Further bird cruelty includes a brief cockfighting sequence.

The majority of the above footage seems quite genuine, but we also get a lot of stuff that is obviously staged and that includes the supposed attack of a snake on a cameraman, or the scene in which a man is curing his hard-on, whilst in another one a man is lifting weights with his own hard-on. A point is made about the sacrifices that one has to go through in order to get married in ancient tribes and these includes whipping and other strange practices. However, we are told nothing of the sacrifices that one is going through in order to remain married in the Western world.

We are told that the crew got access to a Russian roulette game in which they paid to get permission to see a man shooting himself in the head. However, we are never shown the footage. Guess why?

Back to real stuff, we see some amputees, some naked hippies in Copenhagen (Scandinavia is presented as very civilized due to its lack of riots, in one of the many fascist outbursts by the narrator), an impaled man, a gay photographer who has his assistant take some pictures of a couple of naked girls, a supposed pissing contest among university students in Denmark, a little bit of completely uninteresting skateboarding (which somehow the commentary also managed to criticize and put on a bad light), and last but not least, the supposed profession of a shit-taster that eats camel excrement for a living.

There is a lengthy scene about hookers in Manila and another one about amateur boxing, and they both look very real and alarmingly so. I think that you do realize that BBC is not going to broadcast this anytime soon. The usual footage of naked African kids or that of Muslims praying is also presented, as well.

What makes this particular tape stand out as a peculiarity is the fact that it is dubbed in Greek (above an Italian dub that can be mildly heard in the background). This is completely unusual in Greece, as all foreign-language films are subtitled. There are a few exceptions, such as cartoons that are either released dubbed, or in two versions, one dubbed and another subtitled. It is true that several documentaries have been released dubbed as well, due to their educational nature that makes kids who can't read subtitles a target audience, but this was happening with family-friendly docs and never with shockumentaries. What makes this release even *more* peculiar is the fact that it comes in widescreen format and that the print is gorgeous. Colour me excited for having discovered this ge*r*m!

THE MAGNIFICENT SEVEN
1960, USA. D: John Sturges

There's not too much to say about this classic masterpiece that hasn't already been said, but I'll try my best (if only for the purpose of including a mainstream film in the present article). I believe that you know how the story goes.[11] Calvera (Eli Wallach) is a horrible bandit who, together with his gang, is bullying the poor and innocent people of a Mexican village (the film was largely shot on location in Mexico) and steals all their resources (this is a film that was distributed by United Artists, so in contrast to its Italian independent counterparts, there is no raping going on here or anything as remotely nasty, just mean old stealing). One day the villagers decide that they've had enough and ask for advice from the town's wise old man (Vladimir Sokoloff), who suggests that they should rebel against their oppressors. But the problem is that these poor people are farmers and have no idea how to use a gun. So what they do is they approach tough (but good) gunslinger Chris Adams (Yul Brynner, who on a trivia note got actually married on set) and ask him to form a team of professionals that will help the villagers deal with their problems in exchange for the modest pay that they can offer. The team that Chris assembles consists of Vin Tanner (Steve McQueen, who had to stage a car accident in order to take a few days off his day job at the *Wanted: Dead or Alive* TV series), Harry Luck (Brad Dexter, who was cast in this role because Frank Sinatra demanded it), Bernardo O'Reilly (Charles Bronson), Britt (James Coburn, who would later co-star with McQueen in the same director's **THE GREAT ESCAPE** [1963]), Lee (Robert Vaughn, in a role that was famously turned down by both John Ireland and Sterling Hayden), and Chico (Horst Buchholz), who are essentially **THE** (titular) **MAGNIFICENT SEVEN**. Will they be able to train the villagers and along with their help defeat the oppressors that outnumber them and collect the cash, or is this a lost and damned cause?

This is a visually accomplished masterwork which cinematographer Charles Lang (**SOME LIKE IT HOT** [1959]) shot in anamorphic Panavision that you should definitely opt for seeing from a proper copy (that would do it justice) instead of the shit pan-and-scan full-frame VHS that I had to deal with (that completely destroys the experience). But it is also an innovative film in terms of dialogue as well, as it often reminded me the work of Martin Scorsese and Quentin Tarantino (at their "pulp" moments at least). It is not without its faults, though, as some of the aforementioned dialogue comes off rather unnatural and inappropriate for a western (or a period piece in general) and therefore is occasionally unbelievable. The bombastic score by Elmer Bernstein (who went on to compose the music of **THE GREAT ESCAPE**) is now considered iconic[12] and it was even used by Marlboro cigarettes for several years in the company's commercials.

Obviously, the tape that I have in my possession was not released in Greece in 1960 when VCRs were not yet invented, but later on. Unfortunately, mainstream distributors Audio Visual Enterprises not only delivered a bad copy, but an outrageously boring box cover as well.

The film was not an immediate success in the U.S. market and it only caught up when it was released in Europe, where it was so successful that three sequels ensued (**RETURN OF THE SEVEN** [1966] which was written by Larry Cohen, **GUNS OF THE MAGNIFICENT SEVEN** [1969] starring George Kennedy, and **THE MAGNIFICENT SEVEN RIDE!** [1972] starring Lee Van Cleef) as well as a TV series (*The Magnificent Seven* [1998 – 2000]). It has been unofficially remade three times in Italy (by Claudio Fragasso and Bruno Mattei as the horrible **I SETTE MAGNIFICI GLADIATORI** [1983] which is also reviewed in the present article, and by Joe D'Amato as the porn **ROCCO E I MAGNIFICI 7** (1998) and **ROCCO E I MERCENARI** [1999]), and recently "officially" remade by Hollywood as well (**THE MAGNIFICENT SEVEN** [2016]).

INVADERS FROM MARS
1986, USA. D: Tobe Hooper

During a meteor shower, David Gardner (Hunter Carson) sees a U.F.O. landing in his backyard, but it quickly disappears and no one believes him. It is not too long before his parents (Timothy Bottoms and Laraine Newman) and teachers develop weird mannerisms and act all-around suspiciously and robotic, and it becomes apparent that they have either become Martians or replaced by Martian replicas of themselves. The only way to tell the anthropomorphic aliens from the real humans is a wound on the back of their necks. David asks for the help of

---

11 The screenplay was written by William Roberts (who went on to pen **THE BRIDGE AT REMAGEN** [1969]) and it is a (credited) remake of Akira Kurosawa's **SEVEN SAMURAI** (*Shichinin no samurai*, 1954), which premiered in the U.S. as **THE MAGNIFICENT SEVEN**. However the story behind the story (i.e. the screenplay) is far more complicated and it includes a lawsuit by Anthony Quinn, who claimed that he co-developed the concept, but lost due to lack of evidence. Later on Walter Bernstein (who also penned **FAIL-SAFE** [1964]) and Walter Newman (whose debut was Billy Wilder's **ACE IN THE HOLE** [1951]) got involved as well but remained uncredted. Director John Sturges received positive feedback by Kurosawa.

12 It was nominated for an Academy Award in the "Best Music, Scoring of a Dramatic or Comedy Picture" category.

the school nurse (a blonde Karen Black, only a year before Larry Cohen's **IT'S ALIVE III: ISLAND OF THE ALIVE** [1987]) who may be a bit hesitant in believing the kid's wild theory, yet assists him in approaching the military. This is where things get interesting for a while, as you can imagine that a "Martians vs. The Marines" scenario is really exciting and would make for a great pitch in a studio (especially if that studio were the legendary Cannon Pictures who backed this project[13]).

However, not everything in director Tobe Hooper's remake of the same-titled classic from 1953 (which I recently reviewed for *Monster!*) works, as the young protagonist is delivering some really corny lines (and the production could've easily found a more accomplished kid actor). Actually, it is not so much the delivering of the lines themselves but the way these are written by Don Jakoby and Dan O'Bannon (the duo also penned the same director's other Cannon feature **LIFEFORCE** [1985] which is superior to this[14]) as they would be a better fit for an adult character. Furthermore, when you have a sci-fi film in the 1980s whose focus is a boy with an interest for the stars and the galaxies far away, it is impossible to not think of the work of Steven Spielberg and it is absolutely apparent that Hooper was still under the effect of the megalomaniac director's bug (after all, it was only a few years after they had together made **POLTERGEIST** [1982], a landmark not only for the duo's careers, but horror films in general, as well). Actually, Spielberg was in talks to direct this, back when Cannon could still approach such people. Other attempts at grandeur here can be found even in the beginning credits that echo **STAR WARS** (1977), albeit they are too lengthy and quickly outstay their welcome, despite their aesthetically intelligent design. Even some of the alien monsters on display here look like they could be Darth Vader's minions, but the good news is that the practical effects and the visual ones look compelling.[15] To conclude, this could be something outstanding (and it is not bad at

INVADERS FROM MARS

all) but it just never elevates above feeling like an average episode from *The Twilight Zone*.

THE SEVEN MAGNIFICENT GLADIATORS
(*I sette magnifici gladiatori*)
1983, Italy. D: Claudio Fragasso, Bruno Mattei

The Italians were notorious for producing all sorts of rip-offs (sometimes their copying went to the extent of creating new subgenres), but a film that would not only copy **THE MAGNIFICENT SEVEN** (1960; reviewed above) but would do so in a "sword and sandal" entry defied my imagination (and I have plenty of that)…but here it is anyway.

The screenplay was written by hack-master Claudio Fragasso (credited here as the French-sounding Claude Fragass) and it is an identical copy of the aforementioned classic. During the Roman Empire,

---

13 It was produced of course by Yoram Globus and Menahem Golan, on a $7 million budget, and it was one of their first failures as it generated a modest $4.9 million. The duo despised the film and considered Hooper's hiring on this film a mistake.

14 Keep an eye out for this film on a television set that David is watching.

15 The invaders themselves were designed and created by special effects guru Stan Winston, the same period he was handling his landmark work in **ALIENS** (1986).

semi-god Nicerote (Dan Vadis in his last role; he died four years later by overdosing at the young age of 49) is bullying the poor people of a small village just outside Rome. A sword with superpowers that can be held only by "the chosen one" must find its rightful owner (whoever else tries to hold it finds a terrible death by burning) and it does so in the face of Han (Lou Ferrigno), who, along with the help of the gorgeous Julia (Sybil Danning) and a few more magnificent gladiators, will fight for the good of the bullied people.

Okay, obviously this screams "terrible" from the get-go: the costumes are atrocious[16], Lou Ferrigno can't act his way out of a paper bag[17], and the only thing watchable about the performance of Sybil Danning is her generous cleavage. But let's be honest here, you came here to see Ferrigno and Danning kicking Roman buttocks, and you get this in spades, essentially turning this whole cheapo-fest into a very entertaining hour-and-a-half, and this in my book makes for a "good" movie.

Other notable elements include a lengthy catfight between two girls in bikinis, and an unbelievably sexist discussion in which men are portrayed as caring only about sex, whilst women care only about money! No matter how hard I pray, I believe that it is impossible for such outrageous cinema to ever happen again, especially during the present "PC era".

This was executive produced by Yoram Globus and Menahem Golan (under the aegis of their Cannon company's Italian offices), and it was shot back-to-back with their **HERCULES** (1983) which was written and directed by Luigi Cozzi. But who directed the present film? Exploitation film legend Bruno Mattei is the only one credited in the title cards of my copy (an English language dub, with Greek subtitles of course) but some sources (including the IMBb) give credit to his frequent collaborator Claudio Fragasso as well (who also wrote the present film's script). Could this be because the roles on their low-budget opuses were interchangeable? It was produced by Alexander Hacohen, who had also backed Joe D'Amato's **EVA NERA** (1976).

The tape comes with trailers for **FROM HERE TO ETERNITY** (1953), **ST. ELMO'S FIRE** (1985), and **THE KARATE KID PART II** (1986), the latter of which tells us that the film under review was released in Greece three years after completion, which is a bit surprising, considering that a proper distribution plan was conducted throughout the world that involved companies such as MCA/Universal Home Video (who released it on tape in the U.S.) and Vestron Video International (which released it on tape in some other territories). In Greece it was released by Videosonic (one of the top companies in the mainstream field) and it bears the logo of RCA Columbia Pictures as well. But I guess even Hercules can be slow sometimes.

---

16 One Belle Crandall is credited as the costume designer.

17 It seems to me that the only strong man that managed to actually become a proper actor with serious ambition that turned his career into a success story is Arnold Schwarzenegger (now one of the most recognized household names in the history of film).

WESTWORLD
1973, USA. D: Michael Crichton

We are living in a rotten world in which we are restricted by strong bonds and chains; from school to work, and from family to social life, our world and our lives are a gigantic prison. It is constructed this way in order for the public to remain under control. This is why we seek escapism; from music to films, and from travelling to sports, we are constantly looking for our way out. The problem is that escapism is controlled, as well. This is the dark and nihilistic concept in which the movie under review based its story.[18]

Set in the super-futuristic 1983 (a full decade after this was released), this is about the unfortunate goings-on in the Delos company's three ultra-realistic role-playing theme parks: Medieval World (the setting of which is old England), the Roman World (set in, where else, Ancient Rome), and the most popular one, which is called Westworld, in which the paying customers[19] get to experience a real-life western in the American Old West.[20] What is unique about these theme parks (and—ahem!—futuristic) is that other than the visiting humans, every other being is an anthropomorphic robot that you can't tell apart from a living person, aside from a minor imperfection on their hands. The robots are there to serve, and the humans don't treat them too well (echoing the sex tourism that is popular among many rich people), so as it is to be expected, one day the robots rebel. The leader of the rebelling robots is played by Yul Brynner (also in **THE MAGNIFICENT SEVEN** [1960], reviewed above; actually his part here as a gunslinger cowboy is based on his role on that film[21]) who also made it on the box art that I scanned for you. Who will win the small-scale battle between humans and robots?

Although extremely innovative for its time, **WESTWORLD** has not aged very well, and it will definitely put off young viewers today, 44 years after its release. However, I cannot but admire how many things it predicts, including role-playing games. Technically, too, there is a lot to gasp at here, including the soundtrack by Fred Karlin (mostly knowing for scoring TV movies), which is years ahead of its time, with its innovative work of strings. Changing further the cinematic game, this is the first film to use digital image processing, but the terrible "pan-and-scan" 4:3 cropped copy that mainstream distributors Audio Visual Enterprises released in Greece turned the outstanding experience into an unwatchable torture. But you should definitely find a better copy and watch this, as it is essential viewing for sci-fi fans.

18 The screenplay was written by Michael Crichton, who also directed. At first he was negative on the idea of directing this, but he later confessed that the studios would only let him make a genre picture. He is now better known for penning Steven Spielberg's mega-hit **JURASSIC PARK** (1993).

19 These vacations cost $1,000 a day, which is a large sum now, and was unheard of back then.

20 The sets were later used for **BLAZING SADDLES** (1974).

21 In turn, John Carpenter based Michael Myers's nature in **HALLOWEEN** (1978) upon this particular performance.

THE LAST WAR
(*Sekai Daisensō*)
1961, Japan. D: Shûe Matsubayashi

The Greek title on the box art translates as "*Third World War*", but what is written in the title card is translated as "*The Last War*" straight from the English, whilst the translation from the Japanese would be "*Great World War*". This is the backdrop anyhow, as at the front this is a romance story between Takano (Akiroa Takarada from **GODZILLA** [*Gojira*, 1954]) and Saeko Tamura (Yuriko Hoshi from **MOTHRA VS. GODZILLA** [1964] and **GHIDORAH, THE THREE-HEADED MONSTER** [1964]).[22] Be warned, though, that **GONE WITH THE WIND** (1939) this is not; just a family drama about people talking to each other. Sure, this is a Toho production and special effects of mass destruction are employed and they are impressive (considering this was made in 1961), but the strange mixture of genres make this for a particularly difficult viewing.

What also makes it a difficult viewing is the fact that the copy under review is the English dub (a short 76 minutes; the original Japanese copy is supposed to run 100 minutes, but I am not really sure how can one get a hold of it) that comes with Greek subtitles that are not always in sync, making the experience surreal to say the least. To top the pulp experience, the back cover bears a totally illiterate synopsis! The tape was released by VEP (I never found out what VEP stands for, as the acronym was never explained in any of the tapes I own), which was one of the oldest distribution companies in Greece, and other obscure releases by them include John Carpenter's **DARK STAR** (1974) back when nobody knew of it (I am proud to have such an ancient release in my collection).

It was produced by Paul N. Lazarus III (**CAPRICORN ONE** [1977]) on a modest $1.25 million budget (which resulted in a short 30-day shoot in which not too many takes were allowed; however, a few re-shoots were demanded), and was distributed by Metro-Goldwyn-Mayer (MGM). It won awards and critical appraisal, and it grossed an impressive $10 million, which resulted in a tie-in novel, an excellent sequel (**FUTUREWORLD** [1976], which I had seen prior to this one, and I am the proud owner of a copy of its Greek VHS release, which was quite rare even back in the day) and the *Beyond Westworld* 1980 TV series (which I have not seen). Not too long ago a new series called *Westworld* (2016-present) was created for HBO, and from what I've heard it is even better than the film, but I have to see for myself. However, to me the whole idea of the franchise seems a better-fit for a film rather than a long-running series…but we'll see. At some point Arnold Schwarzenegger was set to produce a remake, but his duties as a politician forced him to scrap this plan.

CUJO
1983, USA. D: Lewis Teague

There are not too many things one can write about the film under review, but here we go! Many remember this classic from their childhood as an all-around fun monster movie, but upon viewing it now I came to the conclusion that it isn't really that. It is a family drama that focuses on advertiser Vic (Daniel Hugh Kelly) who may be a loving father to his monster-fearing young son Tad (Danny Pintauro), but is too

22 See our big G franchise feature in *Weng's Chop* #10, p. 7. –Ed.

them alive. This is where things get interesting as the majority of the time we spend inside the car is a masterwork on claustrophobia, and that alone is reason enough for one to see this flick.

The screenplay by Don Carlos Dunaway (**IMPULSE** [1984]) and Lauren Currier (**THOSE SECRETS** [1992]) was based upon the same-titled novel by Stephen King[24] (who has gone on record to say that he was an alcoholic during writing it and does not really remember too much about writing it), this was directed by Lewis Teague (who replaced Peter Medak) and cinematically at least it is pure magic (the shoot started with cinematographer Tony Richardson, who was replaced by Jan de Bont), considering the shots that were achieved. It was produced by Daniel H. Blatt (executive producer of Joe Dante's **THE HOWLING** [1981]) and Robert Singer (associate producer of Dan Curtis' **BURNT OFFERINGS** [1976])[25] on a modest budget of $8 million, and it was trashed by critics. It went on to gross more than $21 million and it is now considered a minor classic among 1980s horror movie aficionados. Sunn Classic Pictures in 2015 announced a remake, and it is now in the works. If you ask me, I can't wait for it and I am super-excited. The tape that I reviewed was released in Greece by mainstream distributor HVH (Home Video Hellas) and it was never rare; I just fancied wrapping-up the present article with something quite popular.

busy with his corporate job that he is neglecting his beautiful wife Donna (Dee Wallace, about whose performance Stephen King has gone on record to say that is the best in any of his book's adaptations) who in turn has an extramarital relationship with her ex-boyfriend Steve Kemp (Christopher Stone, who in real life got married to female lead Wallace during shooting this). Somewhere along all these boring (to horror movie fans at least) storylines we are introduced to the titular dog (yes, it is just a dog, and an adorable St. Bernard at that[23]), which just happens to become rabid and trap mom and son in a car, whilst barking and attacking it, seemingly trying to eat

---

23 Of course several dogs were used, along with a guy in a costume, but everything looks amazingly realistic.

24 King's Previous novel, *The Dead Zone*, was adapted to film by David Cronenberg the same year as **CUJO**.

25 Neil A. Machlis is credited as the associate producer; a few years later he was an executive producer of **WOLF** (1994) featuring Jack Nicholson and Michelle Pfeiffer.

FRIGHT NIGHTS:
HORRORANT 4 INTERNATIONAL FILM FESTIVAL

by Christos Mouroukis

EL ATAÚD DE CRISTAL

Horrorant in 2017 was not only the sole international horror film festival taking place in Greece; it was also the only one to play in six major cities (Athens, Thessaloniki, Larisa, Rodos, Iraklio and Alexandroupoli). Yours truly had the opportunity to attend the majority of the happenings in Athens, and in the week-long event more than 50 features and shorts were presented; here's the report.

PRE-EVENT AT THE WHITE RABBIT:

Horrorant had a pre-event at the newly established The White Rabbit bar in the ever-beautiful neighbourhood of Exarchia in Central Athens, in which a roundtable discussion was held after the introduction by the festival's organizer, Konstantinos Chatzipapas.

The panel consisted of genre film author Dimitris Koliodimos (who has written for *Video Watchdog* in the past, and whose books on genre cinema in Greek are of essential reading), and directors Panos Kokkinopoulos (whose ultra-rare **TA SIMADIA TIS NYHTAS** [a.k.a. **SCARS OF THE NIGHT**, 1990] would be screened at the festival) and Dimitris Panayiotatos (**I NYHTA ME TI SILENA** [a.k.a. **THE NIGHT WITH SILENA**, 1986]).

Koliodimos provided a lengthy and detailed history of the Greek cinema of fantasy and horror; Panayiotatos then delivered an introduction on the definition of the cinema of fantasy and horror, and finally Kokkinopoulos talked about the beginnings of the genre through pulp books, etc.

The event was wrapped-up with a screening of excerpts from Panayiotatos' excellent documentary on Greek genre cinema **XENES SE XENI HORA: 50 ELLINIKES TAINIES MYSTIRIOU KAI FANTASIAS** (a.k.a. **STRANGERS IN A STRANGE LAND: 50 GREEK MYSTERY & FANTASTIC MOVIES**, 2009), which as he said, Mondo Macabro will soon put out on disc, and you should definitely buy it.

After a couple of black beers, I hopped into a taxi and went back home, thinking during the ride that we were off to a great start.

WINNER OF HORRORANT 3:

VAMPYRES

Please refer to my review in *Weng's Chop* #10, p. 216, in my coverage of Horrorant 3.

2015, SPAIN. D: VÍCTOR MATELLANO
AVAILABLE FROM ARTSPLOITATION FILMS

—

OPENING CEREMONY FEATURE:

THE VOID

Taglines: "A new dimension in evil." "There is a Hell. This is worse."

The film kicks-off with a shocking pre-credits sequence in which a young man called James (Evan Stern) runs away from a cabin in the woods, but a young lady behind him does not have the same luck, as she is shot in the back and then has her corpse burned by two menacing-looking rednecks.

Just by chance lazy deputy Daniel Carter (Aaron Poole) picks up James and they rush to a small nearby hospital. Only nurses Alison Fraser (Kathleen Munroe) and Beverly (Stephanie Belding), trainee Kim (Ellen Wong), Doctor Richard Powell (Kenneth Welsh), and patients Cliff Robertson (Matthew Kennedy), Maggie (Grace Munro) and her grandfather Ben (James Millington) are present.

It is not too long before Beverly (a nod to Beverly Garland maybe?) sticks a knife into Cliff's eye and proceeds to remove skin from her face. When she tries to attack Daniel, he shoots her in the face.

Old man and state trooper Mitchell (Art Hindle, about whom no introduction is needed, and is the star attraction here) shows up at the hospital to arrest James. When Daniel goes out to his car to call back-up he is confronted by a hooded knife-wielding maniac who attempts to kill him. Daniel makes a run and he's back in the hospital again. Next thing you know, more people in white robes (not hospital staff, but KKK-looking cultist) have surrounded the hospital, looking even more threatening.

Meanwhile, danger is not only outside, as Beverly's corpse has been transformed into an ugly creature with tentacles! The next additions to the cast of characters inside the hospital are Vincent (Daniel Fathers) and Simon (Mik Byskov), who now hold everyone else at a gunpoint! When the monster eats Mitchell, the group finally looks for what supplies and ammo it can gather for its protection. With danger inside the hospital, and more danger outside the hospital, will they make it? And will an explanation about all this madness be given?

That's the problem here. Explanation is given, and a lot of it. The film has the greatest first half I've seen in the last couple of decades, but in the second half it goes on to over-explain everything that we saw in the first half and connect all the plot dots in order to not come off as another problematic "open to interpretations" affair. However, having said that, writers/directors Jeremy Gillespie and Steven Kostanski

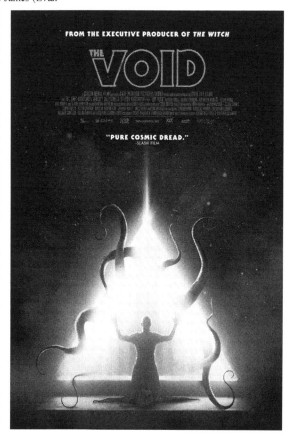

THE VOID

(the duo had previously made Troma's outrageous **FATHER'S DAY** [2011]) still delivered what I will be calling the year's best film. It is true that the first half is better than the second, but by that I mean that the second half is merely great and the first is a masterpiece. True, it loses steam on one or two occasions, but you must believe me, this is not to be missed.

But what exactly is **THE VOID** (2016)? It is the film every reader of this magazine (and especially its sister publication *Monster!*) was dreaming of happening, yet never thought it would: it is old-school, and its practical and creature effects look amazing. Sure, there is some CGI here, showcased mainly when the film is presenting a vision of a dystopian future to come, but that's all about it. The rest is just good old prosthetics and gore; and plenty of them, too. The thing though is that all these look believable, making the ever-stupid argument that practical effects are dated seem more ridiculous than ever. **THE VOID** is the independent masterpiece that will be here to remind everyone that it can be done right and to show everyone how it can be done so. Although this is a throwback to the 1980s or even further back, it should not be confused with all these unwatchable faux-grindhouse homage productions littering the market, as it is a modern feature that can stand on its own two feet without having you alert for catching up with random references and useless movie trivia. With the recent prevalence of CGI (in both blockbusters and cheapies) I thought we would never get to experience something like this again, yet I had the chance to do so, and in one of Europe's biggest cinema screens, too. Colour me happy.

If you are a fan of John Carpenter's **THE THING** (1982), or George Romero's **NIGHT OF THE LIVING DEAD** (1968)[1], stop looking for your new favourite film, as **THE VOID** is here and it is just that. It has played all the prominent festivals (and won Nevermore Film Festival's Best Feature Award), but it should've hit BD by the time this article is printed, so you should go on and purchase your copy.

2016, CANADA. D: STEVEN KOSTANSKI, JEREMY GILLESPIE
AVAILABLE FROM SCREEN MEDIA

—

COMPETITION:

Several features competed for the awards, and these included **ORIGIN** (*Bieffekterna*, 2016), **THE VISITOR** (2016), **BAJO LA ROSA** (2017), **THE NIGHT WATCHMEN** (2017), **GHOULS** (*Vurdalaki*, a.k.a. **VAMPS**, 2017), **IMMIGRATION GAME** (2017), and the ones I reviewed below.

DIGGERS
(*Diggeri*)

Kicking off in found footage-style combined with an overall bombastic approach of modern style, the film introduces us to the world of cosplay and geek conventions. Things soon become more conventional as the story is set. A subway wagon is lost in the darkness. Fast-forward to five days later and a group of teenagers will try to uncover the truth behind the mystery, whilst coming face to face with several Russian legends.

[1] This classic zombie film is also shown on a television screen. You know, it's in public domain, and it is also ever so influential, so it shows up everywhere!

Russian poster for **DIGGERS** (left) and Spanish poster for **RED SUMMER** (right)

Not the festival's strongest feature (far from it), this has interesting cinematography to showcase, along with a premise that if not totally original is still very interesting. I wouldn't say that you should go out of your way and buy this, but if it shows up on Netflix (or whichever platform is providing you with your VOD fix) you might want to check it out if you have 80 minutes to kill.

2016, RUSSIA. D: TIKHON KORNEV

RED SUMMER
(*Verano rojo*)

Two young liberal couples from Madrid decide to spend a sexually promiscuous summer vacation in Mallorca. Unfortunately, they will soon become the prey of fascist Franco descendants that hate city kids and will go on to rape them, torture them, and eventually kill them.

Writer/director Carles Jofre's debut feature may lack in originality—the family of killers is nearly identical to the one from **THE TEXAS CHAIN SAW MASSACRE** (1974) and it comes complete with a "Leatherface" wearing a pig mask (surprisingly justified later on in the story), a grandfather, and a brother; even the girls resemble **TTCSM**'s Sally (Marilyn Burns) and they wear shorts and t-shirts—but it comes in spades in enjoyment.

The thing with these slashers that focus on the torture is that they are usually between 70 and 80 minutes long. After all, how much more violence one could film (as a filmmaker) or watch (as a viewer)? But the film under review does something unexpected and it takes its time, which results in a whooping 105-minute endurance test. And the good news is that it totally works! We are appropriately introduced to the main characters that eventually become interesting (it would be difficult not to be though, as both girls are as hot as Spanish ladies usually are) and the torture and rape later on is a lengthy visual manifesto of the grotesque kind.

I suspect that it was shot on the cheap and on video, but it doesn't much look like it (i.e. it doesn't look like shit, and a good job was done). Also, the use of mainly natural locations adds to the charm, as not everybody lives in the Mediterranean area, and the results will look exotic to most viewers. The conclusion is that there is no excuse for the rest of Italian, Spanish, and Greek genre filmmakers to not make entertaining features like this one.

And on a final note, early on in the film one of the main characters is watching television and the film on the screen is—are you ready for this?—**NIGHT OF THE LIVING DEAD** (1968)!

2017, SPAIN. D: CARLES JOFRE

THERAPY

SINISTER CIRCLE

SINISTER CIRCLE
(*Cementerio General 2*)[2]

This is about a psychologist that returns to the scene of the crime, where some bad Ouija board-related business took place not too long ago. She and her young son will soon become the centre of attention in the Sinister Circle.

This is one of the several recent features that tried to emulate the successful tone of **THE BABADOOK** (2014) and its fault is just that, as it often becomes more "arthouse" rather than "horror". Filmmaker Dorian Fernández-Moris (**CEMENTERIO GENERAL** [2013]) may be wearing his art on his sleeve as a badge of honour, and it will certainly do him good in the festival circle, but he will have to go on all-out horror if he is interesting in gaining a wider audience for his films. The good news is that he evidently has an incredible amount of talent, so his future is up to him.

2016, PERU. D: DORIAN FERNÁNDEZ-MORIS

THE BRIDE
(*Nevesta*)

Nastya (Victoria Agalakova) is an incredibly hot blonde lady (wait until you see her in her underwear) who is dating a mysterious photographer guy to whom she eventually gets married. One day he receives a call from his equally mysterious family and they request his visit. Although he persists that his wife should not come with him, she does. And this is when a long string of supernatural events start happening that involves the photographer's family and Russian traditions and superstitions.

THERAPY

Police officers Jane (Nathalie Couturier) and Simon (Rémy Jobert) get hold of a tape that was seemingly shot by teenagers in an abandoned psychiatric clinic, in which terrible things have happened to them.

Writer/producer/cinematographer/editor/director Nathan Ambrosioni's feature employs a mix of formats (conventional filming, found footage, etc.) and what it lacks in performances (not all of the acting personnel at hand seem to be professional, especially the British performers) it makes up for the mastery in direction. Keep note, as when this feature is discovered by Hollywood executives, its young director will be signed to a major deal to direct the next big-budget superhero epic. For example, the expert way in which the jump-scares were handled had me jumping off my seat and scared shitless on more than one occasion. More than well done, this is bordering on the masterpiece area.

2016, FRANCE. D: NATHAN AMBROSIONI AVAILABLE ON VOD FROM LIGHT HOUSE PRODUCTION

---

[2] It should be noted that IMDb appears to have no less than three (!) listings for this film, all purporting to be separate movies directed by Dorian Fernández-Mmoris, listing it alternatively as **CEMENTERIO GENERAL 2** (2016; which seems to be the most accurate and complete listing), **SINISTER CIRCLE** (2016), and **JUEGO SINIESTRO** (2017). But it's pretty clear that these are all the same film, and hopefully IMDb will clear up the confusion soon. –*Ed*.

Russian poster for **THE BRIDE**

Writer/director Svyatoslav Podgayevskiy's (**QUEEN OF SPADES: THE DARK RITE** [2015]) feature may not have the greatest first half in the world, but it soon elevates into such a bombastic second half full of scares and overall creepiness that it is bordering on the masterpiece area. **THE BRIDE** (2017) is good proof that a film like **THE CONJURING** (2013) can be made outside the studio system, in a foreign country, with limited resources, and be equally horrific, if not more so.

2017, RUSSIA. D: SVYATOSLAV PODGAYEVSKIY

CHILD EATER

Helen Connolly (Cait Bliss) is on a routine night of babysitting young Lucas Parker (Colin Critchley), until it becomes apparent that the monster the young kid is seeing under his bed and inside his closet are not of his imagination or because he just saw a horror movie, but a very real demon that has a thing for taking out the eyes of his victims.

Expanded from writer/director Erlingur Thoroddsen's 2012 short of the same name, this is enjoying a good festival run—it won three Jury Awards at the Fantastically Horrifying Cinema Film Festival[3]—and deservedly so, as it is a polished monster movie (although the slasher clichés are used quite often, but this works in its favour) that you should definitely catch up with when it hits home video.

2016, USA/ICELAND. D: ERLINGUR THORODDSEN
AVAILABLE FROM CHILD EATER PRODUCTIONS

EL ATAÚD DE CRISTAL
(a.k.a **THE GLASS COFFIN**)

Amanda (Paola Bontempi) is a famous actress that was just about to receive an award. A limousine is waiting for her outside her luxurious villa. She soon finds herself locked in the vehicle, with a distorted voice asking her to be obedient. But she does not comply, and it is not too long before a masked man enters the car and beats her up. She now knows the consequences that await her in case she doesn't follow the voice's orders. But who kidnapped her? Who would want to humiliate her in such horrible ways? Who is behind the voice? Will she survive or will she die?

This is director/editor Haritz Zubillaga's first feature (although he is quite experienced with shorts) and it doesn't show a bit, as it is the work of a master craftsman. 90% of the film is set inside the limousine and claustrophobia dwells all around. Bear

---

3 The awards were for Best Cinematography (John Wakayama Carey), Best Actress (Cait Bliss), and Best Film.

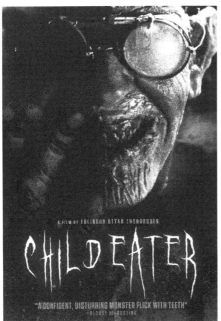

in mind, though, that it is a very strong feature that goes as far as showing rape (even if briefly).

Actress Paola Bontempi was in attendance and during the introduction to the film that she provided us with, she explained how difficult the film was, because for most of the time she had no other actors to interact with. Sure, she is the female lead, but I noticed one other great player. The limousine itself becomes a character here…and a very menacing one, too. Mrs. Bontempi also stayed with us after the film for a lengthy Q&A session. The film itself is a one-woman-show, and to have such a great actress at its disposal that delivered such a strong performance worked miracles for it. Actually, I would say that its luck was dependent on the performance of the female lead, and on that front, it succeeds in spades.

2016, SPAIN. D: HARITZ ZUBILLAGA
AVAILABLE FROM SYNERGETIC DISTRIBUTION

Greek Horror Special:

The Greek Horror retrospective featured five classics in total. These were: **TO KAKO** (a.k.a. **EVIL**, 2005)[4], the screening of which featured an introduction by its director Giorgos Nousias; **RAZOR** (2007), featuring an introduction by its director Filipos Chalatsis; **THE DEVIL'S MEN** (a.k.a. **LAND OF THE MINOTAUR**, 1976), featured an introducing with producer/distributor Peggy Karatzopoulou; **SCARS OF THE NIGHT** (1990); and **ISLAND OF DEATH** (1976).

Sci-Fi Horror Special:

As a member of the Jury I had to catch-up with all the new stuff, so I had no time left to watch any of the classics section (after all, I am a geek who had previously seen all these titles), but just for the record, **THE INVISIBLE MAN** (1933), **RE-ANIMATOR** (1985)[5], **THE LAST MAN ON EARTH** (1964), **RABID** (1977), **THE THING** (1982), **CABIN IN THE WOODS** (2012), **THE BLOB** (1958), **DEAD SHADOWS** (2012), **SPECIES**, and **TETSUO** (1989) were screened.

Greek Horror Shorts:

Several outstanding Greek shorts were screened before the main presentations, and these included *Συχνότητα 13* ("*Frequency 13*", 2016), *Lurking Near* (2017), and the selected ones I reviewed below.

---

4 You can check out my review over in *Monster! Digest* #4, p. 17.
5 Please refer to my review in *Greek VHS Mayhem's Charles Band Special*, which you can find in *Weng's Chop* #7, p. 93.

LyssaVirus

A scientist received funding in order to work on an antidote for a rabid disease, but it soon becomes apparent that he was used in order to make the disease itself, which he hands over to a mysterious man in black. It's not too long before people turn into zombies, and the scientist has to take matters to his own hands, dress in black leather clothes, wear a hat and sunglasses, ride a motorcycle, grab his shotgun, and kill some zombie motherfuckers.

Although clearly not great in execution (also, some of the dialogue comes off as rather unbelievable and too stage-like), and with its limited resources defying it, this has its heart in the right place. And when you are making a short, this is probably all that matters. Well done!

2015, GREECE. D: MANOLIS LEVEDELIS

#Not Alone

A home alone girl is taking a selfie whilst home alone. Once she posts it on Instagram (or some such platform of one sort or another) she realizes that her hashtag #HomeAlone was changed to #NotAlone. Soon she receives gruesome photos that were seemingly taken inside her apartment.

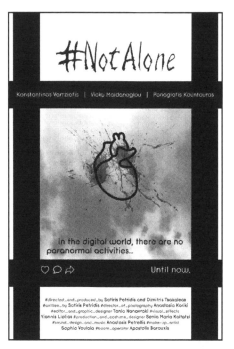

Although this suffers from merely average special effects, both practical and CGI (and it goes fully-blown on both), it was seemingly made with a lot of passion. The fact that it is silent (it has no dialogue whatsoever) is its strongest asset, as the short (only 5 minutes long) experience becomes totally cinematic. It also features one of the most attractive actresses I came across in recent times. Well done!

2017, GREECE. D: SOTIRIS PETRIDIS

—

INTERNATIONAL HORROR SHORTS:

Several outstanding international shorts were screened before the main presentations and these included *Cenizo* (2016), *Beyond Beauty* (2017), *Indios Y Vaqueros* (2016), *Leciones* (2016), *Mia* (2016), *Du Sollst Nicht Lugen* (2017), *Born Again* (2016), *The Butterfly Dream* (2016), *The Incredible Tale of the Incredible Woman-Spider* (2016), *Fils* (2016), *Into the Mud* (2016), *Fashion Victims* (2016), *I See you Everywhere* (2016), *Room 24B* (2016), *Menu* (2017), *Trip* (2016), and the selected ones I reviewed below.

The App

Set in the near future, this is about the titular application which, once you have on your smart phone, gives you suggestions about what to do with every single moment of your life in order to better it. Benito, for example, was a lonely and unpopular middle-aged bald guy with a dead-end job, who now because of the app has a gorgeous blonde girlfriend, a better job, a lot of money, famous friends, etc. One day, though, the app tells him to jump off the balcony. He calls customer service to make sure that this is the right thing to do.

Playing on the fear of technology taking over our lives and how we sign away our right to privacy and give access to of our personal lives to gigantic corporations, as well as making fun of our addiction to smart technology, this short is structured as a comedy, yet it is too frightening to be considered one. Cinematographer Juan Lage's (*Absolutamente personal* [2014]) aesthetics are those of a commercial, yet they work here. In all honesty I can say that it is one of the cleverest shorts I've seen in my entire life as a movie addict.

2016, SPAIN. D: JULIÁN MERINO

Fe

This short is about a priest called by a mother because she thinks that her little girl is possessed. This

one features compelling cinematography and a twist in the end (just what you need from a good short), and it has the distinction of being presented by Tom Holland, whose **CHILD'S PLAY** (1988) is on a television screen at one point.

2017, SPAIN. D: JUAN DE DIOS GARDUÑO

I-Medium

The titular app can get its users/customers in touch with the dead, in this mostly found-footage short that relies heavily on the editing, which is not a bad thing, considering how effective and scary it is. Well done!

2016, SPAIN. D: ALFONSO GARCIA

Nail

An annoying man is moving to his new apartment, and he starts communicating with his equally annoying neighbour by knocking on the wall. But who or what is hidden behind the wall that starts bleeding?

This had potential, but it suffers from a terrible performance by its lead actor. However, writer/director JB Minerva does the best he can, and I am more than curious to see his next film.

2016, MEXICO. D: JB MINERVA

Closing Ceremony Feature:

I, OLGA
2016, CZECH REPUBLIC. D: PETR KAZDA, TOMÁS WEINREB
AVAILABLE FROM STRAND RELEASING

Awards:

Once again this year I was a member of the Awards Jury, so in the closing ceremony I joined festival organizer Konstantinos Chatzipapas on stage and introduced the awards. For most of the awards we had a video sent by the winner in which they thanked the festival; some were really humorous and the audience loved them. Paola Bontempi was in attendance and joined us on stage to receive her award.

Best Feature: **EL ATAÚD DE CRISTAL**
Best Director: Haritz Zubillaga (**EL ATAÚD DE CRISTAL**)
Best Screenplay: Josue Ramos (**BAJO LA ROSA**)
Best Actor: Ionut Grama (**THE VISITOR**)
Best Actress: Paola Bontempi (**EL ATAÚD DE CRISTAL**)
Best Cinematography: Ivan Burlakov (**THE BRIDE**)
Best Special Effects: Jonty Pressinger (**CHILD EATER**)
Fan Award: **THE NIGHT WATCHMEN**
Special Mention: **VERANO ROJO**
Best Greek Short: *#Not Alone*
Best International Short: *The App*

—

On a final note I would like to point out that one of the sponsors of the festival was the Ars Nocturna publishing house, which made its presence known by selling their excellent gothic books. I bought Nikos Drivas' *Return of the Bat*s, which I enjoyed very much.

STEVE'S VIDEO STORE:
THANKSGIVINGSPLOITATION

by Steven Ronquillo (featuring a very special guest appearance by Karl Kaefer)

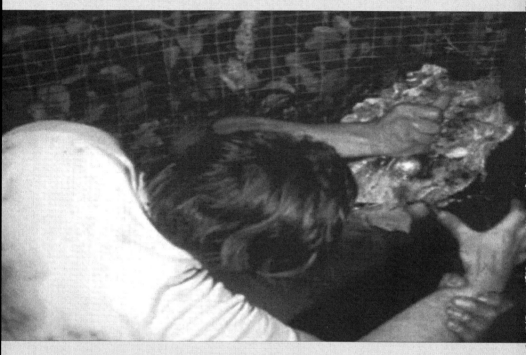

Okay, it's business as usual for a Thanksgiving here at Steve's video store. Danae and Doc are flirting and Karl is bitching about the lack of cheese, as he ate it all. So, it got me to thinking about the same thing we always think about every year: If I kill them, how much time will I get, do I have the holes dug, and why are the dogs so quiet? With that in mind, I thought about the movies that exploit Thanksgiving and how one changed my life for the worse.

(Voice from the background) BETTER!

SHUT UP, YOU!

Ahem. So with that, let's get into Thanksgiving exploitation...with all the trimmings!

Left: Two species stranded on a planet start a new tradition, in Nelvana's weirdo 1979 TV holiday special, *Intergalactic Thanksgiving*

HOME SWEET HOME

Intergalactic Thanksgiving or Please Don't Eat the Planet

This odd one was made by Nelvana, a Canadian animation studio who made some trippy sci-fi in the early '80s with humans, the other aliens. This 23-minute short is about two rockets crashing on a planet, one filled with humans and the other with aliens. So they come together to have the first intergalactic Thanksgiving. This is odd and trippy, but god I love it.

This is the infamous movie with "Body by Jake" Steinfeld as a psycho killer named Jay Jones who injects PCP into his tongue while killing folks over the holidays. This may be one of the most generic slashers ever, but Jake killing a dude who just offered him a drink of his beer is comedy gold. Good god, is this movie silly in a good way, with a Kiss fan named Mistake Bradley (Peter De Paula) walking around being a pisshead and making you glad when Jake kills him. And on a personal note, if you're gonna make a slasher, don't make the cast so hateful you want them all dead. It will bite you on the ass. This slasher is so generic it follows every beat of the Slasher Bible, and outside the drunk's death (it's just a fucking beer, man!), the kills are as bland as a Tony Strauss motivational meeting. But it's so goofy it's worth a watch.

Scan of a production animation cell from *Intergalactic Thanksgiving*

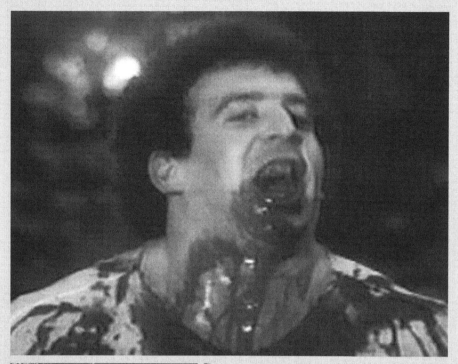

Above: In **HOME SWEET HOME**, Jake Steinfeld injects PCP into his tongue and kills people during the holiday season, perhaps in preparation for a new "Body Eaten by Jake" workout series.

Left: Media Home Entertainment's 1985 VHS cover for the film

BLOOD RAGE
(a.k.a. NIGHTMARE AT SHADOW WOODS)

(Insert metal guitars playing as women in leather bikinis dance around to make the rockin' title seem cooler.) This gorefest starts out in a drive-in where there is so much sex going on that Ted Raimi is selling condoms like a drug pusher! And we have Louise Lasser as Maddy, a woman who doesn't care if her sons are in the back seat because she wants some lovin' now! That makes one of her twin sons so pissed he kills a couple and frames his brother. It really did happen more than you think, but that was the good ol' days at the drive-in. But the non-crazy twin is put in the crazy house, and the crazy one is free. Fade to much later and the non-crazy one decides to escape and be crazy.

> Mark Soper likes to look 'em in the eye and give 'em his very best psycho-face when he stabs 'em in **BLOOD RAGE**

That is the plot of this fun-but-gory slasher with a typical downbeat twisty ending, and Louise Lasser wondering where her check is. It's just okay, but it's set on Thanksgiving, and the gore really flies.

And now for the movie that changed my podcasting life and sent me through five years of hell and pain...

BLOOD FREAK

This is most likely the only X-rated, pro-Christian, killer-weed-addicted turkey monster movie ever. And good god, do I love its saga of Herschell (Steve Hawkes), a biker dude who has sworn off drugs... but the woman who takes him in has a sister with a nice ass. She gets him hooked on weed again and he goes to work eating steroid-induced turkeys and turns into a turkey monster. Most likely based on a true story.

When I started my podcast my first plan was to do a Thanksgiving viewing of **BLOOD FREAK** (1972). So I did a Facebook shout-out and poured out all my hope for someone to do it with me, and Danae Dunning answered and she was awesome. And then I looked back on my life and all the sins I had done... and for my sins they gave me Karl Kaefer!

Yes, **BLOOD FREAK** gave me my co-host for five years now, and god do I regret—err, enjoy it. So here

> The thrilling moment in **BLOOD RAGE** in which a man demonstrates for the camera his amazing ability to clench up so tightly that his '80s short-shorts disappear inside him...

In the delightful X-rated, Christian-minded, anti-drug message film **BLOOD FREAK**, a case of the weed munchies leads to turning into a murdrous turkey monster. 'Nuff said.

he is with his thoughts on **BLOOD FREAK**—the one, the only, the ayatollah of rock and rollah (and cheese!)...*KARL KAEFER!*

"Long, long ago, in a drive-in projection booth far, far away, I experienced the majestic perfection of the only pro-Christian, anti-drug, mutated turkey monster movie in existence...

And there were herbal supplements involved in that first viewing.

But to be honest, I found in subsequent viewings of **BLOOD FREAK** that herbal supplements were not needed to appreciate the film for what it is. And what is **BLOOD FREAK**? Simply put, a "WTF Was That"-level masterpiece.

I was guided in this head-trip of a movie by none other than Howard, the Sherpa head protectionist of the Limestone (NY) drive-in. Howard was a customer at our family music store and had hired me as his assistant. My parents acquiesced (little did they realize), and I found my mentor of drive-in cinematic treasures.

As I look back at first discovering **BLOOD FREAK**, I instantly recognized that, in spite of the bad acting, misplaced camera work, and horrible script, I was truly entertained. And the ex-

No matter how tense or boring or hostile your family gatherings might get, at least you didn't spend this Thanksgiving being strung up, tortured and killed by a bloodthirsty turkey-headed monster, as demonstrated in these two shots from **BLOOD FREAK**. So give thanks, dammit.

planation of this fact came to me years later: **BLOOD FREAK** contains so much misplaced passion that it's nearly impossible to dislike the film.

What can you say about an anti-drug film when the narrator (director Brad Gintner) is making an impassioned speech about the dangers of drugs whilst smoking and going into a coughing fit?

Misplaced passion or stupidity? You decide.

Or when star Steve Hawkes eats hormone-enhanced turkey after smoking a joint and grows a papier-mâché mask that looks like it was bought at Woolworths for $1.99.

Budget constraints or misplaced passion? Or maybe watching **REEFER MADNESS** (1936) too many times?

Or, a movie so Christian (which was partially marketed to the Southern Baptist Church crowd) that it has a pussy shot in it?

Unbelievably, this is the only X-rated film ever to play in churches and Christian drive-ins... and yes, there were Christian family drive-ins when **BLOOD FREAK** was released in 1972.

And all the while I was watching this marvel, Howard would regale me with his version of CliffsNotes, such as how Brad Gintner had starred in several nudie-cuties filmed in Florida.

'Howard, what's a nudie cutie?' I didn't realize that question would require a 15-minute answer.

Or that Steve Hawkes starred in an Italian Tarzan movie and was almost burned beyond recognition by an on-set accident.

'And Karl, don't you think it's weird he's wearing sweaters during the summer in Florida?'

So, given the fact I was stoned out of my mind, you think watching BLOOD FREAK and getting several lectures on the history of drive-ins didn't have an effect on me?

There are several more wonderful films I saw at the drive-in, and even more stories about Howard that I could go on and on and on with... but screw that—Steve just put the turkey on the table! Needless to say, I have the munchies!"

—

Thanks, Karl! Now, as the night grows dark and the food is eaten and as my podcast family is waiting for me, I say good night to y'all, and don't forget...

Always keep looking. There are always new titles to find.
Be nice to the new fans. Because you were once a wet-behind-the-ears fan yourself.
Embrace the past. But don't drown it in nostalgia.

...And always remember: it's our love that keeps these movies alive more than anything else, so keep scanning the shelves!

Intergalactic Thanksgiving or Please Don't Eat the Planet
1979, CANADA. D: CLIVE A. SMITH
LONG OOP, BUT VISIBLE ON YOUTUBE

HOME SWEET HOME
1981, USA. D: NETTIE PEÑA
RELEASED BY HOLLYWOOD ENTERTAINMENT [OOP]

BLOOD RAGE
1987, USA. D: JOHN GRISSMER
AVAILABLE FROM ARROW VIDEO

BLOOD FREAK
1972, USA. D: BRAD F. GRINTER, STEVE HAWKES
AVAILABLE FROM SOMETHING WEIRD VIDEO

"Hey, babe...does this blood-covered machete make me look cool?"

INTERVIEWS

GETTING SICK

AN INTERVIEW WITH GABBY SCHULZ A.K.A. KEN DAHL

by Stephen R. Bissette

What do you do when you get sick?

What do you do when you <u>are</u> sick?

What do you do when your entire life is your greatest fear, incarnate, in the flesh—your flesh?

For many Americans, this is a day-to-day, hour-to-hour, minute-to-minute hard reality—and it is the subject of Gabby Schulz/Ken Dahl's most recent graphic novel, Sick *(Secret Acres, 2016).*

Previous page: Gabby Schulz a.k.a. "Ken Dahl" cuts loose, offering the ultimate monstrous editorial cartoon extravaganza of the 21st century to date in one of the graphic extremes of his recent graphic novel *Sick* (2016, Secret Acres).

This page, left: Cover art for the collected edition of his first autobiographical graphic novel masterpiece *Monsters* (2009, Secret Acres).

I originally interviewed Gabby Schulz a.k.a. Ken Dahl back in 2007, while he was still amid work on his serialized Ignatz Award-winning graphic novel *Monsters*.[1] Gabby Schulz, a.k.a. Ken Dahl, emerged from the 1990s *Factsheet 5* era of intensely personal mini-comics and has kept his hand into slinging the ink, telling stories and making comics (with a few siestas and sabbaticals en route) ever since. Under his "Ken Dahl" moniker, Gabby won the Ignatz Award in 2006 for Best Mini-Comic (*Monsters* #1), and spent a year or so with The Center for Cartoon Studies in White River Junction, VT as the school's 2006-2007 Fellow. He's a kickass cartoonist, a solid musician, plays a mean game of ping pong, and he's also a grand and humble fellow.

Autobiographical and semi-autobiographical comics indeed predated the launch pad commonly attributed to the underground comix era (e.g., Sheldon Mayer's Golden Age *Scribbly*; Sam Glanzman's *U.S.S. Stevens* backup strips in the DC war comics of the '60s and early '70s, etc.), there's no denying the importance of the landmark comix that set a high bar for personal comics and "confessionals". Robert Crumb, Justin Green (whose 1972 *Binky Brown Meets the Holy Virgin Mary* was the first true classic of its breed), Harvey Pekar, Lee Marrs, Roberta Gregory, Howard Cruse, etc. set the stage for the alternative, graphic novel and mini-comics autobiographical boom of the '80s and '90s.

Of course, turning one's personal history and miseries into art and popular entertainment is hardly unique to comics. Novels, painting, sculpture, theater, music, cinema, etc. thrive on the transmutation of life's shit into vicariously-experienced gold, and one need only take a cursory glance at the history of film comedy, for instance, to count the goldmines. From Charlie Chaplin to Judd Apatow, even the most populist of prospectors have found their muses in personal tragedy and reached the masses.

Thus, Gabby Schulz is blazing new trails with his latest effort, *Sick,* which is a companion of sorts to his previous autobio graphic novel *Monsters*, while building upon the bedrock laid by countless cartoonists before him—and his own worthy body of work in the minicomics "scene" of the 1990s.

Monsters made quite an impact. More people see movies than read mini-comics, so bear with me a moment as I offer a cinematic context for *Monsters*: Larry Clark's notorious debut feature **KIDS** (1995) charted a day in the life of a cocky AIDS-infected teen lad eagerly popping as many virgin cherries as possible, while a recent "score", having tested positive, listlessly tracks him down before he can infect more young women. Danny Boyle's **28 DAYS LATER…** (2002) blighted the UK with a hyper-infectious viral "rage" that decimates the island populace in two weeks, erupting from a botched animal activist raid on a biotech lab; **28 WEEKS LATER**

---

[1] That interview was originally published online in five parts at *S.R. Bissette's Myrant* [first edition blog], May 25-26, 30-31, 2007 and June 1, 2007, archived at http://srbissette.blogspot.com/2007/05/gabby-schultz-aka-ken-dahl-interview.html
http://srbissette.blogspot.com/2007_05_26_archive.html
http://srbissette.blogspot.com/2007_05_30_archive.html
http://srbissette.blogspot.com/2007_05_31_archive.html
http://srbissette.blogspot.com/2007_06_01_archive.html

(2007), the sequel, finds the "rage" re-emerging and spilling beyond control. In Terry Gilliam's **12 MONKEYS** (1995), a misanthropic scientist deliberately spreads a contagion to fellow passengers on a commercial international air flight, thus precipitating a global apocalypse. Monsters made it clear that malice, microbiological scientists and misanthropy needn't be involved. All it takes is being horny, homesick, and self-centered enough to ignore the consequences for anyone else.

Monsters concerns herpes, not TB or AIDS (or "the rage" or cultivated bioweaponry). But few other works in any media so thoroughly explores the ethics, issues, empathy (or lack thereof) and agonies of knowing one is infected, facing the conundrum of personal will (and desire) after becoming a mobile vehicle for a contagious disease. Monsters was and is timely in ways Gabby never imagined when he began work on such a personal project.

However deeply the autobiographical Monsters cut into the experience of living with herpes, Sick takes the reader into an even more harrowing experiential journey.

Don't take my word for it: Robert Kirby of The Comics Journal called Sick "a sucker punch of a book" that is not "for everybody ('Trigger Warning' crowd, please take note)." Kirby writes:

> "Upon my first reading I was taken aback at its unremitting bleakness. Schulz has a real talent for identifying those little pockets of dread that punctuate our days and nights, lingering over them and illustrating them with gusto. His gorgeously grotesque visuals, often framed in washes of a nauseous green with accents of raw-meat red, recall somewhat the great Ralph Steadman; while one sequence in particular—Schulz reliving a horrifying childhood nightmare—reminds me of Josh Simmons at his most merciless. Schulz captures the experience of sickness with uncomfortable accuracy: the woozy slipping in and out of consciousness, the sense of health and wellness becoming but a distant memory—and of pain and illness defining all of one's existence. Sick joins other books in the growing genre of graphic memoirs dealing with health issues, among them Ellen Forney's Marbles, John Porcellino's The Hospital Suite, and Jennifer Haydn's The Story of My Tits. While those books offer stories of people who navigated through their physical and mental problems to the point of reaching new possibilities for their lives, in Sick, Schulz's illness is the avenue that leads him to simply confirm all of his worst fears about himself and the world surrounding him: 'The sickness had become me.' This is uncompromising work by a brave and powerful artist."[2]

Ladies and gentlemen, meet Gabby Schulz a.k.a. Ken Dahl.

GETTING SICK

I'd ask, "What have you been up to, Gabby, since I saw you last?" but Sick tells—well, if not all, a lot. Why tear yourself four new assholes in the first few pages of a new graphic novel?

It's my brand! I guess I am just using self-reflection as a starting point for reflecting on the world. If the book seems cruel it's as a reaction to the relentless cult of positivity that has become so mandatory

2 Robert Kirby, May 20, 2016, *The Comics Journal*, "Reviews: Sick," archived at http://www.tcj.com/reviews/sick/

Potent, atmospheric "you-are-there" observational drawing informs the autobiographical content of both Monsters (pictured here, right) and Sick, but Monsters involves communal (such as this festive New Year's gathering) as well as private living spaces.

> Graphic Medicine: the "I am a contagion" dread and self-loathing is graphically manifest—the Self as Sucking Pit—throughout *Monsters*.

and governments can and do read our Facebook pages, and we want to keep our jobs and apartments. I think my generation is more into complaining about things, since we saw the distinct and major shift in life before and after the Internet, before and after global neoliberalism, before and after Dick Cheney, before and after the complete commodification of "cool" and "counterculture," before and after the (first) Cold War, before and after Prozac, and the student-loan crisis, and the housing-market collapse, and GTMO, and rampant mass shootings and drone warfare and the end of the concept of retirement, etc. The generation after me seems to be a lot more comfortable with all that, because it's all they know. They're a lot better at cognitive dissonance, and so spend a lot less time being sour about things and more time practicing what they've been taught about Finding Your Bliss. And maybe that's the only realistic option left for those of us safe behind the Trump Wall: passive acceptance of a collapsing, or collapsed, culture in which your two remaining options are utter, debased subservience, or the gulag.

lately, that is clearly sold to us as a cheap form of social control, and ends up making us secretly more miserable than ever, in part because our anger and mistrust at the things that keep us in peonage aren't allowed release. I just want to pop that huge boil so bad—but I also think it's unfair for me to just complain about other people without making it clear how I participate in that mess.

If Sick *is a "cruel" read—to use your word—the initial target of your cruelty is yourself.* Sick *opens with a horrific situation: your illness and self-isolation, in despair. Was* Sick *based on an actual incident, a real health crisis you faced utterly alone?*

Yeah, it happened pretty close to how I show it in the book.

Oh, man, I am sorry—

It was hard for me to sustain that feeling of just constant unrelenting pain for days and days, but the experience was pretty awful and it surprised me how traumatic it was to have no one nearby to complain to.

Sick *reveals and revels in what so many Americans feel: utter abandonment, particularly regarding bouts with any kind of accident or illness. You clearly communicate your own despair in quite explicit terms; do you see (as I do) the same reflected in those around you, in your generation?*

I don't know! I guess this book is an attempt to take that temperature. It's hard to tell what anyone really thinks anymore, since our bosses and landlords

You cite social media, and yet Sick*'s real-world events, as presented, occur completely apart from any notion of social media: you never reach out to anyone in the book amid the harrowing crisis, having convinced yourself there is no one, nobody cares, and you can't afford any "help" if you wanted to—all of which may well be absolutely true. Yet your eloquence here about your generation, before and after the Internet; and the current generation, which as you (accurately) note seems completely comfortable with the new reality paradigm. In removing social media completely from the equation in* Sick*, were you distilling everything down to an effective means of monologue—to hear your own voice, clearly?*

That's a touchy subject since at the time I was texting a few of my local friends, asking if they could drive me to the hospital, but nobody was able to. One of my roommates cracked my door open and slipped me a bottle of water through it. I guess I was not in a very good place for friends at the time.

Nor were they, for you. Jesus, Gabby—you weren't in "a very good place," period. As I've seen with the students I teach (college-level) and my own now-adult children, there's a generational dread and despair with hospitals, doctors, and insurance as a whole. "Health care" would be a joke in this country if it weren't such a devastating tragedy—and Sick *is unusual in that it's not about your bout with that industry, but suffering in part because of disgust with/dread of the industry (and I do mean "industry"). It's an industry that profiteers off misery; but as* Sick *makes abundantly clear, rejecting "health care" on principle/in despair only feeds misery as well. In your travels, have you found any respite or comfort zones since?*

Well, part of the title of *Sick* refers to how sick our culture is as a whole. Since I've given up on trying to change it, I find the further I get from it, and other people generally, the happier I am. I'm not yet able to get to a place far enough away from civilization where I can't hear some asshole revving his John Deere 800-horsepower prosthetic-dick lawnmower (or, alternately, snowplow), but it would be nice to one day. This is America; I guess I have to buy a car for that.

Okay, but you side-stepped completely my question about the "health care" industry in this country, which seems to be, in part, the focus of Sick. *Let's dig a little in this turf. What have your experiences been?*

Oh, predictably awful—but that's a common story that many other Americans are already covering. I've been on Medicaid a few times in my life by now, and although I guess I should be thankful to have it when I do, it also makes me a cash drain for

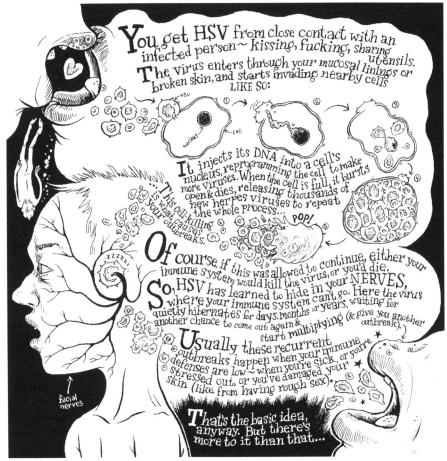

If Greg Irons or Phoebe Gloeckner had drawn an underground comix adaptation of an instructional classroom film like **HEMO THE MAGNIFICENT** (1957), they might have approximated the expressionistic and diagrammatic cartography of Gabby Schulz/Ken Dahl's *Monsters*.

the hospitals, which means I get only the worst doctors, and they dismiss my problems, shoo me out of the hospital as fast as possible, and sometimes use me as a lab rat. A doctor once almost convinced me to get hernia surgery to put a polypropylene mesh into my abdomen. It turned out he just wanted to train some residents in how to perform the operation, and a few years later another doctor told me I didn't have a hernia after all. (The polypropylene patch later turned out to mess people's balls up, too.)

Last year I saw a doctor for shoulder pain and he just lectured me for half an hour about how I was "lucky" that I didn't have cancer like him, and then mildly evangelized at me while a Christian prayer service boomed over the hospital's PA system. Then he tried to get me to slip him $30 cash in the exam room. Chicago is like that.

This year's developments with "Obamacare" or whatever have been pretty amazing though—somehow US healthcare has gotten even worse, in that every American is now fined hundreds of dollars for every month they're not covered by healthcare. Luckily I have a (minimum-wage) job right now that helps me pay for (and be eligible for) a low-tier HMO—but most (about $120/month) of the cost is taken out of my federal tax return. It's such a mess…

The searing cover art for the Secret Acres collected edition of *Sick* (2016)

unnecessary, since it's not life-threatening (unless you're giving birth) and it's incurable. Doctors I've seen have chided me for using "Doctor Google" but most of the doctors I've seen (with my cheap insurance) are doing the same thing when I'm paying them for a diagnosis.

What was the culmination of your experiences with American "health care" that you dug into in Monsters? *I suppose that would have constituted a coda of sorts for that graphic novel.*

I guess it was pretty much the action I described in *Monsters*…a lot of half-baked information about a convoluted disease that left me and others doing a lot of our own research. People are consistently surprised to find that when they go for an "STD test" at a clinic, they're not testing for herpes, and in fact will refuse to test you unless you've been recently exposed; even then some doctors shrug it off as

PROCESS

The power of Sick *as a graphic novel—and as being something more than a mere screed—is that you transcend just attacking our completely fucked "health care" industry and dig into the deeper, more profound cultural maladies. How did you go about visualizing those observations, making your chosen metaphors concrete via imagery?*

It was all pretty intuitive I guess. I just drew what I was feeling. I could have spent a lot more time visualizing how the illness felt, but it seemed like getting too poetic with the imagery would take away from the immediacy; I didn't want to make it too pretty. It did get *really* boring drawing that awful room over and over, and I'll definitely think more in the future about making the setting more appealing visually. But again I just wanted to portray the experience as it was, and that room was boring and sucked.

Well, that comes across in spades; it would have been deceitful to "make the setting more appealing visually." You found other ways to engage my senses, without betraying your candor, the honesty with which **Sick** *communicates. There's a component of musical composition at work in* **Sick***: you had to not just compile and give raw expression to your observations, but organize, choose/build imagery for, and orchestrate the whole into a visual "concert", and you did so quite eloquently. Since* **Sick** *was originally a digital comic, was that something you just allowed to flow as it flowed, or did you preplan and really work through that crucial compositional flow so it would build and build, as it does in the final print edition?*

Not laboring over backgrounds or "atmosphere" was one thing that seemed more appropriate in a webcomic. It was okay for it to be simple. But I think if I left it that way in a book it would have looked too plain, or unfinished. I was also writing the story as I drew it, so there wasn't a lot of "architecture" or large-scale planning to it; in fact I never imagined anything would ever come out of it beyond five or six weeks of venting. I think maybe the book could have been better if I'd thought more about that, but as it was I worked way too much on improving it...five years is too long to spend on an 80-page book!

Let's talk about that five years: the process of doing **Sick***. When did you begin work on this graphic novel, and how long did it take to see it through to delivery of the finished book to your publisher?*

It started out really easily, just a couple weeks after the action it describes, as weekly installments on my website. I didn't think much of it; it was just self-indulgent because I was paying for the website anyway. But then I kept doing it, and it got kind of popular, and then shut down my website with bandwidth issues. Then I stopped doing it for a while. Things got difficult when Secret Acres said they wanted to make a book out of it—I decided to redraw the whole thing, and draw a lot more story for it. And then I got my shoulder injury, and had to stop for a while, and then spent a while wondering how it was possible for anyone to ever publish, in book form, a collection of so much self-indulgent whining from a white man with no real problems...

and so on...for years...the usual cartoonist's process, I guess.

You've done a few things with **Sick** *that are quite different from your earlier long-form work. How did you approach page layouts and flow of imagery in* **Sick***?*

Ugh, that's what made the book so hard to do! The thing about *Sick* that got so many people looking at it was (so people said) its nice use of the "infinite canvas" scroll. And I had no idea translating that language into a finite-paged book form would be so difficult and deflating. It was a series of hard lessons about how restricting paper comics can be, and why the (paper-)comics language is the way it is, by necessity—you just can't simulate the digital scroll experience on paper. At least, I can't.

The concept of an "infinite canvas" doesn't actually exist, by the way—unless you've got infinite money to pay your server for all the bandwidth it takes to infinitely load...

But the whole point of this story was to put craft aside and make it as artless as possible, to just transmit the story of the experience with as little "narrative device" as possible, so as to minimize the pretension. I don't know if I'd do it that way again, though.

The "endless scroll" of the Internet original didn't translate to the published book, **per se***, but I have to say it really worked for me. However tortuous the process of translation from digital format to print, it flows beautifully—would you care to be more specific? What passage really suffered, to your mind, in the transition from digital-to-print edition?*

Thanks! Obviously there are a couple places where it's clearly just made to scroll down and down—like the part where all the various "me"s are tied on a red string, or at the end where the drain's water becomes blood pouring over the world and then becoming the noose rope, etc. It would be really nice to see that all animated, and that feeling that it almost was animated was part of what I thought made the online "scroll" so appealing. It gives me the same feeling you get if you'd been in the Disneyland house of horror as a kid, and the floor slowly drops and the pictures on the wall get longer and tell little horrible stories. *Sick* is basically inspired by Disney.

Don't tell their lawyers that! What passage worked best for you after the changeover?

I dunno, it all looks as good as it could, I guess. Especially the end parts, like the kid in the nightmare. I really hoped that feeling of dread could be

Spelunking the Self: Forever hanging by the proverbial thread, Schulz/Dahl offers mercilessly self-caricatures of his own stages in life from adolescence through adulthood in *Sick*.

communicated by the act of turning the page, like turning a corner in a nightmare.

Sick *is in full color, which also sets it apart from your earlier work. It's so carefully handled, from stem to stern, and quite remarkable. How did that change your work habits and orientation to the material?*

Oh god! The color! Such a nightmare! I had always hated the look of my digital shading, and dread the endless hours tweaking and toning in Photoshop. So for this book I naïvely assumed that, by watercoloring the pages by hand, I could do the maximum possible work on paper, and then just scan the pages and be done, skipping the usual endless digital turd-polishing that I at some point have become so dependent on with my black-and-white comics.

That assumption turned out to be extremely wrong. At some point I realized that you can't simultaneously have full, deep blacks *and* have subtle watercolors read accurately. Either your black areas are gray, or your colors are comically oversaturated or over-thresholded. It was a real nightmare for a while, and Leon [Avelino] from Secret Acres really rescued the book with some Photoshop tricks and a lot of hard work. I really was ready to throw the whole thing out in despair at multiple points. It was a very grim lesson in how tied to digital media we are now, whether we want to be or not—since we send the files to the printer digitally. I'm terrified of watercolors now. I recently drew a few things in just pencil, and like how that looks as well…although I can't let go of this obsolete feeling that a drawing isn't "finished" until the pencils are inked.

I do like watercoloring a lot, still. I just can't imagine drawing comics in straight watercolors, without penciling first, like a Joann Sfar, without the luxury of penciling to hash out the design elements (and fixing mistakes) before committing to a final drawing. I'm a coward, basically. The French would laugh me out of the academy.

Kudos to Leon for the hard work: I think the color looks terrific, Gabby, and the whole really works. Again: what suffered the worst, in your mind, in the transition from digital to print? What can you live with—or, in your brightest moments, do you think still works as you intended it to, color-wise?

The color is definitely as good as it possibly could be; in a perfect world I would have made it a smidge lighter, but I'm guessing these are details people complain about in the production of every full-color book. It's really awful that we have to translate it from paper, to digital, and then back to paper—and that final proofs are too expensive to get for most small-press people (not sure why; probably so people won't ask for endless revisions?).

It interested me, then worried me, how much changes in the framing of a story when you take it from the web to a book—digitally, it kind of seemed okay to go on and on with this (literal, then metaphorical) bellyaching, because pixels are cheap, and we kind of expect petty self-absorption on the Internet. It felt very private, flippant and anonymous.

Cover art to the 392-page diary comics collection *A Process of Drastically Reducing One's Expectations* (2017, Phase Seven Comics), "drawn during a prolonged period of solitude, nightly drinking and suicidal ideation, as I lost a home, suffered from mysterious debilitating pains, and returned to minimum-wage retail life in a new city..." (to quote the artist/author's introduction).

But when you're publishing a book, there's so much more pomp about it. A lot of other people get involved—publishers, printers, the press, distributors, reviewers, retailers. It's a physical object, and there seems to be a higher bar for justifying its existence as a Work of Art.

Also you have to justify killing all those trees, and manufacturing all those toxic inks; the book was printed in Hong Kong, which probably has shit labor practices; and then they have to cart the thing all the way across the Pacific fucking Ocean. Just so a few hundred people can have feels about a comic book. I know the Internet has its own environmental and human costs; but my website's contribution to all that seems pretty negligible compared to a print run. I guess the added importance is intoxicating but, in this case, it's also a bit stressful since I'm not sure something this private and self-concerned deserves to be an actual book. I'm not sure if anyone else other than me will relate with it or find value in it—enough to justify all the effort everyone's putting into it to make it worth the attention as an object in the world. If that makes sense.

Another key aspect of Sick *is how the narrative incorporates primary (and primal) aspects of editorial cartooning. This is pretty rare in graphic novels (though Alan Moore and Bill Sienkiewicz's* Brought to Light *comes to mind); were you consciously melding these cartooning streams?*

Not really; I think it's just force of habit from doing that editorial comic in the *Honolulu Weekly* all those years. To be honest I'm really embarrassed that I fall back on that…it's so artless and dull. But I felt like if I didn't use that kind of shorthand in this book there would just be too many rabbit holes to go down. I wish I had more time to explore all the facets of everything, but sometimes making a comic about the state of the world feels like drawing a world-sized map.

Monsters and Sick *are clearly companion volumes; is there a third in store—and how will you draw it from beyond the grave?*

Woof—I hadn't thought about that. I am thinking about drawing a (ugh) "memoir" of growing up in Hawai'i, as a way of looking at colonialism and whiteness and alienation (again) through the really strange trajectory of my parents.

SEEKING SOLACE

Your latest creation, "The only thing i know," was posted to your 'blog[3], completed for the forthcoming A Process of Drastically Reducing One's Expectations. *First off, is that book a collection of your diary comics, or a collective from many cartoonists you're contributing to?*

Yeah it's a collection of diary comics that I drew from 2013 to 2015, during the time the shoulder of my drawing arm stopped working and I couldn't draw the amount I was used to without a lot of pain.

So, it's all your work; it's a color diary comic collection—

---
3 See *Gabby's Playhouse* at http://www.gabbysplayhouse.com ; "the only thing i know" was posted in April 28-May 9, 2016, archived at: http://www.gabbysplayhouse.com/the-only-thing-i-know-1-of-5/ , http://www.gabbysplayhouse.com/the-only-thing-i-know-2-of-5/ , http://www.gabbysplayhouse.com/the-only-thing-i-know-3-of-5/ , http://www.gabbysplayhouse.com/the-only-thing-i-know-4-of-5/ , and http://www.gabbysplayhouse.com/the-only-thing-i-know-5-of-5/ .

Oh, the diary-comic book—*A Process of Drastically Reducing One's Expectations*—is just black & white!

Ah, the color is just for the online incarnations/excerpts. Your first panel, "It has taken me so long to understand my place in this world," runs like a mantra through your work—you've wrestled with that in so many forms, in so many ways. What was the catalyst for "The only thing i know"?

I think after finishing *Sick*, which is so unrelentingly pessimistic, I realized that I should probably allow myself to indulge in solace somewhere in life—or at least that I should spend less time with nihilistic polemic and find some perspective on life that I believed was worth defending. In the last few years I've spent a lot of time in the woods looking for mushrooms, and although nature can be a nightmarish place of ruthless competing life, there is still a balance and perfection to it that is worth returning to and that I think should be more of a focus in our life and principles. So I tried to be a little positive about that.

"The only thing i know" characterizes itself as "a little love song for this world that made me," which runs counter to much of your previous work in arriving at that conclusion. I know you're working to get yourself out of an urban environment you're unhappy in (Chicago), but are you spiritually in a better place these days?

Sort of. Between the gang warfare, fantastically corrupt politicians, hysterical gentrification, lead-filled water, ubiquitous environmental toxins, late-stage car culture, endless sprawl, crippling winters, and literal Apartheid system, Chicago isn't really the healthiest place for anyone to live. But

> "Civilization is Shit": a meditative sequence from Gabby Schulz/Ken Dahl's "The only thing I know" (2016)

it did at least get me out of extreme poverty (and into the comparatively comfortable baseline poverty) while my arm wasn't working, so I should be thankful for that. I don't know if I deserve to want more, but I am trying to find somewhere I can live that's closer to the woods. If finding peace, or a form of knowledge, or a way to make the intangible real, is what spirituality is about then being in wild places (or nearly wild places extensively curated by conservation workers, in my case now in Chicago) does the job pretty well. I guess that's why people get rich and buy cars and move to the suburbs.

Beyond **A Process of Drastically Reducing One's Expectations,** *now that you've "purged" with* **Sick,** *what have you in mind for the future?*

I suppose I'll get to work on that "memoir" (ugh) now, if my drawing arm holds up, unless some other less-dismal topic catches my interest!

Thanks for making time for this. Here's to you, Gabby!

©2016, 2017 Stephen R. Bissette, all rights reserved. This interview was conducted in June 2016. Deepest thanks to Gabby Schulz/Ken Dahl; all graphics from Sick and Gabby's other work ©respective year of publication, 2017 Ken Dahl, used with permission.

To order copies of Gabby Schulz/ Ken Dahl's work, visit
http://www.gabbysplayhouse.com/books/

Cover art for *Welcome to the Dahl House* (Microcosm Publishing, 2008)

***Sick* Sidebar:**

THE SECRET ACRES INTERVIEW

by Stephen R. Bissette

The following interview with Secret Acres publisher Leon Avelino was conducted between January 31 and February 9, 2017, with a final fact-check and follow-up on December 12-13, 2017. Along with Sick, *in 2016 Secret Acres published* Space *by Robert Sergel,* The Order of Things *by Reid Psaltis,* The Pterodactyl Hunters in the Gilded City *by Brendan Leach, and* The Academic Hour *by Keren Katz and Francine by Michiel Budel in 2017. Visit* http://secretacres.com *for more information and updates.*

Who is Secret Acres, and when and why did you launch your imprint?

Secret Acres is the comics micro-press started by Barry Matthews and me, Leon Avelino. We launched Secret Acres not too long after Tom Devlin, then moving to Canada and to Drawn and Quarterly, shuttered Highwater Books, his seminal comics publishing company. Serving as Tom's flunkies for a while, the absence of Tom and Highwater contributed to a severe depression on my part. Barry, thinking it would cheer me up, suggested we start a comic company. It cheered me up.

What projects were the maiden voyages of Secret Acres, and why did you go with them as your launching pad, so to speak?

Barry and I hunted through thousands of minicomics that we'd found online, at shows, at comic shops and stuffed into 'zine racks all over the country. We fantasized that we'd discover a dozen or so artists and that we'd publish everything they ever did and that would be Secret Acres. We discovered them through mini-comics. We wrote them, stalked them, begged them, and finally earned their trust. We knew well in advance what we'd be publishing through our first couple of years. We published Samuel C. Gaskin's *Fatal Faux-Pas* first because Sam finished-up his book first.

Weather (2012, Secret Acres): Deceptively ethereal imagery by Gabby Schulz/ Ken Dahl

ics Journal, and *Comic Book Resources*. It garnered a Best American Comics selection, two Small Press Expo Ignatz Awards and an Eisner Award nomination. *Flavorwire*, recently, included *Monsters* on its list of the ten most "disturbingly brilliant" graphic novels of all time. It continues to find new readers in its special edition second printing. Gabby rejects any notion of success, of course, but we couldn't be happier.

Gabby/Ken created both Monsters and Sick, of course, but did you and Barry see Sick as a sort of "sequel" to Monsters?

Sick feels very much like its own animal to us. Yes, we're speaking of the animal that is Gabby, but the artist formerly known as Ken Dahl changed quite a bit between the two books. We worried when we first read the complete draft of *Sick* that Gabby would chicken out. As much of himself as he revealed in *Monsters*, *Sick* feels comparatively merciless. Gabby tears down everything in *Sick*, himself, the world, and any kind barrier between the reader and the book. Unfortunately, the world appears to have caught up with *Sick*.

Monsters and Sick are prominent in the current wave of graphic novels concerned with medical and mental health—"Graphic Medicine" by name—and both are also confrontational memoir works as well. How do you go about marketing such loaded material?

Let's consider that a third of all Americans, well over 80 million people, have inadequate health insurance; half of those 80 million have no coverage at all, even after the passage of the Affordable Care Act, which is facing the most hostile legislative attack imaginable. Finding a sympathetic reader for *Sick*, which begins with a look at this national identity crisis, shouldn't be too difficult. There are plenty of bestselling memoirs of illness, but few authors with Gabby's wit, humor, and flat-out genius at cartooning and, as dark as *Sick* gets, there is a dawn. We never expected *Sick* to be a four quad book, and

What was your marketplace and hoped-for readership, and how has that market changed over the decade thus far?

We hoped to be a permanent home for oddball artists and to find a spot within the comics community. None of us looked to build a transmedia property empire. We got lucky and had some surprising successes early on, including *Monsters* by Gabby Schulz, formerly known as Ken Dahl. Our backlist eventually grew to the point that we could get ourselves book market distribution. Somewhere along the way, Secret Acres started taking care of itself. We knew we'd made something good when, year in and year out, familiar folks and total strangers would stop to tell us how much they loved our books. Lots of people have come and gone as we creep up on a decade of Secret Acres, but we found a little family in comics, and family haunts you to your dying day. We wanted to publish comics for comics people and that hasn't changed a bit.

What kind of reception did Monsters garner? Has it continued to reach new readers?

Monsters hit the ground running. Even before it shipped, Diamond, though they classified it as porn, spotlighted *Monsters* as cool. *Monsters* cracked the best of the *Village Voice*, *Library Journal*, the *Com-*

we'd hate it if it were, but the story rewards courageous readers. Sometimes warnings make good advertising.

We're in a whole different world in terms of how comics and graphic novels are produced, as webcomics "published" online, and then (in some cases) move to print publication. How does the online serialization of a work-in-progress like Sick *impact your decision to publish a compilation/collected edition?*

We choose what we publish based on the quality of the work first. Our relationship with the artists we publish plays a huge part in that decision-making process, too. We need to be happy with the thought of potentially being stuck with these folks for years. Looking beyond all that, most of what we've published has been serialized as mini-comics, and we love mini-comics. Webcomics, and the fact they're free, generally, might put a dent in print sales for some publishers, but we haven't seen that to be the case. Clearly, we believe in *Sick* as a story, and we obviously love Gabby since we've put up with his bullshit for a long time now. It's worth it.

Sick *is in full color, and the original files were prepared for digital online presentation; that had to present production issues going toward print publication. Gabby says you folks did a major overhaul/rescue in terms of the color reproduction; what was that process like?*

Producing *Sick* was an absolute nightmare. We ditched the original art, all of what appeared online, at the very beginning. Gabby painstakingly—and we're talking actual pain as in powering through nerve damage from crappy posture—redrew or re-inked the entire thing. The infinite canvas allows for art drawn at wildly different sizes, but print isn't so forgiving. He watercolored every page, beautifully, but reproducing that and the inks proved impossible in four colors. You're looking at a five-color book. It looks great, at least.

Though the events take place "up in the clouds" in *Weather*, the basest human necessities remain the agonizing focal point

There are aesthetic differences between webcomics and print graphic novels: a very different reading process, issues of the screen vs. the page in terms of layout, reading, design, etc. Were there any editorial alterations or revisions in content made during that process? How does the print edition of Sick *differ from the work-in-progress serialized online?*

Believe it or not, Gabby takes edits well. We spent a very long time moving panels around for the sake of clarity. We knew the book would have to be physically large to hold certain narrative beats together. The story lost very little, maybe a gag or two. It expanded in the process. Most everything you see online appears in the book, though heavily altered, along with a ton of new stuff. One thing that drives us nuts about webcomics in print is a tendency for some folks to review what is definitely the webcomic, even including images from the online version, and then call it a critique of the print comic. That ignores a ton of hard work. Making *Sick* into a book relied on Gabby's perfectionism. He never compromises, for better or worse.

With various "Graphic Medicine" academic conferences having taken place in 2017 and more scheduled for 2018, what (if anything) are you doing to reach out to their organizers? Is that a market, per se*?*

Graphic Medicine has been tremendously supportive of our books and Gabby's books, in particular. The year of *Sick*'s release, the conference was being held in Scotland, which made sending Gabby a bit impractical. I wouldn't say Graphic Medicine is a market, but many academics have taught, and ordered, both *Monsters* and *Sick* by virtue of their appearance at the conference. I appreciate the thoughtful essays written by Graphic Medicine's attendees; they've presented both books at the conference, as well, which is a treat for us, given their critical perspective.

How has* Sick *done for Secret Acres, and what other projects are you planning to do with Gabby— and, perhaps, in this genre?

I would publish virtually anything Gabby handed off to us. We don't require our artists, meaning the artists that Secret Acres has already published, to pitch to us. It's rare that we haven't published a comic by one of our gang. Gabby's a huge part of Secret Acres. The comics of his that we've published are some of the finest comics I've ever read, though Gabby would probably argue otherwise. *Monsters* has been a perennial seller for us and I expect *Sick* to stay in print for a very long time, too.

What's ahead for Secret Acres?

Well! Secret Acres will be a solo operation beginning in 2018. Barry Matthews is off to focus on his writing, among other things. Oddly, perhaps because Barry isn't around to stop me, Secret Acres has a record seven books on the schedule for 2018, including *Entropy* by Aaron Contain, *Kingdom/Order* by Reid Psaltis, *Little Stranger* by Edie Fake, *Flocks* by L. Nichols and *Bald Knobber* by Robert Sergel. We're also putting out new editions of Edie Fake's Ignatz Award-winning queer classic, *Gaylord Phoenix*, and Corinne Mucha's much loved *Get Over It!* We've even got some books on the schedule for 2019, but that's a secret for now.

Thank you, Leon, for taking the time for this conversation, and good luck to Barry and to you in this new chapter for yourself and for Secret Acres!

For more information on Secret Acres, go to http://secretacres.com, and for more on *Sick*: http://secretacres.com/?wpsc-product=sick-by-gabby-schulz ...and *Monsters*: http://secretacres.com/?wpsc-product=monsters-by-ken-dahl

---

The Official Secret Acres biography:

Secret Acres was made by Barry Matthews and Leon Avelino. Barry Matthews claims rural Vermont as his place of origin. He pursued and captured an M.F.A. in Creative Writing from Cornell University and was named a Best New American Voice. He has worked for a large dot com ever since. Leon Avelino was born in the Philippines and raised on New York's upper west side. Also possessed of fairly useless degrees, he has been working in comics companies large and small for the better part of his life.

The Secret Acres Bibliography:

Bald Knobber by Robert Sergel
Flocks by L. Nichols
Little Stranger by Edie Fake
Kingdom/Order by Reid Pslatis
Entropy by Aaron Costain
Francine by Michiel Budel
The Academic Hour by Keren Katz
The Order of Things by Reid Pslatis
The Pterodactyl Hunters in the Gilded City by Brendan Leach
Sick by Gabby Schulz
SPACE: An Eschew Collection by Robert Sergel
The Understanding Monster Book 3 by Theo Ellsworth
Palefire by Farel Dalrymple and MK Reed
Eschew #4 by Robert Sergel
The Understanding Monster Book Two by Theo Ellsworth
Get Over It! by Corinne Mucha
Memory Palaces by Edie Fake
Angie Bongiolatti by Mike Dawson
Iron Bound by Brendan Leach
Sequential Vacation #2 by Sar Shahar
Capacity #8 by Theo Ellsworth
Eschew #3 by Robert Sergel
Wayward Girls #2 by Michiel Budel
The Understanding Monster Book One by Theo Ellsworth
Weather by Gabby Schulz
Wayward Girls #1 by Michiel Budel
Only Skin by Sean Ford
Curio Cabinet #5 by John Brodowski
Songs of the Abyss by Eamon Espey
Troop 142 by Mike Dawson
2012 by Samuel C. Gaskin
I Will Bite You! by Joseph Lambert
Gaylord Phoenix by Edie Fake
Curio Cabinet by John Brodowski
Sleeper Car by Theo Ellsworth
Monsters by Ken Dahl
PS Comics by Minty Lewis
Capacity by Theo Ellsworth
Wormdye by Eamon Espey
Fatal Faux-Pas by Samuel C. Gaskin

Deepest thanks to Leon Avelino.

PURGATORY ROAD:
MARK SAVAGE LEADS GENRE FANS DOWN THE PATH TOWARDS EXPLOITATION SALVATION

By John Harrison

After the offbeat modern noir of **STRESSED TO KILL** *(2016/USA, see* Weng's Chop #9, p. 185), Melbourne (Australia)-born filmmaker Mark Savage makes a memorable return to pure exploitation and delivers his best film yet in **PURGATORY ROAD** *(2017). A baroque and gothic southern nightmare, it is by turn wickedly confronting, shockingly violent and—at times—surprisingly moving. As suggested by the names listed at the end of the closing credits,* **PURGATORY ROAD** *pays affectionate homage to some of the filmmakers who clearly influenced Savage in both his appreciation of the art form and the development of his own craft—names like Mario Bava, Pete Walker, Tobe Hooper, Herschell Gordon Lewis, and a number of Japanese directors such as Kaneto Shindo and Kōyū Ohara. And yet it also remains a wholly original piece of cinema in its own right.*

Filmed on location in Mississpi, **PURGATORY ROAD** examines the strong but strange bond between two young brothers, preacher Father Vincent (Gary Cairns) and Michael (Luke Albright), who travel the murky backroads in their grotty, graffiti-covered van with a built-in confessional, delivering sermons, saving souls and taking the odd sinner's life. An opening flashback sequence reveals the boys' father to be a writer of sleazy porn paperbacks with titles like *Pig-Tailed Perverts* and *Trench Sluts* (the nostalgically lurid custom cover art for one of the books cleverly brandishes it as "A Marque de Savage Publication"). When his life's savings are stolen from him by a mysterious woman one evening, father gets his revenge but then puts a shotgun barrel under his chin and pulls the trigger in front of young Vincent, clearly causing the poor kid severe psychological damage and setting him off on a path of redemption and revenge as he obsesses with replacing the money stolen from his father all those years ago, and releasing his anger and guilt by using his mobile confessional to brutally slay any woman who seems beyond saving.

As Michael develops a close relationship with a sweet young waitress (nicely played by Sylvia Grace Crim) and becomes increasingly concerned about his brother and the crimes he is helping to cover up, a young woman in the shape of Mary Francis (Trista Robinson) comes cycling into their lives. With a sly cheeky smile and a demeanour that is sexy and savage with a touch of childlike innocence and curiosity, Mary Francis proves to be the catalyst between the two brothers, and the wedge that finally drives them apart, but not without an explosion of violence and tragedy that culminates in the film taking an unexpected but enjoyably lurid turn during the final act, as it ventures into the kind of Euro-horror territory that directors like Lucio Fulci and Joe D'Amato excelled at.

Bolstered by fine performances, beautiful photography and a wonderfully evocative musical score, not to mention the stunning and often stark southern locations, **PURGATORY ROAD** should cleanse the soul and restore the faith of anyone looking for a new cult favourite to admire and explore. I recently had a chance to catch-up with director/co-writer Mark Savage and female lead Trista Robinson to ask them a few questions about their work on the film.

INTERVIEW WITH MARK SAVAGE

When did the idea for PURGATORY ROAD *first come to you, and what was the genesis of the story?*

I've always loved the idea of circus caravans, enclosed worlds that can be mobile. That probably began with films like **FREAKS** [1932]. Since I was a kid, these caravans of vice and dark secrets have stayed with me.

But **PURGATORY ROAD** was born when co-writer Tom Parnell and myself took a California road trip to Mendocino, a Northern California town that is the setting of the film **DEAD AND BURIED** [1981]. As we drove along the spectacular Highway 1 through Big Sur, our conversation took us to imagining a priest and his brother driving these roads as they took confession from sinners.

At the time, Northern California became the setting of the movie, but as the script developed through about fifteen drafts, the South became the natural home of the story. In fact, the story would not be believable in California. In the South, it *is* believable, and when we were driving the confessional van to locations during the shoot, people would often ask us if the priest is currently hearing confessions.

The concept of a priest who kills sinners was first seeded in my head after I heard the plot of Peter Walker's **HOUSE OF MORTAL SIN** [a.k.a. **THE CONFESSIONAL**, 1976] when I was a kid. I grew up Catholic and not entirely convinced, so the concept of a killer priest was a notion I relished.

You thank a lot of filmmakers during the end credits of PURGATORY ROAD, *and while the film as a whole is certainly unique, you can also spot some cool and clever homage within the film to those directors. It seems like the film itself is almost like a thank you to all the directors who have inspired you over the years?*

Every creative person's work is a synthesis of artistic influences and life experiences. The spirit of independent filmmaking, for me, was always embodied by the late George Romero. The idea of our villain, in **PURGATORY ROAD**, discussing her psychotic life on the radio was inspired by Romero's **MARTIN** [1978]. In that film, this trick was such a wonderful way of conveying another side of the ambivalent vampire character played by John Amplas. Beyond **MARTIN**, other influences were Augustin Villaronga's **IN A GLASS CAGE** [*Tras el cristal*, 1986], a film I admire very much, and numerous Roman Porno films, especially those of directors Yasharu Hasebe and Koyu Ohara. The lighting style was more influenced by European films than American ones.

Another thing I love about PURGATORY ROAD *is the nods to the vintage smut and sleaze paperbacks. Again, it's nothing intrusive or forced, but it forms its own nice little thread within the movie while also appealing to those people who, like myself, have a genuine love for and interest in this form of publishing.*

I collect porno paperbacks of the '70s and '80s: that was their heyday. Although the writing varied in quality, the covers were always incredible and luridly evocative, even when the art was crude or very simple.

I couldn't resist making the father a porno writer because porno writers get so little respect. I've known people who survived writing these porn novels, so I appreciate just how difficult it was back in those days to keep producing. Writing is a tough life, anyway, so pitching the boys' father as a porno writer was an opportunity to give these forgotten soldiers of the written word a little respect.

The covers themselves were painted by an artist named Chris Schaar. I put out a call on Facebook for artists who may understand the porno novel art style. Chris got it very quickly, and contributed three covers based on descriptions and titles I gave him.

You've often expressed to myself and others the importance of casting, and that has been no more evident than in the people you assembled for both PURGATORY ROAD *and* STRESSED TO KILL, *which I think contain your strongest casts and performances to date. In* PURGATORY ROAD, *what*

really impressed me was the way the three leads—and several of the supporting characters—really immerse themselves in their roles and interact so well with each other and bring some genuine weight to their roles. How did you go about assembling the cast for this movie?

I cast the three leads myself. I'd worked with Trista [Robinson] on a creepy oddball web series, *Feels like Forever*, and determined to work with her again one day when the right role came up. She's incredibly talented, and possesses a professionalism that is rare. I did look at some other actresses, too, but few came close to matching her skills and presence.

I met Gary [Cairns] when I helped a fellow director out with a making-of for his film **MALIGNANT** (2013). Gary was the lead in that. We clicked immediately over our sense of humor, so a fast friendship began. Then Gary suggested Luke Albright for the "Michael" character.

I was very happy with this trio, and they added so much to their characters via the preparation process and on the set. If casting is not spot-on, you're screwed.

The rest of the cast came out of a professional relationship with casting director Matthew Morgan. He worked closely with us in Mississippi to provide multiple options for every character in the script. He was a true collaborator.

How did you find filming down in Mississippi? The place seems to have such a strong and unique ambience, it's almost like another character in the film.

Line Producer Chris Smernes, Exec Producer/co-writer Tom Parnell and I fell in love with Mississippi once we started scouting locations. Initially, we were approached by a contingent from the state itself. The state definitely became a character in the film. It truly exudes a unique personality. From the rich landscape to the unique architecture, it naturally frames the story and adds a layer of history and strange texture that was perfect for the subject matter.

What are the plans for the distribution and eventual release date of PURGATORY ROAD?

The film will do a festival run before we push for a limited theatrical run. Then onto smaller screens via VOD, S-VOD, DVD, Blu-ray, and a plethora of digital options. Because of VOD, such films can enjoy an almost continuous run these days, but that also comes with a continuous commitment to marketing.

You seem to be keeping pretty busy these days, which is always great to see. What are your plans after PURGATORY ROAD?

In the last year, we've been setting up a structure to develop and produce quite an eclectic slate of movies which also include several true (but almost unbelievable) stories that are deep into research and treatment stage. The first of these will most probably shoot in the latter part of 2018. But prior to that, we'll go into production on the next movie within the next six to nine months, pending availability of cast. It's quite an exciting time, yet also a difficult time for the business with larger-scale movie production and exhibition stumbling financially. Ironically, these stumbles are allowing for the opening of new doors and new ways to make things work that challenge a pretty tired old status quo.

I'm optimistic, and enjoying the broadening of options.

I believe some of the post-production on PURGATORY ROAD was done in Melbourne, Australia. Do you anticipate ever shooting another feature back in your home city?

Yes, the film's 4K conform, colour grading, and CGI were all done in Melbourne by the extremely talented Kelly Sheeran (he also did **STRESSED TO KILL**), and this relationship will continue. When you've been active for as long as I have, you develop a handful of very special relationships with talented people you know you can trust to deliver the quality that's essential in time frames that are often tough.

I'd love to make another film in Melbourne, and am currently exploring the logistics of an action/magic realism film I'd like to shoot in rural Victoria (along the coast).

Visit Mark's IMDB Page at:
http://www.imdb.com/name/nm0767339

Above: One of the lurid "vintage" pulp covers created for **PURGATORY ROAD** by artist Chris Schaar.

INTERVIEW WITH TRISTA ROBINSON

While New York-born actress Trista Robinson has already established an interesting and varied filmography, she has gained a growing reputation and burgeoning cult following thanks primarily to her work on horror films like **THE HUMAN RACE** *(2013) and* **SILENT RETREAT** *(2016). Coming up, she will be starring in Brian Avenet-Bradley's recently-completed supernatural mystery thriller* **ECHOES OF FEAR**.

In **PURGATORY ROAD**, *Robinson delivers a galvanising lead performance as Mary Francis, a highly disturbed young woman who enters the lives of two troubled brothers and shatters the already taut relationship between then. Bringing an electrifying mix of both sexuality and psychosis to Mary Francis, and being able to deliver a strong sense of character through her eyes and intriguing body language, Trista's presence is one of the primary reasons why* **PURGATORY ROAD** *works so well and effects the viewer so deeply.*

Tell us a little about your background, and how you became drawn towards acting.

I have had an interest in acting since middle school. My first play was *The Wizard of Oz*. I was a munchkin and a flying monkey. In my mind, as a monkey I would soar across the stage. In reality I ran around in circles in brown sweatpants. I have an aunt who is an actor. She does theatre in Pittsburgh and was valuable in my development as an actor. I lived and worked with her during my last year of high school.

What attracted you to PURGATORY ROAD? *What was your initial reaction when Mark first pitched the project and you read the screenplay?*

Trista Robinson as the disturbed and dangerous Mary Francis

I was attracted to **PURGATORY ROAD** because it is very well written, unique and unpredictable. Also, although I loved Mary Francis, I couldn't quite figure her out. She is such an enigma and it took a lot of work to figure out her arc since she is so visceral and strong throughout the script. I was excited to work with Mark on this. I loved the script and character right away.

How did you prepare to play such a challenging role as Mary Francis? Did you reference any characters from either fiction or fact when developing her? She is a pretty interesting and multi-layered character; I sense a Manson girl vibe about her at times.

I prepared for the film by retreating with the script. I hid away for a little while to cram and figure her out. Her arc was so tricky to me. She was such a badass, almost mythical character. I needed to find out what made her human. Who did she love? What changes was she going through? What were her fears? When we were shooting in Mississippi, we had very extreme weather. Tornadoes! (Whoa, is this a *Wizard of Oz* full circle moment?) I had to hunker down in my hotel room for several days and I took advantage by watching documentaries about female killers. This extra time and research affected my choices on set. It helped solidify what I suspected was important. The humanity I had been searching for.

It is funny that you mention a Manson girl vibe. That was not intentional, but in one scene, while watching the film I did pick up on that myself. Although, in that scene Mary is playing a role herself. She plays many roles.

How did you find Mark Savage to work with as a director? Did he allow you to improvise and develop your character in tandem with him, or is he someone who already has a pretty clear and set image in his head of what he wants?

Mark and I get on quite well. We have similar sensibilities and communicate easily. We are often luckily just naturally on the same page. He trusts his actors and allows for a lot of freedom, so I feel comfortable and fulfilled. He is open to ideas so I run things by him and don't ever feel intimidated or stifled. He also explains his direction so I find that educational.

One thing Mark pays particular attention to with his movies is the casting, and in PURGATORY ROAD *he has assembled a particularly strong line-up of performers; there seems to be a real sense of natural chemistry between Gary Cairns, Luke Albright and yourself that really bind you all together and make the film that much more effective and engrossing to watch.*

Thank you so much! I don't know if there is a question there, but this compliment made me really happy.

What was it like filming down in Mississippi? It always seems like one of those locations that au-

tomatically adds an air of atmosphere and authenticity, a look and feel that you can't fake.

Mississippi was a wild adventure. It is hard to explain. I mentioned the extreme weather…I mean, it was extreme! I had never seen anything like it! Lightning storms all night and weather sirens going off and rain and wind battering my hotel window. It was dramatic and exciting. The people were sweet, with the loveliest accents and the town was quaint and the food was yummy! I would have explored more if the weather had been different.

Tell us about your own taste in cinema. What genres do you like and what ae some of your favourite films and individual performances?

I have a soft spot for indie horror since it is what the bulk of my work is and I know the passion and work that goes into it. I also favor obscure documentaries. I would be remiss if I did not mention **THE WIZARD OF OZ** (1939) as one of my favorite films, since it is the theme of this interview. I constantly rotate my favorite films, but some great contemporary horror flicks are **THE BABADOOK** (2014), **HUSH** (2016), **DON'T BREATHE** (2016), **THE INVITATION** (2015)[1], **GET OUT** (2017)…I mean, there are so many! Those films are chock full of memorable, brilliant performances!

You co-produced the 2016 TV movie MELONIE'S GAMBIT, which you also starred in. Is producing/directing something you would like to do more of in the future?

I sort of fell into producing that project by necessity. The writer/director is a friend and it was a low-budget shoot and we just needed to get stuff done. Often on indie shoots, where I am friends with the filmmaker, I wind up doing more than acting. Indie filmmaking is hard and I work with my friends to accomplish the best possible outcome. It was kind of him to give me a producer credit. I didn't ask for one. I just did what needed to be done for our project.

Visit Trista's IMDB page for a full list of her credits: *www.imdb.com/name/nm3199188*

---

1 See review in *Weng's Chop* #10, p. 238.

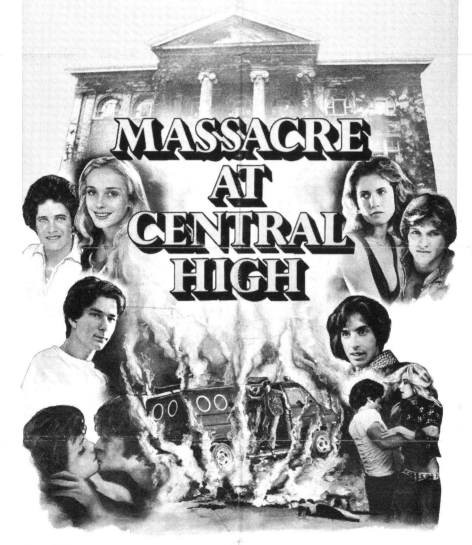

Original theatrical poster

MASSACRE AT CENTRAL HIGH

VENGEANCE AND VIOLENCE AMONGST THE CLASSROOM CLIQUES OF 1970s AMERICA

by John Harrison

*Conceived by producers Harold Sobel and Bill Lange as little more than a cheap exploitation film that would hopefully pack in the grindhouses and drive-ins for a couple of weeks before being relegated to the bottom of a triple-bill, Rene Daalder's **MASSACRE AT CENTRAL HIGH** (1976) ultimately proved to be a disappointment at the box office during its initial run. Reviews were also ho-hum, and in the days before the mass-marketing of home video cassettes, the movie looked destined to spend its life rotting away in some forgotten film vault, before a chance screening in 1980 at the Thalia Cinema in New York caught the attention of New York Times reviewer Vincent Canby, whose subsequent write-up was so glowing the film suddenly found itself in demand by repertory and arthouse cinemas—as well as college campuses—across America.*

After being teased by an exciting television trailer for the film (it was rated R in Australia—restricted to adults over the age of 18—and I was only 12 at the time), my interest in **MASSACRE AT CENTRAL HIGH** was rekindled by Danny Peary's interesting essay on the film in the second volume of his *Cult Movies* series (Dell Publishing 1983), and I finally caught up with the movie via its local Australian VHS release on the Merlin Video label. To my surprise, I found the film more than lived up to its reputation as well as my own expectations, and it has since developed a niche amongst my favorite and most interesting American low-budget exploitation films from the 1970s.

Set within a denim and t-shirt teenage world seemingly free from adult interference (although more than half of the action takes place within the walls of the titular high school, no teachers or "grown-ups" appear in the film until the final sequence, and even then they exert no discernable influence), **MASSACRE AT CENTRAL HIGH** takes as its basis the familiar theme of the new kid at school and his struggle to be accepted without having to change the person he is. David (Derrel Maury) arrives for his first day at Central High in California and instantly catches wind of the stifling atmosphere inflicted by ruling rich-kid bullies Bruce (Roy Underwood), Craig (Steve Bond) and Paul (Damon Douglas). Unfortunately, David's childhood friend Mark (the prolific Andrew Stevens, son of Stella and writer/producer/director and/or star of seedy direct-to-video low-budget exploitationers like **NIGHT EYES** [1990], POINT **OF SEDUCTION: BODY CHEMISTRY III** [1994], **ILLICIT DREAMS** [1994], **VICTIM OF DESIRE** [1995], etc) is also part of this dominating clique, and David's refusal to either join them or give into their ways immediately causes tensions between the two.

After David sinks a few mean right hooks into Bruce, Craig and Paul for attempting to rape two pretty students ('70s cult fave Cheryl "Rainbeux" Smith and future **EIGHT IS ENOUGH** star Lani O'Grady—both now sadly deceased), the trio retaliate by crushing his leg under the wheel of a car which he is servicing in his garage. But rather than forcing him into line, this merely tips the brooding (and now limping) David right over the edge, as he sets off on his path of revenge by planning spectacular deaths for those who crippled him. Bruce plunges to his doom—and gets fried to a crisp by

a power line, to boot—when David snips a wire on his hang glider. Craig takes a nighttime dive from the high board into the school's swimming pool, only realizing too late that it has been drained of water, while Paul is trapped in the back of his van and rolled backwards down a treacherous coastal mountain road. But rather than liberate the school, the death of the three bullies only allows those who had previously been repressed and beat-upon to come out and try to assert their own dominance, and David decides that mass slaughter is the only way to get through to these people.

Featuring elements and themes which would later show up in films like **CLASS OF 1984** (1982) and **HEATHERS** (1990), what helps set **MASSACRE AT CENTRAL HIGH** apart from the standard exploitation fare is the assured direction and intelligent, thoughtful screenplay by Rene Daalder.[1] The Dutch-born Daalder, whose foreign upbringing no doubt helped him to form a unique insight into his interpretation of the American teen, came from a musical background and went on to have a sporadic but diverse film career which included orchestrating the famous "mass shooting" sequence perpetrated by Sid Vicious while performing "My Way" in **THE GREAT ROCK 'N' ROLL SWINDLE** (1980) and working as visual effects consultant for the Michael Apted thriller **BLINK** (1994). He also spent some time as a protégé of notorious sexploitation filmmaker Russ Meyer, making his career a rather interesting one indeed. Daalder's screenplay for **MASSACRE AT CENTRAL HIGH** makes a lot of observations about the sociology of high school hierarchy, of the pressures to conform and fit in, and the ability of the few to wield power, fear and persuasion over the many. The ruling bullies think nothing of raping two female students in an empty classroom in the middle of the day, and have their own table (complete with fruit platter!) reserved for them in the school's outdoor eating area. And despite all the murder and mayhem happening around the school and to its students, there seems to be no investigation into it all, and no police presence. The lack of adult characters in the film can be viewed as a comment on the ignorance and ineffectiveness of authority figures in situations like this. When you are a part of that world of the high school student, you are often left to deal with its associated problems on your own (and most likely, at that rebellious age you are not likely to seek adult interference even if it is available, preferring to show your burgeoning independence and deal with things on your own terms). And on a much more somber note, the rise in tragic school mass-shootings which followed in the wake of the incident at Columbine in 1999, has given **MASSACRE AT CENTRAL HIGH** something of a prophetic and much more sobering tone over the ensuing years.

Also appealing are the performances from most of the central cast, in particular Derrel Maury (a familiar face on 'Seventies TV shows like *Happy Days* and *Emergency*), and Kimberly Beck, who creates a strong impression as Mark's girlfriend Teresa (who doesn't think twice about stripping off to take a late-night skinny dip in the ocean with David). As a child and young teen, Beck appeared in episodes of *The Munsters*, *I Dream of Jeannie*, *Land of the Giants*, *The Brady Bunch* and others. Exploitation fans remember her best for her performance opposite Linda Blair in the fun disco schlock of **ROLLER BOOGIE** (1980), and as the surviving female lead in **FRIDAY THE 13TH: THE FINAL CHAPTER** (1984).[2] Other cast members of note include Rex Sikes as Rodney (see interview) and Robert Carradine (youngest of the famous Carradine clan) as Spoony, the lanky stoner who ends up flattened by an avalanche of dynamited rocks while enjoying an orgy in the great outdoors with Rainbeaux Smith and Lani O'Grady!

Although some of the dialogue appears a little forced and clunky, Daalder at least refrains from overdosing on 'Seventies slang expressions. He also fills the film with a number of exciting set pieces (in particular, the various creative deaths), all of which are well-captured in a grimy low-key way by

---

[1] The onscreen credits as well as all the publicity material for **MASSACRE AT CENTRAL HIGH** spell Daalder's first name as Renee, no doubt helping fuel some early speculation that the director was a female. Credits on all of his other projects spell his name as the more traditional Rene, which is how I have referred to him in this article.

[2] See our coverage of the entire *F13* franchise in issue #10, p. 71.

cinematographer Burt van Munster (who would go on to find fame and considerable fortune as the producer of the groundbreaking and highly influential reality TV series *Cops*). The hang-gliding sequence is particularly well-shot and effectively dizzying (I imagine it would be even more so on a big screen).

Also worth mentioning is the soundtrack score by Tommy Leonetti, which is highlighted by the sappy TV movie-esque ballad "Crossroads" that plays over the film's opening credits and was released as a 7" vinyl single on the RCA Victor label. The New Jersey-born Leonetti, who was the stepfather of the film's female lead Kimberly Beck, established himself as something of a media personality in Australia during the late 1960s and early '70s. He hosted his own late-night television variety show in Sydney called *The Tommy Leonetti Show*, which ran between 1969-70, and his song "My City of Sydney" was used as the nightly sign-off music for channel ATN7 until well into the 1980s. Leonetti passed away of cancer in 1979 at only 50 years of age. According to an online interview with Derrel Maury (for *The Terror Trap* website), Rene Daalder was originally planning to compose the soundtrack for the film himself, utilizing his background as a musician and record producer, and had even composed a song called "David's Theme" for it, which was a lot more eerie and somber than what they eventually used. The film's producers, however, nixed the idea in favor of

Despite initial failure at the box office, **MASSACRE AT CENTRAL HIGH** soon caught a second wind and has held a strong cult following, due not only to its exploitation appeal as a revenge film, but also its relatable characters.

bringing in Leonetti, and Daalder was reportedly so upset by the decision he refused to watch the movie in its entirety for many years.

While it has surfaced occasionally on VHS throughout the years, and has been released as a bare bones DVD in some countries (utilizing a worn and dull print), **MASSACRE AT CENTRAL HIGH** has sadly so far failed to appear on Blu-ray or on any kind of decent DVD release. Synapse did announce a forthcoming Blu-ray back in 2015, and even posted some screen grabs to illustrate the restoration job they are doing on it, but as of October 2017 no further news or release date has been announced. Hopefully, it won't be too long before **MASSACRE AT CENTRAL HIGH** receives the deluxe hi-def special edition treatment, as it's a film which deserves some attention and to find a wider niche amongst fans of provocative exploitation cinema.

As an interesting aside, **MASSACRE AT CENTRAL HIGH** was also released in a re-edited version, under the amusing but highly misleading title of **SEXY JEANS**! The only addition which the crazy lusty Italians made to their print was the insertion of some near-hardcore XXX footage, which is spliced into the film whenever a sex scene takes place in the original print. The fact that they are inserts is made quite obvious, as the faces of the characters are never shown during these more explicit moments, and the naked bodies on display seem to be just a little too old and hairy to be high school students! The film has also been screened in the UK under the title **BLACKBOARD MASSACRE**.

Interview with Rex Sikes

(Rex Sikes plays Rodney, one of the main bullied high-schoolers in **MASSACRE AT CENTRAL HIGH**.)

Tell us a little bit about your background and upbringing—where were you born and raised? What initially drew you to acting?

I was born in the Midwest and moved to Los Angeles first chance I got. My parents put me in dancing and acrobatic classes as a three-year-old, acting classes by four or five and I loved performing. I made movies with friends as early teenagers. I travelled and performed as a "mind-reader" from about the age of 8. Around 18 or 19 I joined the Screen Actors Guild after some years working non-union features. I think I was drawn to acting because I so loved early movies and I glamorized the show business of the '30s and '40s. Loved the mavericks of the '50s like Dean, Brando and Clift, and was in love with the idea of being a film star. I liked the craft, I liked the movies, and I like the idea of Hollywood glamour. I think mostly I figured I would get more girls as an actor—only I learned I should have been a rock star instead. Even the dingy bar bands seemed to meet more girls than actors ever did, especially in Hollywood where everyone is an "actor". I hope this is honest enough. I believed I would get benefits I wouldn't in any other way by being in the film business and it was a business I did love anyway.

How did the part in MASSACRE AT CENTRAL HIGH come about? Was it an open audition, or did you get recommended for the part? Was Rodney the role that you originally went for?

MASSACRE AT CENTRAL HIGH came about by an interview. My agent called one day and told me to go on audition at a director's home in the Hollywood hills for some movie. I got there and waited quite a while as the director Rene Daalder was busy with some actress. Turned out that actress was Kimberly Beck. I was lucky enough to sit with the man who was the cinematographer, Bert van Munster (later of *Cops*, *The Great Race* TV show and more), who looked over my acting portfolio. Rene eventually freed himself from his task and met me. He said,

Left: Lurid Italian poster for **MASSACCRE AT CENTRAL HIGH**, under its re-edit title **SEXY JEANS**, wherein near-hardcore footage was spliced-in to extant sex scenes

Rex Sikes (left) and Derrel Maury (right) as Rodney and David, two of the bullied teens at Central High

"Hello, talk to me." I said, "I like your view," and he again said, "Talk to me." I again gave the same reply. I think my agent told me I was going up for some tough guy part—so I acted a little brusque during the interview—a practice that was not a good one to have been utilizing. In an interview with George Lucas for **STAR WARS** (1977) I pretty much told him he was full of shit and when he got his shit together they could call me. Needless to say the call never came in. I had to learn how to be better and nicer the hard way apparently—and to not *be* the bad guy when my agent told me I might be playing a bad guy. Oh well, live and learn. Readers who might be interested in a career, listen to this advice: be charming, charismatic, engaging and save the "character stuff" for the reading. Don't live it, act it when called upon to actually act or audition.

Anyway, Bert kept telling Rene how photogenic I was and showing him different photos of mine. He was a fast ally from the start. Rene dismissed me. I drove home only to arrive about 40 minutes later to a call telling me to return to the director's home. I got there an hour or more later because it was now dinner rush hour. It was winter, I believe, because I believe it was dark. What I remember was him sending me into another room to read lines for Rodney and to come out when I was ready. I did and when ready he and I read together. I don't think I read anything else. He may have had me read more than once, I don't recall, but sometime after our couple read-throughs he looked at me and said "You have the part." I'm sure I said thanks and must have left shortly after that. For some reason I drove down into Studio City from Laurel Canyon stopped at the landmark now no longer there, Tiny Naylor's Coffee Shop, and phoned my agent to tell him the news. There were no cells phones then—we survived by plugging these strange devices mounted on walls with dimes and then eventually quarters...I think they were called "pay phones" *(laughs)*—pay phones and answering machines or answering services made up a large portion of an actor's life—getting off the freeway to call your machine or service or agent. Spending your life behind the wheel of your car or by bus getting to interviews and then stopping somewhere to call and report or check your service. I digress. I phoned my agent said, "I got the part," and he said, "We will see." Often times in Hollywood everyone says yes because they don't want to be the one who told you no (in case you become a big star), so they say yes and you only learn later that for some unforeseen reason the gig fell through. Elation for a little while and then disappointment. That is why so many, including myself, become jaded, or a nicer term to describe it is "cautiously optimistic". Anyway, at some point my agent confirmed it with me in the following weeks. Eventually we all met at offices on Sunset Blvd. for a cast and crew meeting prior to first days of shooting. Jeffrey Winner was cast on that Saturday. The rest of the cast and I that were conversing at that time felt awful for the actors. A few came in for the same role and all left without it, save one—and that was Jeff, who played Oscar.

To me, Rodney was always one of the more interesting characters in the movie. Initially, you empathize with him because he is being put down by the ruling school bullies, then you feel happy for him when David kind of takes him under his wing, befriends him and helps him fix up his car, then eventually you come to despise him when you realize that he is just as manipulative and power-crazed as all the other kids at the school. It was a good transition and you played the part really well, conveying in turns both sympathy and loathing.

I agree that I thought Rodney as one of the "picked on students" had the most interesting character and story arc. Yet, oddly enough he is one that is frequently left out of reviews. The focus of course is on what transpires between David's character and the bullies—rather than what transpires between David and the "picked on students". Looking back on the movie I do think it was cast perfectly for what it was/is. Everyone brought something and all seem right in their roles, at least to me. It was a privilege then to make this "little low-budget movie" and work with the cast and crew. It is disappointing that so many like the movie and that it has trouble in getting a new release. There are plenty of fans but for some reason the company that made it sits on it. Strange indeed. Anyway, Rodney was an interesting character and I hoped that people would

feel for him, empathize with him, and then get upset or be disappointed when he changes and thirsts for power. After all, he was such a dweeb, but an innocent dweeb at first.

Do you recall the locations you used throughout the shooting of the film? How long did you work on the production?

The production was either four or five weeks (I am sure at least under six weeks), and I worked either three or four. Don't actually remember. I can't even remember the first day of shooting or the last. I just have memory snippets of pieced-together moments though I am very clear about when I got my nose broken during rehearsal, prior to shooting the scene poolside where I describe how I found the body in the empty pool. But other than a few set moments and a few dinners after the day's shoot ended my memory is not that clear. We shot at a variety of places. We shot at the beach of course, Mulholland Drive atop Hollywood for much of the roadway shots. Griffith Park provided the parking lot and school grounds and some driving scenes. An abandoned Catholic High School we used for some interiors—the food fight outside I believe, Rodney's car getting trashed by the bullies, Hollywood High School provided the library and a Jewish Community Center provided the pool. There was the garage somewhere and I think that was it.

What was life like on the set? Were you still studying at that point in your life? MASSACRE AT CENTRAL HIGH had such a strong ensemble cast of young actors. What cast-mates did you feel most connected to?

I think life on the set was fine. Everyone seemed to get along as I recall. We worked together. I made many friends, sadly many whom I have lost touch with, and some whom I remain in touch with. I still speak with Derrell Maury (David) and with Tom Logan (Harvey) and Andrew Stevens (Mark) and Kimberly Beck (Theresa). I would love to say hello to Robert Carradine and Steve Bond and Jeffrey Winner and Dennis Kort, because it has been to long without at least a hello. I saw Damon Douglas shortly before he died and I was shocked to discover he had when I called his home to speak with him nearly two years later. Sad, very sad. Ray Underwood died and I found out years later from a fan of the film. I had briefly reconnected with Lani O'Grady shortly before she died and was saddened to learn about Rainbeaux (Cheryl) passing well after the event. I have reconnected with Rene, would like to connect with Bert again and others from the crew I have not seen or spoken to in so long. I think for that short while, we became a little family, and some of those connections remained. That frequently happens on film shoots because if you are involved in a significant way as cast or crew you work intently with others for a period of time—you go out, blow off steam together, gripe or praise together. Must be tough to be on a TV series for a number of years and then one day not have to show up and everyone goes elsewhere to different separate projects. Anyway, life on set was good as I recall and we all hung out quite a bit during the shoot at least.

I was probably closet long-term to Tom Logan. We did quite a bit together after we finished **MASSACRE**. And I would see the others around. I enjoyed spending time with Rainbeaux. I would see Kimberly on shoots at Universal, Lani went on to *Eight Is Enough* and I would see her there. Derrel I saw some, Damon and Andrew…Bobby and I spoke or saw each other at times. Again, we all kind of drifted but they were all good people (and are still good people) and important in my life to me. I like speaking with Rene these days and wish we could again work together, I think that would be an incredible amount of fun. We got together at his home within the last year or two and he has gone on and done some incredible things. What I have learned in retrospect is keep your friends and associates close. I have lost and forgotten more people in my life than I remember. In some cases I have reconnected but in many cases we have moved on, you know, having families changes everything too. And people move from L.A. I am fortunate to have reconnected with another director friend, Robert M. Carroll, who directed **SONNY BOY** (1989) after many years. We did a film called *Pale Horse, Pale Rider* (1980) with Charlene Tilton that his wife Dalene Young wrote from the short story. The girl who doubled for Charlene I have lost contact with—her boyfriend at the time was Darwin Joston, who starred in **ASSAULT ON PRECINCT 13** (1976) as Wilson. In some ways the longer you are in this business the more opportunity to reconnect with others you might have met or known along the way, because as big of an industry as it is, it is also a small pond. It is a very strange or odd kind of thing I can not quite explain myself.

What was your opinion of the finished film, both at the time of its release and in retrospect?

Well at the time I was hoping for a "**REBEL WITHOUT A CAUSE** reception". I think I truly hoped it would be far better-received than it was and that it would have had an impressive run. I don't think any of those hopes were based in reality, just wishes for being in a hot property. You know if it makes a splash, producers, directors, casting directors and all the rest may see it and you can get known from it. But if not, you are constantly re-selling yourself, which you do have to do anyway even if the film comes out big. But show biz really is a lot about visibility. You raise the ladder, the more visible you are and become. That is why if you do an IMDb search for most "stars" they have quite a film or TV history prior to the public knowing who they are as a talent, but they may get known inside the industry. Some people have done scores of TV pilots that never sell, like George Clooney, and/or even series, before the public gets to know who they are. So yes I was hoping it would come out big. And I am surprised by the fans and the loyalty to our little movie through the years, especially since it disappeared thanks to how the producers manage it. Yet people like it and it used to play on cable all of the time.

There are things I enjoy and things I cringe about watching it then and now. They had a showing in L.A. I had hoped to make this past year; I couldn't go at the last minute but Derrell did and he said it was well-received by the audience. Of course they were probably fans who hadn't seen it in years so… who actually knows. I do think it speaks to the kind of mentality of high schoolers—we all think we are so grown up and so cool at a relatively early age and only as we grow older do we sometimes, if we are lucky, realize we aren't so cool and we don't know as much as we thought we did. I think Rene struck gold when he scripted the dialogue for his characters. As kids we try to act tough and cool and I think the dialogue now shows that off brilliantly, but it is a subtle point for most film-goers of that genre. I am not certain they look at it as such and may think of it as merely schlock—which it is—but that is too-often how we behave, making ourselves more important that we are, the mini Gestapo running the school yard, the nerds, etc. So I think he was spot-on whether by design or by accident. And the subtle social messages conveyed in all of it stand out now after having lived longer than when I was young and making it. At the time I think we thought it was about a number of deaths at a high school, not how the peons will struggle to rise to power when their oppressors are removed.

But that too is part of **MASSACRE AT CENTRAL HIGH**'s charm. You can find messages and meaning in this little low-budget exploitation film. Given with what happened in film with the rise of the slasher film and graphic violence, I am a little surprised that new viewers don't find it disappointingly un-violent. In retrospect I think it should be viewed more today—especially since people say it predicted punk and foreshadowed things like Columbine, because people should really see the futility of violence. David's demise is because he cared about someone. His twisted form of justice is what the wackos who do such disgusting and inane things think will bring about change. It doesn't—it just hurts people, devastates people horribly and then life goes on. David is twisted, stating, "Since I couldn't bring them back I had to do in the others," or whatever the words were, but in the end he decides someone is worth saving…hell, everyone is worth saving. So people should probably watch it today (as other than an exploitation film or allegory to power abuse) as what a waste of time it is to be violent. People should find more constructive ways to make changes in their world. Right, but then I am being optimistic and **MASSACRE AT CENTRAL HIGH** was just a movie after all. Entertainment is what it is all about and selling tickets and products and making money. Had **MASSACRE AT CENTRAL HIGH** made a *fortune* it would have had a bigger shelf life. Still, it is interesting to see the acclaim it got from critics including Roger Ebert. I have been lucky enough to appear in films that get yanked because of the changing political climate. I have been in a few that you may never see because they are not and have not been politically correct to show these days. Hopefully, nothing like what happens in **HOSTEL** (2005) will ever actually happen in a hostel. It is only entertainment—but because sickos exist we fear (sometimes realistically) that they may copy things they see or read, and the fact is they often do. But this is a *big* discussion about the responsibility of the creator of art and commercial product…so I have to let the readers and viewers address these issues for themselves. It is complicated. I can't let my children watch a lot of the films I am doing these days because they are violent or gory. I wouldn't let them because sadly they will encounter those elements soon enough growing up, through media. And hopefully the viewers will only use it as horror movie escapism and not as a model for how to behave in their future.

Rex Sikes today

Writer/director Rene Daalder is something of an enigma, and his output, at least in feature film terms, has been sporadic at best. What kind of a director was he to work with?

Working with Rene was fine. It was fun…frustrating at times, but I think that is true of working with any director. You have to place yourself in their hands—it is their visual vision of a work they are creating and you and they may not agree. And as an actor you need to realize your place in the production—what you are hired to do. Too often I think we get a role and we think it is all about "me" when it is truly all about the production. Depending on frames of mind, people can have quite a lot of disputes. As for Rene I think we got along well. There were moments we disagreed, but we never argued over anything. Others may or may not have had that experience with him but I cannot say. As stated I would be happy to work with him again after all these years if there was something we could both work on together.

While it seemed to do reasonably well at the drive-ins and grindhouse cinemas upon its initial release, the film seemed to disappear for a few years, before home video and a write-up in Danny Peary's Cult Movies Volume 2 *led to a reappraisal of the film. When did you first discover that the movie had developed something of a cult following?*

I was told by video store owners right after its video release sometime in the '80s I guess that it had become a top-rented video, so I knew early on that it had a life, plus it was always on HBO, Cinemax, TBS, TNT, and USA for quite some time. Then it vanished, and some claim the Columbine tragedy for that, but I think it has something else to do with the producers and I am not sure what. That is only my opinion and have nothing to base it on other than people seem to be clamoring in whatever small way for it, and if it could make money you would think they would be making money from it, so why aren't they? But since that time—it has been more recent—within the past five years or so that people such as me to do interviews or write to me about it, and I became aware of the cult following. It is nice to be a part of something people enjoy and want more of. Wish someone could give it to them.

The same year you made MASSACRE AT CENTRAL HIGH, *you also appeared in Larry Buchanan's strange Marilyn Monroe biopic* GOODBYE, NORMA JEAN *(1976), starring Misty Rowe. Any memories of working on that film?*

Actually I think I made **GOODBYE, NORMA JEAN** in the early part of the year (January or February) of 1975. It was sometime before **MASSACRE AT CENTRAL HIGH**, although it may have come out later. I don't recall the premier if there was one…which there must have been—I don't remember parties or anything, other than Frank Curio, who was the producer's son, got me either an audition or meeting for the movie. I owe him for that and lost touch with him years ago. Misty Rowe was very nice and I used to see her afterwards at Paramount on the TV series *When Things Were Rotten*—I believe it was about Robin Hood, and she played Maid Marion. When we shot our scene she mentioned that some actor in a scene they shot previous to ours had gotten carried away and roughed her up, and she was happy that I was professional. They cut my hair (long hair was in back then), a 1940s haircut which embarrassed me to no end until it grew back. I'd go to the Rainbow Bar and Grill or the Roxie or other bars and apologize to the women I met telling them I normally had long hair. I was silly and vain, but it bothered me for a long time that I was unfashionable out on the Strip when I should have been thinking how lucky I was that I got to portray a 1940s masher guy in a movie. Live and learn, right?

Thank you for taking the time to share your memories of MASSACRE AT CENTRAL HIGH *with us.*

Thank you! I love Australia I have been there a number of times, but not in some while. And thanks to everyone I have met, stayed in contact with, and lost along this fascinating journey.

1976, USA. D: RENE DAALDER
AVAILABLE FROM CORNERSTONE MEDIA

ANIMATED ANGUISH

The Jimmy ScreamerClauz Interview

by Mark Reynolds

Jimmy ScreamerClauz began receiving attention a few years back for his ultraviolent and sexually explicit computer animated films, starting with the experimental 2008 feature **REALITY BLEED-THROUGH**. After making a handful of shorts, he was catapulted to instant notoriety with his 2012 sophomore feature, **WHERE THE DEAD GO TO DIE**, and in 2016 he released his third feature film, **WHEN BLACK BIRDS FLY**, a psychedelic dystopian creation myth and exercise in sensory overload that actually packs a surprising bit of emotion under lots and lots of crazy. Astonishingly, while most CG features are the work of dozens or even hundreds of artists, Jimmy's films are the result of a demented one-man force.

I spoke with Mr. ScreamerClauz recently about **WHEN BLACK BIRDS FLY**, as well as his work on Flying Lotus' directorial debut, **KUSO (2017)**, which recently premiered at Sundance. We also talked about "fat sandwiches" and the best hamburger I've ever eaten, but I edited that part out, so you'll just have to use your imagination there.

I have the world's creakiest office chair here, so I'll try not to move a lot.

Oh, I probably do too.

We both spend a lot of time sitting in them, I'm sure.

Oh, I spend too much time sitting in it. And then I broke the arm off it somehow, so sometimes I fall out of it if I turn too fast.

These are the physical dangers of animation. That and diabetes.

Oh, I do eat a lot of sugar. But I'm somehow not overweight. I still maintain my girlish, trim figure.

How do you swing that one?

I don't know, because I don't exercise, and I eat horribly. I'm convinced I have worms of some sort.

Better living through parasites.

There's probably several of them, because there's never just one!

I have a friend who had, I think it was a dairy allergy, and he was looking into some sort of parasite that people will willingly and experimentally put in their stomachs. They're called helminths.

So is this supposed to be a new weight loss thing or something?

No, I think it was a dairy tolerance thing.

That would be even weirder!

Fortunately his wife found the idea unappealing enough to where he didn't start eating bugs.

It's like, "I already gotta take your worm, I don't want another one!"

So how's everything going? You've been really busy recently.

Actually, I finished up doing that music video [for Butcher's Harem] and the thing for **KUSO**, so now I'm kind of not doing anything. I'm kind of just floating along.

So let's start with KUSO. How did you get involved with it?

Have you ever heard of a short filmmaker named Mike Diva? I guess his most popular thing that people would know is that he did the Japanese Trump propaganda movie.

Oh yeah—he does those crazy, '80s-style things.

Yes, and then he did one for Hillary as well. So I'm friendly with him, because I worked on one of his movies years ago, called *Thresher* [2014]. He was hanging out with Flying Lotus one day, who is the director of **KUSO**, and he was just like, "You wanna see some fucked up animated shit?" [*Laughs*] At that point Flying Lotus only had about 45 minutes of **KUSO** done, so he contacted me on Twitter, and said, "Hey, I'm doing this really crazy movie with David Firth," who is the guy who does *Salad Fingers* [2004-2013] and all that.

And he was also a voice in WHEN BLACK BIRDS FLY*.*

Exactly. So I was like, "You know, I know David Firth as well," and there were just a lot of little connections like that, so he was like, "You gotta work on my film!" And he sent me the 45 minutes he had, and it was really, really awesome. It was probably…

how do I explain it? It's probably *the* closest thing to a cult movie in this day and age that I could put my finger on. Everything *tries* to be a cult movie now, they all try to hit those points, but this is the first thing I've seen in years that I would one hundred percent consider a cult film.

So then he was planning to shoot one more 45-minute segment, because it's a series of interconnecting shorts that weave in and out of each other. They don't play out fully, so you'll see ten minutes of one and it'll weave into something else, and you'll see another ten minute chunk, and there's like four or five like that. So he invited me out to LA to be on set and help shoot that segment. So I got to see all the last half of the movie being made.

So you were involved in the actual shoot, then.

Yup. I was there and I have one little tiny cameo in it. I don't have any lines or anything; I'm just sleeping in a hospital waiting room.

I did a lot of little jobs on set, too, like I threw a fetus at Buttress's face, and I pumped cum out of some alien midgets, and I made shit one day to throw at Buttress, as well.

Just another day at the office.

Yeah. And then I did a little two-minute animated segment for it as well, and I did the sound and music and stuff for that part.

It recently premiered at Sundance, last month, so I flew out for that, and I got to hang out in the house with everybody. It was a great time.

I read about the screenings—I'm looking forward to it coming to New York so I can see it.

A breast-centric sequence from Jimmy's segment in **KUSO**

It's definitely super-gross. It's got some scary parts, but it's more of a gross-out humor kind of film. Like really over-the-top, gross-out, poop and shit and fetuses and all the nastiest stuff you can imagine. But it's also got this really high artistic value to it, almost. It's almost like watching Jodorowsky and *Adult Swim* shit mixed together. But super filthy.

I don't remember what it was that I read about it, but it wasn't the walk-outs that interested me. I'm fairly unshockable, so a lot of movies that are "shocking," if there's nothing beneath that, I just get bored.

Oh yeah, there's definitely layers beneath this, and it's got a lot really cool stuff. Like I said, it's the closest thing to a cult movie I've seen come out in years, and I think that a lot of people are gonna dig it, and a lot of people are gonna hate it, and that's exactly what makes it a cult film.

As far as the walk-outs go: I was only at the premiere, the very first screening—we were supposed to have a second one, but Sundance actually got hacked, believe it or not, and then they lost power for a whole day, so everyone's screenings got cancelled for a day—but I went to the premiere, and there weren't really any walk-outs at all. In fact, I got up from my seat to shoot Flying Lotus' intro, and when I tried to go back to my seat somebody had stolen it, and I kind of started getting in a little argument with him, so I was just kind of like, "Oh, never mind," and I ended up having to stand in the back for the whole film. So there definitely weren't any walk-outs there. But from what I hear, Sundance has these things called press screenings, where only the press is allowed to attend—not even Flying Lotus was allowed to go. And apparently all the press walked out and then reported on each other, like snitched on each other, like, "Oh, all the press is walking out on this movie, it's too intense." So that's what the articles were about—the press just ratting on each other, really. So it's funny how that stuff works, huh? [*Laughs*]

Did you write your segment, or co-write it? How did that work?

We kind of went back and forth with ideas. There's not really any dialogue in it, so there wasn't really so much a script. He would give me a general idea, and then I would do parts of it, and then he'd say what he liked about it and what he didn't like about it, and then we'd add on another segment to it, and we just kind of built it shot-by-shot.

Does it have the same kind of "look" as a lot of your own projects?

Yes, but it's not so much character-based this time. It's like more like weaving in and out of really scary tunnels. And then some DMT-tripping set-pieces, and some big set-pieces of a bunch of little things going on that you fly through. It's like one long fly-through motion kind of scene.

Should I even ask what tunnels you're flying through?

[*Laughs*] I think you can guess what tunnels they are! Let's just say that if you read any of the articles, and they talked about George Clinton's butthole being in the film…let's just leave it at that.

I was beamed up. Beamed up to the mother ship. It was a very cool experience. And I'm not usually the type to work on other people's films so much, like I never seriously got that work, but I'm really proud I got to work on that film, and I met a lot of cool people, and made a lot of new friends, so it was a very good experience overall. And I got to go to Sundance, which I know I wouldn't with one of my films. [*Laughs*] So it was nice going there, seeing how that all works.

You don't think Robert Redford would say, "Hey, get that ScreamerClauz kid!"

Well, you know, they *did* play **KUSO**, so now I feel like maybe they *would* take me, if they're willing to play *that* filth, for the love of God! And I don't know if you looked up what **KUSO** means, but it's Japanese for "shit." So that's what the title of the film means.

But it's classy, because it's in a foreign language.

Exactly! That's the joke.

I think that, as big-budget as Sundance has become, a lot of the lead features are probably more offensive than KUSO.

You know, it's really funny, because David Firth was at Sundance with me as well, with all of us, and me and him just walked around for a whole day trying to see a movie, because there was nothing really going on and it was just me and him for a little while. So we walked around for hours trying to see a movie, and we sat down in this little café, and I put the Sundance app on my phone, and we were sitting there reading the description of every film. And every film, every single goddamn film had some sort of—how do I say it—like, do-gooder tie-in. Everything was either a documentary about AIDS, or a drama about domestic abuse, or something about the rain forest, or something about recycling. There was no fucking movie, just like a movie-movie, to go see for an hour and a half. So we're sitting there, scrolling through the list, just rejecting it one by one, domestic abuse, AIDS, rain forest, blah blah blah. So then the only other thing we could do with the passes we had were to go to the panels and the Q&As, and the discussions. So we just walked into some random panel, and it's packed, people everywhere, and little couches that we could sit on and stuff. And we're sitting there and they all just start talking about the environment. And not only talking about the environment, they started showing clips from movies that pertain to the environment. So they showed like five minutes of that Pixar film, **WALL-E** [2008], and then they stopped it and were like, "You see? This is Earth! This could be earth any day now!" And somebody literally said, "We've been hanging out with Al Gore, and we've been getting all the inside info that they don't let out to the public." Me and David were just sitting there, like, "Jesus Christ."

Then we went to the music café that was across the street, and the girl was onstage singing a Jesus song, and then after the Jesus song it was like, "We have to stop the pipeline!"

So literally everything was just somebody trying to change the world, but they weren't, because they were, you know, in Utah. [*Laughs*]

A festival full of PSAs.

PSAs, but also trying to get you to buy Lamborghinis and high-luxury items. Like, consumerism at its peak, but save the rain forest at the same time.

You're living in Pennsylvania now, but you're from Brooklyn?

I was born in Brooklyn, but I moved to PA [*"pee-ay"*] when I was ten, so at this point I'm way more PA than I am New York.

Are a lot of the musicians and collaborators you work with based there, too?

No, not really. Everyone I work with is kinda scrambled all over the place.

How have you met your collaborators?

HEART STRING MARIONETTE
A Tale of a kid, a samurai mime and a stripper.

I met M dot Strange because he was having an audition to do voices in his film, **HEART STRING MARIONETTE** [2012]. At the time, all I had was *Tainted Milk* [2009], so I sent him *Tainted Milk* as my audition tape and he actually liked it a lot, and then we became friends and I did end up in **HEART STRING MARIONETTE**.

Butcher's Harem, Bushpig and Cumblood—who are in all my films and I just did a music video for them—I know them because we both did speedcore music years ago, so I've known them for like ten years just from doing that.

I guess Ruby Larocca and Victor Bonacore, Joey Smack, all those guys, they're semi-local. They all lived in Jersey, and now they're kind of spread out.

Brandon Slagle and Devanny Pinn, they were also, at the time, local East Coast actors, but now they're out in LA, so I don't see them as much, but when they come back east is usually when I record with them.

So you're doing effects for Brandon Slagle's new movie, too, CROSSBREED *(2018)?*

You know, it's funny with Brandon Slagle, because he always hires me to do effects, then I somehow never end up doing them, but then I somehow end up with credit for them still. So there's like five credits in his films that I never actually did anything for. I always say yes—I never say, like, "Fuck you, Brandon Slagle, and your films." I always say,

"Yes, my friend, I will animate anything you want for you," and then he says, "All right, man," then he gives me credit on IMDb, and it just never happens.

So do you think Vivica A. Fox, the star of CROSS-BREED, *will do a voice in your next movie?*

Who knows? Anything could happen! [*Laughs*]

So let's step back a bit. What drew you to animation? Were you an animation fan, or did you get into it because it is hard to make these kinds of movies in live action?

I grew up really into MTV and Nickelodeon animation, like the '90s stuff. That's what I grew up on. I'm 33, so in the '90s was when my exposure to most things—

Like Liquid Television—

Yeah, like *Liquid Television*, and *The Maxx*, and *The Head*, and *Cartoon Sushi*, all those shows. And on Nickelodeon I was really into *Rocko's Modern Life*, *Ren and Stimpy*, and even *Doug* and *Rugrats*, all of those early '90s Nicktoons.

But I was also super into horror films, like *really* into horror films. I lived in a small town in PA, and you ride your bike two miles, and there's a little plaza of stores. In the '90s there were two video stores in that little plaza, and they both had different shit somehow, that's just how the VHS boom was back then. So I would ride my bike there every couple of days. You'd get five movies for five dollars, for five days—it was the five-five-five deal. So I'd ride my bike there every five days and get five horror films, and just see everything I could.

I was also super-into industrial, weird, techno/electronic music. So those were the three things I grew up really into. I eventually found ways to just combine them all into one set of talents, skills.

You filmed a live-action feature at some point, right?

The very first film I tried to do, with Brandon Slagle, actually, was called **REALITY BLEED-THROUGH**, and it was kinda half-and-half. But it was only After Effects animation. I didn't know anything about 3D yet, and that was actually the film that introduced me to 3D. I tried to do one or two shots in Maya, which ended up being way too hard for me, so I scaled back to Cinema 4D for the next movie, which was *Tainted Milk*.

I kinda always wanted to do live action, but it was hard to do with no money, especially with the ideas

I had. With animation I can get people for a day or two, just to do voices, and the rest of the time will just be *me* doing it.

I sorta realized after doing **WHERE THE DEAD GO TO DIE** that nobody had ever really done an animated horror film before. If you think about it now, you can't really come up with any.

There are a few shorts I can think of, but as far as features, nothing comes to mind immediately.

They just recently did **HELL AND BACK** (2015), which is like half horror, but then it's a comedy as well, so there's no straight horror films that aren't comedy based. There's some anime stuff, but even then it falls more into the action realm with horror elements, know what I mean?

WHERE THE DEAD GO TO DIE

There's a lot of comedy in your stuff, though.

There's definitely humor in all my stuff, but there's also been darker parts and horror-ish stuff. Quirky stuff. It's not slasher film stuff, exactly, but horror stuff.

I think non-horror fans can have a limited idea of what horror is. There is so much that is scary. I think most David Lynch movies are scarier than most "horror" movies, because reality just gets bent, and that, to me, is scary. It's not just masked people running around killing other people. There are more existential scares—

Yeah, it's psychological.

Absolutely. And the jump scares in THE EXORCIST (1973) are scary, but it's primarily a sad movie, a movie about a woman losing her daughter, and that makes it so much more effective.

Definitely.

I found out about WHEN BLACK BIRDS FLY when Cartoon Brew did a write-up on this crazy animated movie made completely by one person. I watched the trailer, and at the scene where the kids are eating the fruit in Eden and the faces start changing, I said, "I gotta see this movie."

I'm glad that worked.

Absolutely. But the look is pretty punishing. It's very saturated and contrast-y, so honestly, I expected that it would take a couple of sittings to watch. I ended up watching it straight through—I was surprised at the story's depth and emotion. It took you about three years to do that?

Yeah, roughly three years. I finished **WHERE THE DEAD GO TO DIE** in September 2011, that's when I sent it in to distribution, and I spent most of 2012 just recording voices and writing the script, and that's probably all I did that year. So 2013 to the end of 2015 was when I worked on that film.

Did you storyboard it out?

I would do chunks of it. If I tried to do too much of it—like, stuff would change so much, there would be stuff I would write and then I would figure out that I couldn't really animate it right, especially by myself, so I would do some re-writing. I had to do the film in order for the most part, like I didn't stray from going out of order.

Just to keep everything straight?

Mm-hm. There would be parts I would go back to later, but I would mostly do it straight through, and I would storyboard the chunks I would be doing at the time. I kind of set myself up for a month. I would say, "I'm going to storyboard what I'm doing this month." And when I'd get to the end of that, I would start the next scene like that as well. And then there'd be a lot of times where I'd get stuck, because I wouldn't know what to do, but I couldn't move on, either, because it was so scrambled, everything was such a mess.

The stupidest way to make a movie is the way I made this film. That's why it took so long. It wasn't really the animation or the rendering. There would

WHEN BLACK BIRDS FLY

just be so many times where I'd be like, "Fuck! How do I do this?"

What sort of things? Are you talking about narrative twists, or technical how-do-I make-this-thing-happen-on-screen, or…

Well, for one thing, it was way too long. If I'd done the script the way it was written it would have been a three-and-a-half hour movie. But I was just like, "Fuck it! Let's just animate it and see what happens!" And then you get halfway through the film, and it's already two hours long, and it's like, "Fuck. Now what do I do? Do I cut stuff at the end…do I split it into two movies? How the fuck do I do this?" So I'd just have to stop and figure that out. Like, how do I cut two hours from this movie and still have it make sense?

You didn't want to do a volume one and volume two?

I almost did. There was a year where I thought that was what I was doing.

[Spoiler alert, next paragraph]

There was a year where, you know the part when the OSWA soldiers come in and kill the mother? That was going to be the end of part one for a long time. And then volume two was going to pick up from there and have a whole bunch of other stuff in it that I didn't end up doing.

There's a chunk of exposition that happens right at the end, written on the screen. Is that why?

No, that was always there. There was just a lot of stuff in between that, and the whole Caine and Evil One back story was a lot longer. There was a lot more stuff with the worm baby cave. There was more stuff in heaven, more characters that ended up getting lost that I recorded voices for. God was gonna talk at one point and have an actual voice and personality. So there was a lot of stuff that ended up changing. There was going to be a lot more of those animal people, like there was going to be a whole village of them, and they were all gonna have separate little stories.

Like I said, it was just the stupidest, backwards-est way to make a movie. It was way too freeform and way too all-over-the-place and I just had to somehow condense it down.

I like the way it came out, except for the ending—I wish I would have done the ending differently, more towards the way it was scripted, but it was just too big.

*One thing that people don't understand is that animation takes **forever**.*

Yes.

You have to have kind of a damaged personality to do it [both laugh] because it's tedious and it's boring and takes forever but when it's done it's absolutely magic. What is your workflow for doing this as a one-man-band? You're using a lot of motion capture, right?

Yeah, it's like 90% mocap and I do a lot of it on my own, and what I can't do I pull from stock elements, stuff you can buy.

So you're using a Kinect setup?

For **WHEN BLACK BIRDS FLY** I used the Kinect, but now I have the Perception Neuron motion capture suit. I didn't use that until after **BLACK BIRDS**, so the first movie I actually did with it will be this Butcher's Harem video.

Now, your short film Recluse (2016)—*was that done after* WHEN BLACK BIRDS FLY?

It was, but I was still using the Kinect.

I hadn't seen **Recluse** *until recently. It starts out pretty funny, and then takes something of a turn...*

That one I did—I was trying to get **BLACK BIRDS** into film festivals—which didn't end up working out, by the way [*laughs*]—so there was a six-month chunk where I was just sitting there waiting to hear back, so that's when I did that short. I timed it so I could release it the same week that **WHEN BLACK BIRDS FLY** came out, thinking that a lot of people would see the short and then buy the movie, but then nobody ended up seeing the short [*laughs*], so now I just have this sort of lost short just floating around that nobody's really seen.

To me it seems like WHEN BLACK BIRDS FLY *is doing pretty well—I keep seeing new articles and reviews of it.*

People seem to like it, definitely a lot more than the first one, but it's definitely not selling very well. So anybody out there, you should buy it! [*Laughs*] But it seems to be getting good reviews, and people seem to like it, and it's definitely opened some more doors for me, and I've made some friends off it. So, yeah, it's been good so far.

Have you seen a difference in how it's received between animation circles and non-animation circles? There is kind of a warts-and-all approach to it—hands sometimes go through bodies, that kind of thing—so I'm wondering if you see that animators appreciate what goes into it more and are more forgiving, or if they're actually less forgiving, or...

It's definitely the opposite. People in the animation community seem to really, really hate me. A lot. [*Laughs*] Which is fine. But then horror movie people, the horror movie crowd, seem to be more into it than the animation crowd, at least as far as I can tell. The thing about animation is that so much of it is geared towards children—like 95% of it is geared towards children—so all those people who are really into animation are really into children's films. So a lot of them don't even like horror films at all. So even if my films were animated beautifully, with Pixar quality, the fact that they're so filthy and wrong, they would still hate them. So, what's the difference, really?

But at the same time, adult animation, especially horror animation, is such an underserviced niche, it's nice to see it when it comes out there.

Like even with *Adult Swim* stuff, when they start getting really weird and fucked up, and then you go read people's reviews of them, it's the same complaints people have about my movies. Like, if you read the reviews of *Mr. Pickles*, or *King Star King*, like all those really avant-garde, violent ones, people say the same shit they say about me, except they can't attack the animation, because it's actually well-animated. [*Laughs*] So that's the thing with my stuff—the animation is an easy thing to target if you already don't like the film. People who like the film say, "Oh well, the shitty, creepy animation makes it weirder," and they kind of like that aspect of it. So, no matter what you do, somebody's gonna like it, somebody's gonna hate it, so I just don't care.

I wouldn't call it shitty—

Oh, it's shitty.

There are some warts, but there are moments that are really effective, like the girl dancing in Recluse, *or in* BLACK BIRDS *when the father is chasing the worm down the street, because the animation is so suddenly "human". Well, I guess that's actually a case for motion capture. But combined with the rough animation it's even more unnerving.*

Yup. There you go. [*Laughs*]

I also have to say, I thought some of the funniest moments of WHEN BLACK BIRDS FLY *were some of Marius' expressions, which I feel like sometimes you zoomed in, and tweaked a blend shape a little too far or something, and then left it there because it was funny.*

[*Laughs*] Yeah, that's why I did it!

I knew it all along.

Yeah, I was still using Poser characters for those movies. I've upgraded—I use iClone characters now.

I was wondering about all the modeling. What about the sets and props?

For sets I usually find stock stuff that I can alter, or I build them. I'm not a modeler—I'm not gonna lie, and I'm not gonna pretend that I am. But this is the way *I* look at it [*laughs*]—bear with me, here—it's like, all those directors from Pixar, or Dreamworks, or all those dudes who direct those big movies, none of those motherfuckers are sitting around modeling their own characters, either. They got teams of fucking intern-slaves to do that. Jimmy has no intern-slaves, so he's gotta steal stuff from other places. So fuck you. [*Laughs*]

One thing that people don't always think about with animation: if you're making a movie, and

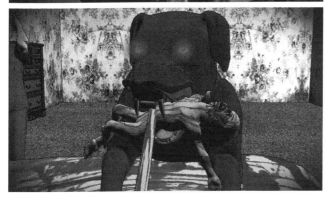

Above: Some of the completely unhinged imagery from Jimmy ScreamerClauz's equally unhinged animated feature, **WHERE THE DEAD GO TO DIE**

need a couch in your movie, you say, "Hey, Props, get me a couch," and they do.

Exactly!

In animation, 3D or otherwise, that couch does not exist. It—everything—has to be made. Plus, Pixar has teams of two or three hundred people.

Exactly. So when you're doing stuff by yourself you've gotta cut corners wherever you can.

Your team of two or three hundred people just work for iClone.

I just don't employ them. I pay them ten dollars here and there when I need a couch. Then you slap your own textures on it and say, "Look, I made my own couch, because I'm a genius." And people go, "That couch looks really good," and I'm like, "Yeah, I know. I did that shit. You like it." [*both laugh*] Then they go, "Whoa! Would you make a couch for *my* movie?" and I'm like, "All right." Just tack five bucks on there, like, "Oh yeah, I need fifteen bucks for that couch."

Are you animating on other people's projects?

I really try not to.

I know you've done voice work, and some music.

Just here and there. Like, I did the **KUSO** thing. I did that thing for Mike Diva years ago...that's probably it, honestly.

You're still doing music for other people's movies, right?

Yeah. I did the first *American Guinea Pig* movie [**BOUQUET OF GUTS AND GORE** (2014)]. I do music for Brandon Slagle here and there—he actually does end up using that stuff. And Victor Bonacore's films I've done music for.

You're still making music, then, as ScreamerClauz. You released an album not too long ago, right?

The last album I released was in 2012. I did it the same time I did **WHERE THE DEAD GO TO DIE**, 'cause when I signed the deal with Unearthed, they were like, "Hey, you should put out an album, too!" I'm like, "I don't know. Are you sure?" And then I did. And nobody bought it. So it's just sitting there in boxes somewhere.

Actually I started working on another album, but it's different. It wouldn't be under ScreamerClauz—it'll be under a different band name. It's not gonna be speedcore. It's gonna be really weird techno music. I want to make a *really* stupid techno album, like a *really* retarded one, so that's what I'm trying to do. So I've been learning how to do, like, synthwave, dubstep, and stuff, and make it really dark and dumb and retarded, and find the most fucked-up samples that I could just cram in there somehow. I'm going to get some people to just come in and do some vocals on it.

Working with animation, do you feel more free? If you had an unlimited budget and crew, would you still be wanting to make the movies you're making, just live-action?

The next one I do I'm definitely gonna make somehow partially live-action. What I'm thinking about doing is like a live-action-faces-on-3D-bodies sort of thing. So that's what I'm probably going to try for my next film. But, yeah, I would like to make live-action stuff, but never having any money or resources, doing the solo animation stuff just made sense to me.

Would it still be full of, you know, women being torn in half and victimized—

Definitely! Why would I get rid of that? [*Laughs*] If anything, if I could do that better? Hell yeah!

"And the Academy Award goes to…"

I don't do that content because of the low budget! It's just what I see when I close my eyes at night.

That accompanies the screaming babies…

Exactly. If I don't wake up in a pool of sweat and screaming, "God help me," why even bother waking up at all?

How much of the "look" of your films comes out in post-production? When you're compositing, how much of the look changes from what was rendered?

I color-correct the shit out of everything in After Effects. I don't do a whole lot of compositing, though—I try to do as much as I can in Cinema 4D. And I've actually started using Unity now, too. Like, 90% of this new Butcher's Harem video is all Unity, with a screen shot script, so it's screen shots, and in 4K.

They've gotten some really nice real-time rendering out of Unity recently, too.

I haven't figured out how to push it quite as good as their demo films yet, but I'm getting pretty good results. I can get it to look almost as good as Cinema 4D. Cinema 4D still looks a little better, but I'm *almost* there.

The only thing I really did with compositing for **WHEN BLACK BIRDS FLY** was all the psychedelic skies, and that shit really bogged me down, because I had to composite them all and I had to motion track them all, so that was kind of a pain in the ass, so I'll probably never do it that way again. That was a *huge* pain in the ass. That drug on for months, too, just sitting there, putting all those hearts and things floating in the sky.

And so many Marshall Applewhites…

There's always Marshall Applewhites everywhere.

So where did that Heaven's Gate love come from?

I was always really obsessed with that story. How old was I when that happened? I had to be, like, eleven, twelve years old, and I was super into aliens, really into that show, *Sightings*, and all my library books from school were always about UFOs and ghosts and bigfoot and shit, so I was really into that.

And that was the first time I had seen the mainstream news that my parents watched actually talk about aliens. And in the craziest, kookiest way possible. "Oh, they cut their dicks off so they could get on the spaceship." So I was always just really obsessed with that story, and then years later, when I started getting into bootleg VHS tape trading, that was one of the first things I sought out, the Marshall Applewhite recruitment tapes, which is just two hours of a camera staring straight into his crazy face, saying, "The earth is about to be recycled. But if you join us, you can blah blah blah," just ranting on and on. So it just became kind of a recurring joke for me. I just started putting it in everything, because I was so obsessed with it. Really for no reason whatsoever, other than that. I don't think there's anything he's been left out of so far. He might not be in *Affection*, actually, I can't remember right this second.

Was he in Mickey Mouse's Mystical Journey *(2016)?*

You know, he might have been left out of that one, too. Goddess Bunny was in that one, though, and the alien autopsy.

I thought that one was really funny. It's pretty recent, right?

Yeah. That was just for the **WHEN BLACK BIRDS FLY** VHS. There's two of those Disney distortions. There's one before the film and one after, and the one from YouTube is just a chunk of the one—it's a little longer on VHS. That was just some mashup shit I did.

I don't know if you saw the VHS cover of **WHEN BLACK BIRDS FLY**, but it's a parody of **THE LITTLE MERMAID** [1989] VHS, with all the dicks in the castle. So when I made the VHS I wanted to do some sort of Disney thing to go with it, so I did two of those Disney distortions.

One of the funniest "subliminal sex messages in Disney movies" theories I've heard was from this guy who was really one of those hardcore, Jews-are-reptiles, conspiracy theorist-types. He said that Disney did that so that people would get all riled up when watching them, and then go home and make babies, because that meant more consumers for Disney. Of course, the flaw in that is that they're probably watching it because they have a child, and if they have a child, then—I dunno, I would think they wouldn't like it by then.

[*Laughs*] I did my high school senior thesis on subliminal messages in Disney films. The priest getting a boner in **THE LITTLE MERMAID**, **THE LITTLE MERMAID** cover, the "sex" in **THE LION KING** [1994] the **ALADDIN** [1992] thing, where he's like, "Good girls take off their clothes."

There's only one of them that's like one hundred percent real, and that was in **THE RESCUERS** [1977]—

Yeah, I was about to ask you about that one!

That one's the only one that they one hundred percent were like, "Yeah, we fucked up."

That's because there wasn't such a thing as a pause button when they made it.

Yup, it was only in movie theaters back then.

What do you have coming down the pike?

[*Laughs*] I'm doing an animated bumper for that porn site, eFukt. So I've just been doing that, and I've been writing what I want to be my next feature film, and working on that stupid techno album.

What can you tell us about the next feature film?

I don't really have enough of it to really say anything about it yet, except I want it to be... I'm going like a post-apocalyptic route, almost like a quest film sort of thing. But really fucked up and weird. From what I've gathered so far, it will be more disturbing than **WHEN BLACK BIRDS FLY** for sure. **WHERE THE DEAD GO TO DIE** is still a little hard to gauge, because the thing people find so disturbing about that one is the child angle. So I don't really have *that* in this film. So that's why it's sort of hard to gauge that sort of thing.

So it's going to be like a soft PG-13.

[*Laughs*] Yeah. Definitely. Bring the whole family!

So I guess the obligatory last question is: what do you see these days that is exciting to you?

Wow. I've not really seen anything great in a number of years, I'm not going to lie. So, I wouldn't even know what to recommend at this point, that's new, anyway. Sorry. Everything sucks, kids!

WHERE THE DEAD GO TO DIE
2012, USA. D: JIMMY SCREAMERCLAUZ
AVAILABLE FROM UNEARTHED FILMS

WHEN BLACK BIRDS FLY
2016, USA. D: JIMMY SCREAMERCLAUZ
AVAILABLE FROM BAG MONSTER

A Brief TED V. MIKELS Interview

by Christos Mouroukis

Ted V. Mikels was born Theodore Mikacevich on the 29*th* of April, 1929. He started directing features in the early 1960s when he debuted with the arty **STRIKE ME DEADLY** *(1963)*, which he followed up with the cult hit **ONE SHOCKING MOMENT** *(1965)*. In the late 1960s he also directed **THE ASTRO-ZOMBIES** *(1968)*, which spawned three sequels, and **GIRL IN GOLD BOOTS** *(1968)*, about which we'll be talking below.

In the 1970s he found success in the drive-in market with films such as **THE CORPSE GRINDERS** *(1971)*, **BLOOD ORGY OF THE SHE-DEVILS** *(1972)*, and **THE DOLL SQUAD** *(1973)*. In the 1980s he directed **TEN VIOLENT WOMEN** *(1982)* about which we'll also be talking below. In more recent years he helmed a variety of straight-to-DVD releases, including sequels to his own movies *(***THE CORPSE GRINDERS 2** *[2000])* as well as new films *(***CAULDRON: BAPTISM OF BLOOD** *[2004])*.

Sadly, Ted V. Mikels passed away on the 16*th* of October 2016. This short interview was conducted on the 14*th* of August 2012 via email and it was originally published in Greek by Michalis Sideris in my book Conversations with Cult Movie Creators; this is the first printing in English, and is dedicated to his memory.

---

*GIRL IN GOLD BOOTS **(1968)** was a road film disguised as a cult movie. Why did you choose this approach?*

Actually, I had no intention of making a "road film". I have always totally avoided whatever theme and genre that all of my other compatriots were making. Everyone was telling me to make a biker movie, so I went totally the opposite way. Go-go dancers were the way I chose. Consequently, I became more and more involved with songwriters. So in **GIRL IN GOLD BOOTS**, I have seventeen new and original songs and musical numbers. Many people have asked if I had the soundtrack for sale. I couldn't put that together because I had far too many sources.

Nicholas Carras, one of the greatest composers, did the score for me. I sent him to Berlin where he had a full philharmonic orchestra to produce the music he created for the move. At shows and conventions, very often I have been told by both men and women that **GIRL IN GOLD BOOTS** was their most favorite movie of all time. To this day, 46 years later, it is still very popular, and still one of the best sellers for my U.S. distributor, Alpha, (*oldies.com*). I made it to be different from what everyone else was doing.

Can you explain why TEN VIOLENT WOMEN *(1982) had such a troubled distribution history?*

TEN VIOLENT WOMEN only had difficulties because of a distribution process that hurt me badly. Up until I was ready to market the movie, I had released all of my previous movies through my own distribution company. I had seven employees, and my offices were at Columbia picture studios, and Samuel Goldwyn studios in Hollywood, where I worked for thirty years. Wanting to give up the distribution process and concentrate more on directing my movies, I gave release rights to a new group just starting up, and unfortunately they were not experienced enough to handle the marketing and distribution. They passed off the only eight 35mm prints that were ever made to another distributor. Unfortunately for me, that distributor was not honest with me. His company made a lot of money playing New York theaters until the eight prints were worn out. I did not ever get any of the money due me as owner-producer-creator of the movie. Meanwhile, the laboratory that had the original negative went out of business and the negative was lost, never to be found again. So I was literally "cheated" out of my movie, with no way to proceed without any prints or negative. The movie is very popular with home video, and last quarter it was at the top of the list of my distributor's best sellers...

When you made TEN VIOLENT WOMEN *were you inspired by the W.I.P. (Women in Prison) genre's films? Were you targeting that particular market?*

When I made **TEN VIOLENT WOMEN**, I had no idea of what a "women in prison" movie was. I had never seen one. I had input from several pretty

actresses, and we dreamed up story material to add to a script my friend James Gordon White had written called THE VIOLENT SEX. I added my personal thoughts to the process and changed the direction of a rather serious script into what I called a "caper" movie, with a different slant. I wanted a bit of tongue-in-cheek entertainment—girls robbing jewelry stores with water pistols, etc. I meant for it to be part serious and part fun as a movie.

Were you aware that GIRL IN GOLD BOOTS and TEN VIOLENT WOMEN were released here in Greece on VHS and they are now very hard to find?

I was not aware that **GIRL IN GOLD BOOTS** and **TEN VIOLENT WOMEN** were ever released in Greece. I had never licensed anyone to release them, so in a sense, they were pirated from me. That has happened to me continuously around the world. You put in a year of hard work, blood, sweat, tears, and all the money you can put together, then someone takes your creations, makes money from them, and I get nothing. It has happened again and again. Very discouraging.

Although you have been making cult films for approximately half a century, you were gravitating to primarily entertaining subjects, instead of extreme violenc,e for example. Why this approach to your body of work?

I think my approach to making films was that of an entertainer. At age five, I was bugging everyone with magic tricks, then learned to play accordion—later professionally—then ventriloquism, then fire-eating and Houdini escape tricks. I put it all together with a full two-hour magic show I called "Open Sesame". I did this show until I felt it necessary to film it, and that is when I turned my desire to entertain into making full-length feature films. Entertainment was my approach. Violence, unless it was totally campy, was not my way. I have six children, twenty-five grandchildren, twenty-one great grandchildren, and did not want to make any movies we could not all be proud of.

Recently, apart from original movies, you are also making sequels to your greatest franchises. Is that a market dictation or you felt that there is more to add to those particular stories?

Making sequels is not so much wanting to add more to the stories, but to continue on with a successful franchise, making newer renditions of my most successful movies. Many folks ask me when I am going to do a sequel of this movie or that movie, and in each case, it is one of their favorites. I try to listen to that. I know it is difficult to summarize 64 years of movie-making, but I think I am able to claim making more movies as writer, producer, director, cinematographer, editor and distributor, all as one man, than anyone else in the business. Thank you, Chris, for inviting me to do the interview.

My friends and Famous Monsters, Part 1...

Cortlandt Hull
A Conversation in Wax

by Chris Nersinger

This is the first in a series of articles/interviews with friends and colleagues within the entertainment industry—including Cortlandt Hull, David Shecter and Daniel Griffith—all who have gone on from their childhood dreams and fantasies to making them a realty, all the while never losing sight of one thing: a magazine, and a very special one, at that. It was and still is near and dear to our hearts, and I say our hearts because it was a childhood tradition, especially for those of you fortunate enough to have grown up in the late '50s, '60s and '70s. It was the age of monsters, horror hosts, drive-ins, Creepy Crawlers, trading cards, comic books, Grape Nehi, A&W, Snyder Dutch Pretzels, and Bub's Daddy gum (sour apple!). There was a magazine that was kept under your bed and pulled out at night when everyone else was asleep—and no, I'm not talking about Playboy, although that might have been there, too. This one was bound full of non-glossy paper filled with fantastic frightful images, serving up news and editorials devoted to creatures both big and small, slimy or oozing, dedicated to the splendor of horror and science fiction celluloid: the legendary Famous Monsters of Filmland.

Before delving into the aforementioned conversations with my friends I wanted to provide some additional information regarding *Famous Monsters* and just how important this magazine was. It debuted in 1958 and had a run that lasted 25 years. Published by James (Jim) Warren of Warren Publishing and affectionately edited by Forrest J. Ackerman, or as everyone knew him, Forry. It was the love of these two men that would have a long and reaching influence over three generations of "monster kids" including the likes of Joe Dante and John Landis, and was even the very inspiration for an iconic '80s cult favorite, **THE MONSTER SQUAD** (1987), directed by Fred Dekker. *Famous Monsters* helped further the careers of Vincent Price, Peter Cushing, Roger Corman, even the Big G himself, Godzilla, and many more. Their on-screen adventures were covered between the pages of this endearing fan magazine, making instant fans of every reader while helping us discover the classics that we missed during the initial releases such as **THE WOLF MAN** (1941), **FRANKENSTEIN** (1931), **IT CAME FROM OUTER SPACE** (1953) and **EARTH VS. THE FLYING SAUCERS** (1956). Every issue was loaded with behind-the-scenes pics and complete plot synopses, plus in-depth coverage of a highlighted movie within the issue. Also covered were upcoming releases, TV broadcasts, and the far and few fan events that existed at the time.

This installment, the first segment of hopefully many more to come, focuses on Cortlandt Hull, curator of the original Witch's Dungeon Movie Museum in Bristol, Connecticut…

Cortlandt was born in 1953 and has spent the majority of his time in Bristol, CT. He was not your typical kid; when it came time for family vacations, instead of heading to the beach or camping he would head to places known more for their attractions. However, when the family was settled in at the hotel he would be always be searching for a monster movie on TV or a wax museum nearby. But when it came to the wax museums he was never satisfied, because none of them had a decent section devoted to movie monsters. In fact, no wax museums had anything even closely resembling anything from the movies. What they did have was a dungeon or chamber of horrors, with statues of Jack the Ripper and the like, wax figures mainly based in reality and not fantasy…that was about all you got. This is something that would always be in the back of Cortlandt's mind well into his early teens, and would prove to be a driving force later on.

Now, for most kids his age that grew up during the '50s and '60s, there were horror hosts showing the collection of *Shock Theater* packaging from Universal Studios on TV and the above-mentioned *Famous Monsters* satisfying those cravings for a late-night dose of werewolves and vampires…along with the Aurora model kits that hit in the '60s (my favorite was the mad scientist lab). Cortlandt was blessed with other factors in his life that would forever drive him in the direction of a lifetime of creating and being surrounded by classic movie monsters. For one, his great uncle, Henry Hull, was the first on-screen werewolf, and one of the greatest of them all. Hull's movie days predate **WEREWOLF OF LONDON** (1935) by several years, including work on a D.W. Griffith film, **ONE EXCITING NIGHT** (19220, a precursor to the "Old Dark House" films of the later '20s and '30s. A little-known bit of trivia concerning this particular film involves a scene with a storm. Griffith was one to spare no expense when it came to getting a shot the way he wanted it to go, and this movie was no exception. To create the intensity of the storm, two airplane propellers were brought onto the set, which made for some pretty realistic footage and at times dangerous working conditions.

Henry appeared in 76 films between 1917 and 1966, his last in **THE CHASE** (1966), starring Marlon

Cortlandt's tribute to his uncle Henry Hull, the **WEREWOLF OF LONDON** himself!

Brando and very young Robert Redford. Always surrounded by other stellar cast members, Uncle Henry made numerous guest appearances on Television, many of which were in western TV series including *Bonanza* with a record of four appearances—no one else ever appeared more than once as a guest. Cortlandt really enjoyed his uncle, who would tell Cortlandt many stories over the years about his days in Hollywood, including what it was like to sit in the make-up chair under the supervision of the legendary Jack Pierce, as well as working with Vincent Price on the set of **MASTER OF THE WORLD** (1961). Henry Hull was also a well-known performer of the stage. He gave an amazing portrayal of Edgar Alan Poe and Mark Twain on Broadway in one-man performances and he did his own make-up, as well. In fact, most performers and actors did their own make-up until the mid-'30s when that became unionized.

Uncle Henry co-starred in Tod Browning's last film, **MIRACLES FOR SALE** (1939), which also starred Robert Young as the lead, along with supporting actors William Demarest (*My Three Sons*) and Gloria Anne Holden (**DRACULA'S DAUGHTER** [1936]). Cortlandt mentioned that he actually has the skull from the film—a prop that is prominent in the story, with eyes that light up. And still works today!

During the interview, Cortlandt asked me to include some information that would clear up a rumor that has been circulating since the filming of **WEREWOLF OF LONDON**; something that has bothered him and his family for years.

For more than half a century the thought has been that Henry Hull refused to let Jack Pierce apply the full make-up for the werewolf, allegedly because Hull did not want to cover himself completely with all the facial hair required and that he was a difficult person to work with, which couldn't be farther from the truth. Now it is true that Pierce wanted to use the full make-up for a werewolf appearance, something similar to **THE WOLF MAN**, starring Lon Chaney. However, the reason behind Henry refusing to have the full facial application was due to the script. There are two scenes in which Henry's character is recognized by his wife, and it would not have made sense for Henry to have been filmed any other way than a version that allowed several of his human features to appear noticeable to friends and family. Especially since there is a line where the wife says that she knows he is the werewolf due to his distinct features. So, case closed and a rumor quelled. Henry Hull was being most professional and loyal to the script. *The Werewolf Filmography* (2017 McFarland Publishing), written by Bryan Senn, also confirms this as told to Cortlandt by Uncle Henry.

The one other introduction to the limelight for Cortlandt was via his aunt, Josephine Hull, who appeared with Cary Grant in **ARSENIC AND OLD LACE** (1944) as one of Cary's not-all-together aunts. Josephine was not only an actress but a director of plays, a very successful career that spanned 50 years and she was groundbreaking as a female in what during that time was very much a male-dominated business. She won a Best Supporting Oscar for her role in **HARVEY** (1950) as the aunt of Elwood P. Dowd (Jimmy Stewart), a role she had played for 10 years on Broadway (it is one of my favorite films). Two of the characters she created each took up 10 years of her life in long-running productions. Now *that* is commitment and dedication—a trait that runs in Cortlandt's family, and one that is evident in Cortlandt himself.

Part of Cortlandt's Dick Smith display at The Witch's Dungeon

Now, in my household growing up, it was *Batman* who ruled the TV dial; it won out on both nights during its initial run between 1966-1968, but over at the Hull household it was *The Munsters*. As a result Cortlandt was catching only the second part of *Batman* each week. Keep in mind that this was when he was starting the museum and *The Munsters* were perfect for keeping his mind open and forever expanding his vision of classic monsters... plus the makeup was superb and accentuated by the choice of filming in black and white. It would be a few years before he ever saw the beginning to those *Batman* stories, when the show surfaced again in syndication.

Monsters were not the only things Cortlandt was interested in: cartoons were another. His favorites included Warner Bros.' Bugs Bunny and Hanna Barbera's Tom and Jerry. Cortlandt being friends with master animation director Chuck Jones, once asked Chuck, "Did you think the kids would accept the Road Runner cartoons?" Chuck stated that kids were not a consideration, since these shorts were shown in the theaters for adults, playing with A-pictures; adults wanted laughs too, and Walt Disney already offered a softer option for younger kids. Speaking of Disney, two of Cortlandt's favorites are the classic short *Lonesome Ghosts* (1937) and *Trick or Treat* (1952), the latter showcasing Donald Duck vs. his nephews and a witch on Halloween night (the witch voiced by the quintessential female voice artist, June Foray, best known as Rocky the Flying Squirrel and Witch Hazel from Warner Bros.). June would later provide the voice of Zenobia the Witch, who presides over Cortlandt's very own Wax Museum. On a sad note, before this article was finished June passed away at the age of 99. She would have been 100 years young in September. She was a marvelous person, who also became a very dear friend to Cortlandt. June will be missed, and leaves behind a tremendous body of work.

Over the years Cortlandt developed an amazing array of artistic talents including drawing, painting and sculpture. But these skills that developed were cultivated thanks to Cortlandt contacting some

Top: Entrance to The Witch's Dungeon—enter...if you dare! **Above:** Ben Chapman (left), Julie Adams (center) and Cortlandt Hull with the **CREATURE FROM THE BLACK LAGOON** display

well-renowned make-up artists at 20th Century Fox and organizing the family vacations to California to visit the movie studios, all with the support of his parents. These trips gave Cortlandt the foundation to establish his very own wax museum at the age of 13, The Witch's Dungeon, which opened in 1966, and this past October marked 51 years in operation. Imagine at the ages of 13-16 being tutored by the likes of Dick Smith, Don Post Sr., Verne Langdon (a huge influence in the creation of the Magic Castle in LA) and John Chambers (**PLANET OF THE APES** [1968] and *The Wild Wild West* TV series make-up), all of whom had a hand in Cortlandt's continuing education in what today many consider almost a lost art. It was this tutoring that would lead to life-long friendships the likes of which probably would not

be possible today, with so many policies studios have today and the security that has been put in place at studios, and that is an unfortunate reality. One of the key things that was driven home for Cortlandt was that you can make a statue, but if you want to bring "life" to your creation you have to master make-up, for that is the essence of being…its soul, so to speak.

Through the years, the museum has grown in size and stature. It predates Disney's The Haunted Mansion by three years and is the longest-running Halloween attraction in the country. The "monsters" take over the Bristol Play House during the last part of September and through the month of October. It boasts over 25 statues of classic monsters of the movies, all in settings taken right out of the very films that featured these endearing and eerie characters. What makes this gathering of ghouls and goblins unique is that it is the last museum with live hosts to escort you victims—I mean *guests*, of course—who would want to see any mysterious circumstances befall you… especially before dinner. The hosts are

in black and white (including makeup) and the monsters and the sets are in glorious color, reminiscent of the Aurora model kits from the '60s and early '70s, adorned by the artwork of John Bama. Speaking of color, one only has to look to the late, great Basil Gogos, who recently passed away; known for his artwork that adorned many a cover of *Famous Monsters of Filmland*. He became a very good friend of Cortlandt's through attending several monster movie-oriented events and they often had booths next to each other. Cortlandt's choices of décor, along with the lighting used for the monsters' domains, owe as much to the coloring technique of Basil as to those Aurora models. The sets have an eerie glow to them thanks not just to the colors but the hues within those colors, and unique lighting that emphasizes the dressings and the statues, making them very much "alive".

Lending a bit of the macabre and otherworldly dimensions to The Witch's Dungeon, as mentioned earlier, June Foray provides the voice of Zenobia, the Gypsy witch. She welcomes those who or dare to enter this enchanted realm of fantasy, all with the hopes of returning on the other side. However, she is not the only celebrity to lend their voice to the spreading of doom and gloom on this journey into werewolves, vampires, Dracula and the Frankenstein monster. No, there have been others, including one of my all-time favorites, the very King of Horror, Vincent Price, and good ol' Luke Skywalker, Mark Hamill. Past celebrity stopovers include the likes of Forry J. Ackerman, John Bama, Ron Chaney, Sara Karloff, Bela Lugosi Jr. and even the lady of horror herself, Elvira, Mistress of the Dark.

The museum has had its fill of publicity from *Entertainment Tonight* (*ET*) in the guise of Leonard Maltin not once, but twice covering the wax figures and their surroundings. This led to the beginning of a close friendship with Leonard, and when it came time for help with Leonard's book on Disney's animation, one of his sources was none other than Cortlandt. The Witch's Dungeon and Cortlandt were mentioned in *Famous Monsters* in one way or another in several issues. He also made an appearance on *To Tell the Truth* (a series that has run in various incarnations from 1956 to the present) back in the early '70s, when he was guest on one segment. For those who are not familiar with the show, it consisted of a host (at the time of Cortlandt's appearance, it was Gary Moore) with a celebrity panel of four. In general the panel featured regulars Kitty Carlisle, Peggy Cass, Bill Cullen, Gene Rayburn and special guest Rita Moreno. Jack Cassidy and Nipsey Russell would alternate with the regular panelists. During the episode the panelist are given clues by the guest and two imposters (or challengers, as they were referred to), and the panelists have to weed out the false clues to determine who is the real person of interest, someone with an unusual occupation or experience. The challengers are allowed to lie, but the one who has that said occupation has to tell the truth. To make this segment more interesting, Cortlandt, through a lot of lobbying, won out on being able to not only appear in make-up of his design but also was allowed to make up the other two contestants. This was no easy feat, considering that everything is unionized and normally this against union rules. But what he proposed made sense to all, since he was invited based on his skills in make-up and for The Witch's Dungeon. Ironically, I was a guest audience member during that time period and got a whole $1.00 for clapping the hardest—to an 8-10 year old that was pretty good change in those days.

The Witch's Dungeon became a reality not only based on Cortlandt's talents, but due to help from a very supportive father who was in the construction business. He designed and built for his son a Swiss Chalet to house the creations that would be brought to life thanks not only to Cortlandt's talents, but also his mom, who was a gifted artist in her own right and a designer of costumes. She also worked for the local playhouse, but that is a whole other story. Many an actor spent nights dining and watching movies at Cortlandt's house, because it was the best food in town and after long days and nights rehearsing and performing it was a home away from home, and this is where everyone would relax and watch a good old movie. It was nothing to find, say, George Chakiras of **WEST SIDE STORY** (1961), kicking back on the sofa watching cartoons and eating popcorn waiting for the main feature to start.

This is where we conclude the first part of our feature story regarding Cortlandt Hull, one who has led a charmed life, and most deservedly so. If you ask Cortlandt, he will only be more than glad to convey that thought, as he has said so often, "I may not be overflowing in the green stuff, but I lead what I would say is a life rich in friends, memories and experience." And I'm sure he wouldn't trade it for the world, or anything else, for that matter. Cortlandt is a very humble person, and what is refreshing is he has never changed in that department. I am very fortunate and proud to consider Cortlandt my friend.

So next time when we catch up with our monstermaker we will delve deeper into his amazing stories of celebrity friends, the Oscars and a talent for restoring vintage carousels, which is something of a lost art. Until then, always keep looking over your shoulder…remember, 'tis the season of witches and goblins and things that go bump in the night. And if you do happen to run into one or two, just tell them Doc Nersinger sent ya. They just might let you off the hook…literally. I cook with a lot of garlic, and if they think for even a moment you were at my place for dinner…well, there are a certain variety of those creatures of the night that tend to shy away from that particular herb. But mmm-mmm good for us!

Visit The Witch's Dungeon's website:
http://www.preservehollywood.org

**The Witch's Dungeon
Classic Movie Museum
will re-open for their 52nd year
on Friday, Sept 28th, 2018**

REVIEWS

(Left to right) Bud Abbott, Lou Costello, Glenn Strange, Lon Chaney Jr. and Bela Lugosi in a Universal continuity still for **ABBOTT AND COSTELLO MEET FRANKENSTEIN**

ABBOTT AND COSTELLO MEET FRANKENSTEIN

Reviewed by Chris Nersinger

The first time I saw this wonderful excursion of fantasy—a mixture filled with just the right amount of scares and of course crackerjack comedic timing from Bud Abbott and Lou Costello—I was somewhere between 8 and 10 years old. This was a time when Saturday Morning was still king with shows like *Scooby Doo, Where Are You!*, *Groovy Ghoulies*, *The Hardy Boys/Nancy Drew Mysteries* and *H.R. Pufnstuf* in rotation, *Chiller Theatre* presenting the classic horror films on the boob tube, *Famous Monsters* magazine at the newsstands, and kiddie matinees for $1.00 at the movie houses (Godzilla reigned supreme at the majestic Rivera Theater). Basically monsters, especially the classic ones, were not only in every media type including print comics (*Boris Karloff Tales of Mystery*, for one), and it was a proving ground to us "kids" that monsters could be funny and scary. And so it was that I and my good friend Steve caught wind of this double-feature playing at our local high school one upcoming Saturday morning. We grew anxious as the magical day approached. Mind you, we were constantly reminded during the week-long wait due to local stations running commercials. But finally the day arrived. Good old R.L. Thomas High—they had an awesome auditorium/theater and every student knew it…the place was packed.

On the bill was, of course, **ABBOTT AND COSTELLO MEET FRANKENSTEIN** (1948), and it was paired with this crazy film called **LEMON GROVE KIDS MEET THE MONSTERS** (1965), which is a fantastic tribute to The Bowery Boys by the late Ray Dennis Steckler (who passed away in 2009, and is destined to be the subject of a future *Weng's Chop* article). **LEMON GROVE** played first and was pure escapism—if you have ever seen a *Bowery Boys* flick, this was right on the money, like a *Monkees* episode without the songs—and its zaniness got us psyched in anticipation for the main attraction. The audience went crazy when the lights went down and the opening titles appeared, it couldn't have been more appropriate and fitting that the titles were animated, as just like the real-life counterparts Abbot and Costello, who are like watching a cartoon at times. So it was again when watching **ABBOTT AND COSTELLO MEET FRANKENSTEIN** on Blu-ray, time for me to relive that experience all over again.

The film opens in pure classic style as Wilbur (Lou Costello) is trying as best he can to accommodate a customer at baggage pick-up for a train station and answering a phone at the same time. We all know Lou is not capable of multi-tasking and with Chick (Bud Abbott) on his case, this scene is loaded with one-liners, pratfalls and sheer tomfoolery, especially when Lou attempts to retrieve a woman's handbag from a dolly loaded with other assorted luggage…and guess where her handbag is, right smack in the middle of the dolly. Everything ends up on top of Lou.

The main story revolves around Wilbur and his wonderful, childlike brain. And guess who wants it? None other than Dracula (played by Bela Lugosi for only the 2nd time in his career). Drac needs Wilbur's brain for the Frankenstein Monster, this time played by Glenn Strange (Strange had started out as a stuntman and then progressed to playing screen villains). Well it's up to Chick and Lawrence Talbot/Wolfman (Lon Chaney Jr., who was the only actor to ever have played all of Universal's classic monsters) to stop them and save Wilbur. The movie features some excellent sets and special effects, including Dracula morphing into a bat, a castle complete with secret passages, a dungeon and a mad scientists' lab, all in glorious black and white…and thanks to the Bluray presentation it has never looked better. Universal had a major hit on its hands with this one, and due to its great box-office success it lead to several Abbott and Costello encounters with monsters, including Boris Karloff as Dr. Jekyll/Mr. Hyde, the Mummy and the Invisible Man.

The extras include an audio commentary and a making-of documentary with guests galore, among them Bob Burns, Chris Costello (Lous' daughter) and hosted by film historian David J. Skal. I always make a point to watch the making-of documentaries and audio commentaries when they are available because there is so much to learn from, and this release is no exception. For example, Abbott and Costello did not want to make this film initially, and to keep the energy level up on the production there were many practical jokes and pie fights, much to the dismay of Bela Lugosi, who was said to have a great

Top: Theatrical quad poster for **ABBOTT AND COSTELLO MEET FRANKENSTEIN**, featuring the then-instantly recognizable (to US audiences, anyway) comedy duo front and center, fleeing in terror from the Universal monsters on the sidelines. **Above:** In the Japanese poster for the film, it's the world-famous Frankenstein Monster that gets all the prime real estate rather than the comedic leads.

ABBOTT AND COSTELLO MEET FRANKENSTEIN | 1948

sense of humor, although not when the pie was on him...literally. Remember, Bela was a very professional actor and took his craft seriously. Also, this has a digital HD copy which means you can watch it on your designated streaming carrier.

Well, I'm not going to spoil your time in re-discovering this masterpiece that blends scares, chills, and comedy, other than to say this is a great movie to introduce your kids to monsters without the graphic blood-letting. You will all be laughing through a great big bowl of popcorn!

1948, USA. D: CHARLES BARTON
AVAILABLE FROM UNIVERSAL

AMITYVILLE: THE AWAKENING

Reviewed by Christos Mouroukis

Tagline: *"Every house has a history. This one has a legend."*

This film kicks off with an introductory scene featuring a reenactment of the infamous DeFeo murders that shook the foundation of 1970s true crime culture. The action then moves to the present day and finds a troubled family, namely single mother Joan (Jennifer Jason Leigh) and her daughters Belle (TV actress Bella Thorne), Juliet (Mckeena Grace from **INDEPENDENCE DAY: RESURGENCE** [2016], which I recently reviewed over in *WC*'s sister 'zine *Monster!*), while her only son James (TV actor Cameron Monaghan) remains in a coma. It is not too long before strange occurrences start happening in one of the most famous allegedly haunted houses.

What is this film? Is it a sequel, a remake, a reboot, a prequel, or what? It does acknowledge the real-life events that serve as the background for the infamous book and media frenzy, and it even acknowledges the first film (**THE AMITYVILLE HORROR** [1979]), its first sequel (**AMITYVILLE II: THE POSSESSION** [1982]), and the first remake (**THE AMITYVILLE HORROR** [2005]) when DVDs of these films are shown and discussed by the performers. But it also ignores all the other semi-unrelated sequels. But does it matter really? It is just a film and it should be judged on its own merits and faults and stand on its own two feet. After all, with so many official and unofficial (and sometimes cases of something being both) entries in the franchise, even die-hard fans have stopped caring about what is what, about timelines logic, and focus on the films as individual entries. If you need a detailed article on the lesser known *Amityville* films, please refer to the article that I wrote in this magazine's previous issue.[1] The good news is that **AMITYVILLE: THE AWAKENING** (2017) works, and because it is actually that good, it surprises me that it had such a troubled distribution history.

Sure, writer/director Franck Khalfoun (**MANIAC** [2012]) didn't invent the wheel, and in many ways, this looks like routine Blumhouse Productions fare...and it is one, but bear in mind that these films are what most people (me included) consider the scariest output from current mainstream U.S. horror cinema. I would even go as far as to say that this is the greatest *Amityville* film we've seen since **AMITYVILLE 3-D** (1983).

Originally conceived as a found-footage film (tellingly, the original working title was THE AMITYVILLE HORROR: THE LOST TAPES), luckily that idea and the original screenplay (by Casey La Scala and Daniel Farrands) were scrapped and Bob Weinstein via The Weinstein Company's Dimension Films opted to go for a more traditional route with the services of director Franck Khalfoun, who brought on board his more conventional script as well. Delays were not only evident during its inception and making; the film went through a distribution hell, when its release date and method was postponed and changed so many times that it became a *Chinese Democracy*-kind of joke amongst horror news websites and fans alike. Add to that the fact that, while it originally received an R-rating, it was cut in order to obtain a PG-13, and everyone was (rightfully) expecting a mess. After seeing the final product, I am glad to say that, although the wait is not justified (this is no masterpiece, to be

[1] See "Amityville Horror Cinema: The Lesser-Known Films" in issue #10, p. 65.

fair, despite how entertaining it is), what we have here is, by all means, a good film, which should be loved by fans of the series. It is also very modern, in the sense that it relies heavily on up-to-date jump-scares, which is an element that could have drawn new and younger audiences as well.

Overall, with so many rehashes flooding the market, and with your peaking becoming increasingly difficult, it is safe to say that whether you are a longtime fan of the series or a newbie, you should watch this and be scared for a solid 90 minutes. Add to that the rocking soundtrack is more often than not very appropriate, with its gothic overtones, and you've got yourself a winner!

2017, USA. D: FRANCK KHALFOUN
AVAILABLE FROM LIONSGATE

AUGUST UNDERGROUND

Reviewed by Christos Mouroukis

This film is about depraved serial killer Peter (producer, director, and co-writer Fred Vogel) and his unspeakable murderous mayhem, all of which is filmed by his best friend whom we never see, as he is the one holding the camera (co-writer Allen Peters), in this found-footage atrocity that is definitely not for the easily shocked...and this time we mean it.

First of all we are introduced to a naked and bloody girl (AnnMarie Reveruzzi) that the leading duo is keeping in a filthy basement. She is tied up there, and a close-up reveals that her left nipple has been cut off. Her dead boyfriend is also lying around. They soon throw a bucket full of piss on her head, eventually showering her with it. Presumably they have also kept her hungry, and they tease her appetite with an apple.

The dynamic duo then picks up a random girl off the street (Alexa Iris) and promise her a ride to her destination. Peter asks her to show him her tits for $20, which she does. She is then asked to show her vagina, which she also does, and goes as far as inserting a finger in it as well, although this is obscured; surprisingly the film never becomes hardcore, at least in porn terms, because in gross terms it certainly does, many times over. Peter then goes outside the car with the girl. She kneels down and performs oral sex. He then attacks her, and leaves her behind, nearly dead.

The two guys return to the basement, where the cameraman picks a porn magazine off the floor, grabs some of the first girl's shit, also from the floor, and feeds it to her. In another sequence, the two protagonists attack a supermarket's attendant and two customers, forcing them to perform a variety of humiliating acts (including ass-sniffing).

The film ends with a sequence featuring the two leads, and their escapades with some drugs and two prostitutes (Erika Risovich and Randi Stubbs), one of which ends up dead, whilst the other one escapes.

Calling the film misogynist would be an easy way out for reviewers, but it would also be irrelevant, as a lot of the violence onscreen is targeted toward

males, too, including the kidnapping of two tattoo-artist brothers (the film's special effects artists Aaron LaBonte and Ben LaBonte), who end up slaughtered in the basement.

At 70 minutes this still feels much too long, but it is so well-done that you'll have a hard time believing it was staged and that the filmmakers managed to pull off such antics for a mere budget of $2,000. If you love seeing a chubby protagonist throwing up because he mutilated one body too many, then look no further, as this will become your new favorite film. After all, the best way to describe it would be **HENRY: PORTRAIT OF A SERIAL KILLER** (1986) for the perverted.

I hope I did it justice with this review, because it is honestly a unique piece of cinema, even though it is a video. Most online reviews that I came across focus on how experimental the whole thing is, but I think that this is misleading. First of all, found-footage films or extreme films or a combination of both are not the rare thing that some commentators make them to be, but aside from discussions on originality, this is unique for a much more important reason: it was made by young artists without too much previous experience. Found-footage scenarios may be a good way for someone to kick-off his cinematic career inexpensively, but to go to such extreme with the violence is simply outstanding, and for that I am taking my hat off. The fact that many people are involved both in front of the camera and behind it, essentially blending so many roles and capacities (in true low-budget and guerilla filmmaking fashion), creates a blur between reality and staged cruelty (sometimes you will find yourself wondering what's real and what's staged) that comes across as a completely honest piece of cinema, even if totally absurd, and for that, it is fascinating.

2001, USA. D: FRED VOGEL
AVAILABLE FROM TOE TAG PICTURES

AUGUST UNDERGROUND'S MORDUM

Reviewed by Christos Mouroukis

In real life, violence could be viewed by some as an exclusive asset of the governments and the rich (they are one and the same, since sadly, money is more powerful than politics) and is used in monopoly fashion against the oppressed. Luckily, this is not always the case in films, where the world of fantasy can turn things upside-down. I don't endorse violence in real life by any means, but since violence exists, if it is only an asset of the powerful, then it becomes a totalitarian tool. Extreme cinema usually makes an interesting alteration to this, especially when these films are helmed by passionate artists, rather than careful auteurs. Such is the very case of the film under review, and the violence comes from

it is still not as seedy as the first film, and it contains a lot of filler, including some tired effects such as hammering skulls. It is even less misogynist than most films of this kind, because on one hand the violence is targeted left and right and is by no means gender-specific, whilst one of the killers (arguably the meanest one) is a girl.

Director Fred Vogel has been arrested on charges of transporting obscenities (and a short investigation accordingly ensued), and although the charges were dropped, you have to admire the man's guts. You also have to admire his ability to deliver such stuff on a mere budget of $300. They say that you cannot catch lighting in a jar, nor does it strike twice, but amazingly Vogel managed just that with this sequel. If you thought that the first film was an experiment (and to an extent, it seems like it was) that just happened to work by accident, you should definitely catch this one as well, even if only to see that although Vogel is no master auteur by any means, he does have a pattern in making these films which is consistent (not to mention persistent) and makes his signature (like it or not) apparent.

2003, USA. D: JERAMI CRUISE, KILLJOY, MICHAEL TODD SCHNEIDER, FRED VOGEL, CRISTIE WHILES
AVAILABLE FROM TOE TAG PICTURES

AUGUST UNDERGROUND'S PENANCE

Reviewed by Christos Mouroukis

The murderous couple returns (again producer/director Fred Vogel and co-writer Cristie Whiles) for a series of antics that they record on video, only this time it is shot 16x9, whilst the first two films were shot in 4x3. Curiously, this decision seems peculiar; because there was a lot more mayhem in the first two films (so normally you would expect 16x9 widescreen greatness) and there is a lot more story here (so normally you could live with 4x3). But it is not as illogical as it sounds. These films follow a linear timeline that present the main characters' actions in chronological order, and although I believe that the change of format is not mentioned anywhere, it would only make sense if in the early days of digital video it was 4x3 and then the protagonist bought (or stole) a better camera or simply switched to 16x9. Maybe I am reading too much here because I am nuts about formats, but Vogel seems like a coherent director and I don't think that such an aspect was left to chance.

every direction, essentially creating a feeling of uncertainty that completely destroys all expectancies, and putting the audience in such position that we can't help but get surprised every few minutes, not to mention how unprotected and vulnerable we feel, which makes this an unexpected roller-coaster ride for the demented.

Peter (returning Fred Vogel, who also co-wrote and co-directed, and handled special effects with special makeup effects artist, producer, and production designer Jerami Cruise) is this time joined by his cutter girlfriend (co-writer/co-director Cristie Whiles) and her cutter brother (co-writer/co-director Michael Todd Schneider), and the three of them go on a killing and spree, again of found-footage nature, as each of them keeps exchanging roles in torturing and camera operating duties, because apparently, the depraved camera guy from the first film was not available. It's a shame, as he's missing a lot here, including breaking and entering, raping and gangraping, dicks cut off, plenty of drug use, slashing, corpse fucking, and what's more, the kids appear to personally know another serial killer (co-writer/co-director Killjoy) with whom they are on friendly terms, apparently showing off their collections of mutilated body parts to each other.

Watching this will have you ask yourself what is the point of the entire thing, but consider that you signed on for a **PARANORMAL ACTIVITY** (2007) with gore. As such, it is not a bad thing, but

This time around they attack a hobo (although they don't kill him), indulge in cocaine consumption with their friends, and do some home invasion business when they break into a family's house where they proceed to hit the father with a hammer (a favorite act in this film series), rape the mother, and abuse the kid. Home invasion films or films that simply have such a scene may be shocking even when traditionally filmed, because this is a real danger that can touch everyone and as such is so much more creepy than a fantasy monster; but it becomes even more cruel here, because the reality of the found-footage aspect is added on, making this look like a documentary of your worst nightmare. I survived all three of those films without too much problem because I am thick-skinned when it comes to watching violent films, but this particular scene tested my endurance. And just when you thought that it couldn't get worse, the aspect of the kid was introduced. The film may not be mean in itself because there are great amount of artistry involved here (plus you can tell that the filmmakers are fans that just have fun with the aesthetics of the grotesque), but even as such, having a film that just depicts atrocities in a low-budget rollercoaster fashion, this outstanding scene is definitely able to shock unsuspected casual viewers, although I am not sure how one would sign on watching these films without being warned by the several online reviews.

Other events that might be of interest to you include the slaughter of a human fetus, and the semen-painting of a tied-up and apparently tortured female. There is a scene here in which a live mouse is fed to a small alligator. This technically is no animal cruelty, but I am over-sensitive with animals and it appeared shocking to my eyes. There is also a gorgeous white cat, but luckily nothing bad happens to the kitten.

There are two more differences that I noticed in relation to the first two films—one good and the other not so much. The good thing (which is quite an outstanding achievement) is that for the first time the viewer gets to relate with the lead character. Yes, this may be perverted because you spend most of the time seeing them slicing up victims. But what could be this third installment's downfall—namely the amount of time we spend of seeing the main characters doing not much (and sometimes nothing)—actually works in its favor, because you can't help it but start caring about them and their obviously disturbed minds and antics. The bad thing is that this was reportedly made on a bigger budget than the first two combined ($5,000); this amount of money is definitely not much by any filmmaker's standards, but I couldn't help but notice how the first installments achieved more spectacle with less means. Still, this minor detail helps the story department, which although I think was improvised, comes across as more carefully planned than the ones in the previous entries.

2007, USA. D: FRED VOGEL
AVAILABLE FROM TOE TAG PICTURES

BLOODY MUSCLE BODY BUILDER IN HELL

(*Jigoku No Chimidoro Muscle Builder*)

Reviewed by Jeff Goodhartz

"Sayonara, baby"

It took fourteen years for director Shinichi Fukazawa to complete and edit his 8mm pet horror project, and another five years for it to earn a simultaneous release in theaters and home video in its native Japan. That's a ton of time for a man to devote his

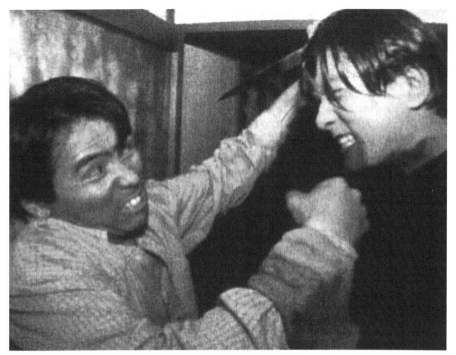

Fourteen years in the making, Shinichi Fukazawa's 8mm pet project, **BLOODY MUSCLE BODY BUILDER IN HELL**, delivers the goods with gusto

life to, but one gander at **BLOODY MUSCLE BODY BUILDER IN HELL** (*Jigoku No Chimidoro Muscle Builder*, 2012) and you'll realize that it represents a labor of love in its truest sense…and you've just gotta love a title like that!. This is the kind of thing that harkens back to the pre-CGI days of '80s home video, where virtually any intrepid independent filmmaker with a few bucks and a backer or two can shoot and release a horror epic to haunt your local video store.

After an opening sequence showing a man murdering his possessive (no pun intended) lover, we fast-forward some three decades and follow the man's unemployed bodybuilding son, Naoto (Shinichi Fukazawa himself). Naoto aimlessly splits his time between trying to get over his latest breakup and building up those biceps until one day, he receives a call from an ex (Masaaki Kai), who out of the blue asks him to assist her investigate a haunted house (yes, the very one that dear old adulterous Dad once owned and committed his crime in). Joined by a professional psychic, our three would-be adventurers arrive at the now-derelict destination, and the psychic immediately senses that something ain't quite kosher. That feeling is confirmed when he is possessed by Nato's bitter deceased stepmother and from that point on, all hell doth break loose. It is only when things appear bleakest that Naoto comes to understand what his greatest weapon is to combat the ghoulish spirits: his muscles and his beloved weights.

BLOODY MUSCLE BODY BUILDER IN HELL has been dubbed the Japanese **THE EVIL DEAD** (1981), and that's certainly apt, but for maybe an even more accurate comparison to Fukazawa's labor of love (if more so in execution than concept), look toward the cult favorite, **EQUINOX** (1967/1970).[2] Like that 1967 college project (before producer Jack Harris got his hands on it), this production feels much the same, where bare-bones story and character development serve as a platform to lay on as much over-the-top low-tech, (and in this case, gore-drenched) eye candy as could be conceived and/or afforded. Taking its cue not just from the aforementioned influences, but also from the likes of Stuart Gordon's **RE-ANIMATOR** (1985)—in the form of a threatening and somewhat overly talkative disembodied head—our dedicated auteur lovingly slathers on enough horrific and sometimes hilarious grue in the second half of his 62-minute opus to satisfy any of us old-timey VHS viewing types. Sure, it's highly derivative stuff, but joyously so; its enthusiasm is never less than infectious. If there's one missed opportunity here, it's in

---

2 You absolutely must read the extensive coverage of **EQUINOX** in *Monster! Digest* #14 (p. 8) if you have any kind of self respect. *–Ed.*

the father/stepmother/son arc. The vindictive female spirit targets Naoto because she mistakes him for his father (and her ex-lover). There is zero Oedipal material on display, which is something that was either lost on Fukazawa or more likely was simply territory he chose not to cross into (this being a "fun" flick, after all). Perhaps it's just as well, thinking about it.

With its tongue placed firmly in its poker-faced cheek (something the Japanese excel at), **BLOODY MUSCLE BODY BUILDER IN HELL** adds up to lots of B-movie fun. At the very least, this entertaining Indie would make for a fun supporting feature to the likes of Nobuhiko Obayashi's **HOUSE** (*Hausu*, 1977). Now let's just hope it doesn't take another decade-plus for Fukazawa to follow this one up.

2012; JAPAN D: SHINICHI FUKAZAWA
AVAILABLE FROM TERRACOTTA RELEASING [R2]

CELLAR DWELLER

Reviewed by Michael Hauss

Check out this awesomely bad New Line poster for **CELLAR DWELLER!**

"He who has wisdom wonders not of the beast, for nothing in hell lives without man's consent. Woe unto you who give the beast form. To contemplate evil is to ask evil home."

If ever there was a film that I would personally label a guilty pleasure, this film would be it. Somehow, through some cringe-worthy scenes, questionable acting, and wooden dialogue, this film still manages to entertain. While the much-used premise of comic creations coming alive (used heavily in both animated cartoons and in film) was the thin plot thread this awkward production hung its flimsy hopes upon, that concept, although promising to break at any minute, held together long enough to get through the short 77-minute run-time. Although the film is technically a horror film, I felt as if the production may have been angling for a comedy-horror mix, but the comedy just did not come across as funny; an aborted comedy-horror film that may have been funny to someone, but not to the viewer.

The film starts out in pulpy splendor, with the comic book artist, Colin Childress (Jeffery Combs), unintentionally invoking a creature that possessed the attributes of a vampire, werewolf, ghost and a demon, into the physical world from his comic book pages. Childress is in possession of an ancient leather-bound book called *Curses of the Ancient Dead*, from whence he uses passages to include in his comic book *Cellar Dweller* (obviously based on the famous 1950's E.C. comics). The problem is that by using the curses, he has brought forth a hideous creature that attacks a scantily-clad woman, come to life from the rough draft of his latest comic masterpiece. Thinking quickly, he flips out his trusty Zippo lighter, and attempts to beat back the monster with fire. Childress quickly realizes that the fire can destroy the monster, by simply burning the pages from whence it sprang. The fire spreads

The **CELLAR DWELLER** him--er, *it*self, in one of the many generous glimpses at the impressive monster FX makeup created for the meagerly-budgeted film

quickly about the basement, and before Childress can act or over-act (as seems to be the case here), he is engulfed in flames and perishes.

Then the movie abruptly shifts gears, thirty years into the future, and Jeffery Combs is gone from the film, never to reappear. (Yeah, *the* Jeffery Combs, who appeared in the classic horror films **RE-ANIMATOR** (1985) and **FROM BEYOND** (1986), both productions predating this film…and they use him for all of ten minutes or so.) We are introduced to Whitney Taylor (Debrah Farentino), an aspiring comic book artist, who has come to the old residence of Colin Childress, which has been changed into a place called ThrockMorton Institute of the Arts, an artist colony. Whitney excitedly proclaims to the head of the institute, Mrs. Briggs (Yvonne De Carlo), that she wishes to create a comic book in the tradition of *Cellar Dweller*. Whitney is not welcomed warmly by Mrs. Briggs, and is told in no uncertain terms that her comic book aspirations are below the standards of the institute, but the facilities admissions committee has forced her to find a place for Whitney at the illustrious ThrockMorton.

The secluded institute has no phones, no television, and no ties with the outside world. The basement, from which blood-curdling noises emit, was the one-time studio of Colin Childress, and is strictly off-limits. The odd (to say the least) artists of the colony are introduced one by one, and how any of these talentless hacks, aside from Whitney, were accepted at this so-called art institute is beyond me. The colony artists include Phillip (Brain Robbins), who does finger-painting, Lisa (Miranda Wilson),

the performance artist, Norman (Vince Edwards), the ex-detective-turned-writer, and Amanda (Pamela Bellwood), who is a video artist, and a bitter rival/nemesis from Whitney's past.

Each of the characters are well-trodden tropes of various horror films, and the dialogue is so wooden and heavy-handed, that the cast had a hard time reciting their lines at times, especially Debrah Farentino as Whitney, who seemed to be trying to hold back from laughing throughout the whole production, until the end and her dramatic, tearful turn (which unfortunately, after a movie that was all along unsure of its direction, made the dramatic finale fall flat on its face). In what is probably the most bizarre turn in the film, the Norman Meshelski (an unrecognizable Vince Edwards) character, a one-time detective, who has turned to writing, is a middle-aged man, dressed like a 1930s *noir* detective, who chomps on a fat cigar and drinks whiskey while plugging away at his typewriter in the best Mickey Spillane fashion…and this was set in the 1980s for Christsakes!

Of course, the lure of the basement is too much for Whitney, and to her surprise and our bewilderment, the basement studio, although covered in layers of dust and spider webs, is exactly like it looked pre-fire. So, if the fire did not happen, then either the whole opening was a false step, or the monster wrote the area back to its original look pre-fire, to lure Whitney in. Either that or the young girl who was killed in the basement was killed by a deranged Colin Childress, and all the rumors are true, that he was a homicidal maniac. Once Whitney persuades

Mrs. Briggs to allow her to move into the basement, using the logic that if she did so, then her old room could be used for another more deserving student, she jumps right in on creating her comic, with the help of the ancient curses book. As Whitney draws her comics, the monster comes to life and attacks the colony's members. At first the rough draft pages are drawn by Whitney, but then the pages begin to draw themselves and Whitney and Phillip, who have begun to have feelings for one another, figure out what is going on and must find a way to stop the creature from killing all the colony's members.

CELLAR DWELLER (1988) was filmed in Italy and was produced by Empire Pictures, best known for producing and distributing the abovementioned Jeffery Combs vehicles **RE-ANIMATOR**, and **FROM BEYOND**, along with many other films, headed by the famous (or infamous, depending on how you view his career) Charles Band. John Carl Buechler, the director, is probably best known for directing the films **TROLL** (1986), and **FRIDAY THE 13TH PART VII: THE NEW BLOOD** (1988)[3], but, is probably more venerated as a special effects wizard on many low-budget flicks, including a fair amount for Empire pictures. Yvonne De Carlo as Mrs. Briggs seems exasperated at the dialogue and the cheapness of the production. De Carlo is best known for her wonderful performances in the classics **CRISS CROSS** (1949) with Burt Lancaster, **THE TEN COMMANDMENTS** (1956), and *The Munsters* (1964-1966), where she played Lilly Munster. But De Carlo, also appeared in such exploitation gems as **SATAN'S CHEERLEADERS** (1977), **GUYANA: CULT OF THE DAMMNED** (1979) and **THE SILENT SCREAM** (1979), among others. This was the big-screen debut for Debrah Farentino, and it shows in her apparent anxiety-fueled performance that almost bordered on hysteria at times. Farentino continues to act, mostly on television. Brian Roberts, who plays Phillip, gave up acting and has become a successful producer, but not before appearing in that groan-inducing television series *Head of the Class* (1986-1991). Roberts did appear in the follow-up to the successful film **C.H.U.D.** (1984), appearing as Steve Williams in the inferior sequel **C.H.U.D. II: BUD THE CHUD** (1989).

Now, **CELLAR DWELLER** is no more than an average flick, at best, that plays its hand fast and stupid. The monster is nicely realized, and it boasts some good, entertaining kills, courtesy of director John Carl Buechler and his crew of special effects artists. The acting is atrocious across the board, and at times it appears that the cast had a hard time performing their lines with a straight face, especially, as previously stated, the Whitney Taylor character, who was seemingly in on the joke of this production, a joke us viewers were never allowed in on.

1988, USA. D: JOHN CARL BUECHLER
AVAILABLE FROM SHOUT! FACTORY

C.H.U.D.

Reviewed by Chris Nersinger

Tagline: *"They're not staying down there, anymore!"*

This is one of those "they just don't make them like this anymore" flicks: a mix-em-up creature feature featuring as it baddies zombie-like radiated-

---
3 See *Weng's Chop* #10, p.79.

Above: A close-up look at one of the monstrous Cannibalistic Humanoid Underground Dwellers living in the tunnels below NYC

Right: A group of C.H.U.D. gather around a puddle of the toxic goo that begat them

homeless-turned-cannibalistic-creatures who love munching on the living, and if you happen to survive…well, once you're infected you know the rest.

C.H.U.D. (1984) is a prime example of great '80s horror made with a small budget, but thanks to smart direction, excellent location shots, a very creative special effects team and a cast of solid actors early on in their careers who have all achieved a rare thing: a modern cult classic that has aged well like a fine glass of wine. A film that can be watched over and over and still feel like a first-time viewing while at the same feeling like an old friend who has come to visit. This is the type of film I watched with my friends when I was growing up, hiding behind the couch and taking turns squinting with one eye open during the scary scenes, and sipping a cool mug of root beer and munching on a bowl full of Dutch Snyder pretzels. Well, better to do the munching than being the one munched on.

The titular acronym "C.H.U.D." stands for Cannibalistic Humanoid Underground Dwellers (also for Contamination Hazard Urban Disposal in the film), and the film takes the grim premise that if we can have mutated giant alligators or rats in the sewer systems, why couldn't the same thing happen to the all-but-forgotten homeless people that we encounter in our everyday lives who just seem to just disappear? Then add a big urban setting like New York City with all the underground places like abandoned areas of the subway system, and you've got yourself a party. Remember CBS' *Beauty and the Beast* TV show? There was a whole other world under New York, and who knows—maybe it's true! I grew up in Rochester, New York with an entire subway system that was shut down and abandoned, with tunnels that still to this very day run underneath parts of city…so who knows what really is down there?

So on that note, the film is off and running with a woman named Flora Bosch (Laure Mattos) oblivi-

Pitor, played by Itay Tiran, has an unfortunate "episode" at his own wedding in Marcin Wrona's **DEMON**

ously walking her dog until...one minute she's there the next she's gone. Monsters are coming up from their subterranean refuge and they're hungry—extremely so. But what are they? Maybe this has something to do with the ever-growing number of homeless that have been disappearing, missed by no one at first...no one except for Daniel Stern (no one does manic better) as rebellious, caring preacher A.J. "The Reverend" Shepherd, who is more than worried when several of his regulars start missing and the ones who are left want to arm themselves. But why? At first no one seems to care until neighborhood police Captain Bosch (Christopher Curry), spurred on by his wife's disappearance, tries to get to the bottom of a city-wide conspiracy that involves a government cover-up (they're the best kind, of course). When the Reverend starts pressing for information, the green ooze is about to hit the fan...and believe me, when these underground dwellers get shot or cut it just sprays everywhere—we all know that chemicals mixed with a radiated source never spawn anything good! There is one tense scene that has The Reverend and "tunnel-life photographer" George Cooper (John Heard, in a great subdued performance) stumbling across these creatures as they are congregating around some awful-looking liquid almost as if they are worshipping it, like some kind of ritual. Ugh! Also look for a young John Goodman and comedian Jay Thomas as two rookie cops on the beat.

C.H.U.D. has long been considered a cult horror classic (the term "chud" has since become slang for a stupid, ugly person), and the film has been beautifully restored by Arrow for this first-time Blu-ray release. The disc is just overflowing with extras, including a fully illustrated collector's book with writing from Michael Gingold, an extended shower scene (I mean, that's reason enough to buy it right there), plus an audio commentary with Daniel Stern, John Heard, Christopher Curry and director Douglas Cheek, which itself is worth the purchase. The whole commentary track is hilarious, and you can tell these guys are still friends and had a lot of fun making this film. There's also an isolated score audio track with interview/commentary from composer David A. Hughes, an interview with production designer William Bilowit...and even more!

So run, hide, dodge and duck to get this into your monster-loving hands, and no matter what you do, don't ever stand close to a manhole cover again! Whatever a C.H.U.D is, it boasts crazy fangs, pointed teeth, glowing eyes, radioactive blood, three-fingered hands with sharpened claws...and it's famished!

1984, USA. D: DOUGLAS CHEEK
AVAILABLE FROM ARROW VIDEO

DEMON

Reviewed by Jacob Gustafson

Over the last few years we've seen a shift in the horror genre. More and more, horror films are becoming personal, subtle and, for lack of a better term, "arty". Horror is becoming smarter, too, which is never a bad thing. With major hits like **IT FOLLOWS** (2014), **THE VVITCH: A NEW-ENGLAND FOLKTALE** (2015), and **GET OUT** (2017), we're seeing low-budget, high-quality horror films that satisfy not only our love for shock and scares, but also our love for intelligent, artful storytelling. Made in Poland, **DEMON** (2016) is one such "arthouse" horror film that is the nexus point between the understated European sensibility and the world of horror.

DEMON begins with Piotr (Itay Tiran), our leading man, on a ferry, being taken to what will be his

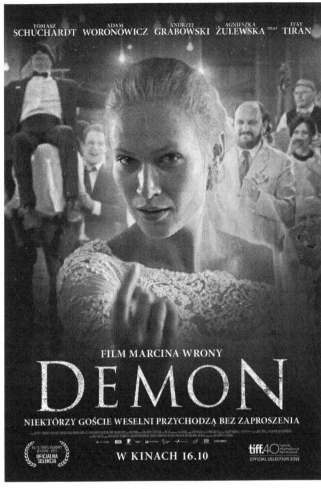

Polish theatrical poster

new home. He is getting married to a Polish woman after meeting her in London. His grasp of Polish is still a little shaky but he has decided to go all-in and move to the country to be with his bride Zaneta (Agnieszka Zulewska) on a piece of land owned by her grandfather and willed to her. Excited for his new life in a new land, Piotr arrives at the home and begins to clear away some branches and small trees to make room for the wedding which will be officiated on the property. Using a backhoe he accidentally knocks down a small tree. The uprooted tree reveals a partially exposed skeleton of an unknown animal. Immediately disturbed, Piotr decides to tell no one and cover up the skeleton. The wedding is the next day and Piotr isn't feeling well. Excited about his new life, he ignores his ill feelings and welcomes his new family. He has a Polish-Jewish wedding with lots of music, drinking, and merriment. As the night wears on Piotr's ill feelings crescendo into a full-blown epileptic fit that leaves him vastly different than when the wedding began.

DEMON manages to blend the supernatural elements within the film without going full-blown "throwing people around with giant possessed mouth gaping", as is so common in American horror of the last decade. Instead, the film focuses more on how Piotr's strange behavior unnerves the guests, including the local priest, who wants to have nothing to do with it. Zaneta's father spends most of the movie trying to convince the wedding guests that nothing is going on and that everything is totally fine, while Zaneta is left in the dark wondering where her new husband is. Rather than focusing on special effects and gore, the film's primary concern is to keep the story as grounded as possible to make Piotr's possession seem more realistic, and thus more frightening. As has been the case with many European horror films of the last decade, the film is more subtle than your average American horror flick, which may leave some viewers either confused or bored. No, there isn't any gore or any dramatic lighting. The film utilizes natural light and subtle music to convey the slow overtaking of Piotr. Again, "subtlety" is the key word here, for the most part. That being said, **DEMON** had me fully engaged during its runtime. I was fascinated by how the film unfolded although I'll admit at certain points I did want it to speed things up a bit. All of the actors deliver great performances, but the standout of course is Itay Tiran as Piotr. The whole film hinges on his performance and he delivers a great one. The film is populated with relatable and memorable characters and, more importantly, ones that don't grate. There is a lived-in quality to the film, and that's due to the great performances and writing for the characters. I felt as if I had been dumped in the middle of these characters' lives. Because of this, the story isn't overt and requires a bit of simple detective work on the part of the viewer. It's a bit like walking in on a conversation that's interesting so you listen and try to piece together what each person is talking about.

Don't get me wrong—I love special effects-driven horror films with lots of monsters and crazy over-the-top moments. But sometimes I also enjoy a quieter horror film, too. **DEMON** is more challenging than your average horror flick. The film doesn't spell everything out and so the viewer has to be attentive and pay attention to what each character is doing, and why. It's a creepy film that gets by without makeup effects or jump-scares. If you're looking for a rip-roaring horror flick with lots of action, this isn't that film. But if you're intrigued by the quieter arthouse horror films that have been coming out of late, **DEMON** is a unique film within the horror genre and worth your time.

Sadly, director Marcin Wrona committed suicide in 2015 before the film was available to most horror fans. Reportedly, he took his own life while at a film festival in Poland where his film was screening. He will never know how well-received this film has been and we as fans won't get a follow-up.

2015, POLAND/ISRAEL.
D: MARCIN WRONA
AVAILABLE FROM SONY

DERANGED: CONFESSIONS OF A NECROPHILE

Reviewed by Tim Merrill

*"There once was a man named Ed
Who never took a woman to bed.
When he wanted to fiddle,
He'd just carve out the middle,
And just hang the remains in the shed."*

The annals of American hillbilly history are riddled with deviants, misanthropes, and right pigfuck bastards, and the crown prince of them all was one Mr. Edward Gein.

Ed was a man of simple pursuits, like practicing interpretive dance, prancing under the Wisconsin moon decked-out in his freshly skinned "ladyhosen", beating a coffee can drum while howling to the sky. He was also quite resourceful with his hands, and took to crafting both furniture and clothing out of his neighbor folk, showing he was into "recycling" long before it was hip. Before Ed could show Martha Stewart a thing or two about home furnishings, the local law came 'round his rural farm on a wild hunch, and they found a Jane Doe (a deer, a female deer) cleaned and hanging in the barn.

Hobby time was over, and Ed was hauled off to the Central state mental hospital in Waupun, Wisconsin to weave baskets for the rest of his days. Little did he know while chilling in the nut hatch, his exploits became the stuff of legend, and people became terrified of the stories of the "Butcher of Plainfield". The crimes of Ed Gein became so infamous that they seeped into the collective consciousness of countless writers and filmmakers, starting with Robert Bloch and his 1959 novel *Psycho*.

As Bloch's novel would go on to become Hitchcock's 1960 classic film, there would continue to be an endless stream of movies that were influenced by Eddie's antics. There's little doubt in the minds of horror fans that if it wasn't for Ed there would never been a **THE TEXAS CHAIN SAW MASSACRE** (1974).

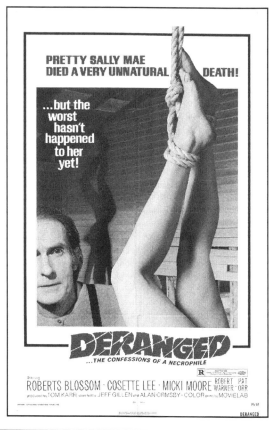

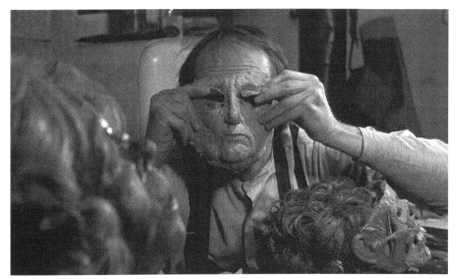

Ezra Cobb puts on a brave face for Mama in **DERANGED: CONFESSIONS OF A NECROPHILE**, loosely based on the story of Ed Gein

There's a real irony in this that doesn't sit well with some. While Hooper's film, released in October of 1974, would go on to be regarded as a seminal classic, it proved to be nominal in its ties to the crimes in Plainfield. The movie that many swore to be "true" was anything but.

Now, eight months prior to the release of **TTCSM** in February of '74, directors Jeff Gillen and Alan Ormsby released **DERANGED: THE CONFESSIONS OF A NECROPHILE** (originally just titled **DERANGED**). Despite being criminally eclipsed by Hooper's film, **DERANGED** is the closest faithful dramatization of what "truly" happened. Now *not* to say that **TTCSM** is a pale imitator at all, but this was the first film to have the "dinner scene", and the first to present its lead in a dead skin mask. There's no denying that **DERANGED** did not receive its due recognition, and was unfairly relegated to a life in the grinds and drive-ins, until it was, rediscovered by a Florida Company in the late 80s and released on video.

Shot throughout Southern Ontario, Canada for a $200,000 budget, the film stars Roberts Blossom as Ezra Cobb, our homicidal lead. Most will remember Blossom from his role in **HOME ALONE** (1990) as old Mr. Marley, and especially as George Lebay, who sells Arnie (Keith Gordon) the demonic car "Christine" in John Carpenter's titular 1983 film.

It's absolutely eerie how close Blossom plays Ezra to Gein's true character, and it's practically impossible to imagine anyone else playing the part. What's even more amazing is that both a young Christopher Walken and Harvey Keitel both tried out for the role.

The film takes a narrative approach similar in introduction to Whale's **FRANKENSTEIN** (1931) and Lewis' **BLOOD FEAST** (1963), by warning audiences of the horrors which are to come. Canuxploition fans will quickly recognize Leslie Carlson (**BLACK CHRISTMAS** [1974], **VIDEODROME** [1983], **THE FLY** [1986]) as the intrepid reporter who acts as a narrator in telling the gruesome tale of Ezra Cobb.

Ezra is a timid mouse of a man, only raised by two things, his Ma (Cosette Lee) and the Good Book. Throughout his life Mama acted as his moral compass, and Ez could not make a move on his own without being warned about the dangers of alcohol, and "evil women". Mama always reminded Ez that the wages of women were "gonorrhea, syphilis, and death". Ez plays the good son and tends to the farm, and to his ailing mother, but when mother finally kacks over (while he feeds her pea soup, during one of the most wretched moments in the film), his last thread of sanity finally snaps. Ezra's boat finally sails adrift, leaving him rudderless and insane. Blossom embraces the role, and plays Ezra so timidly, yet so far gone. He's pathetic and childish, yet nuttier than a shit-house rat and totally goes toe-to-toe with Tony Perkins when it comes to homicidal mama's boys.

Without his doting mother a boy will tend to wander, and do "unspeakable things". Despite Mama taking a dirt nap, Ez can't seem to get her domineering voice out of his head, so he does what any good boy does: he pulls out his shovel and brings Ma home where she belongs before any of nature's critters can dig in. Unfortunately, after a year under ground, Mama doesn't look like the picture of good health, so Ezra is forced to return to the cemetery to find some "touch-up parts" to make Mama pretty again. Thanks to the gnarly early effects work of Tom Savini, we get to see Ezra at work, giving away his "beauty secrets" and peeling off the face of a Sunday school teacher, not to mention spooning out her eyes and brains into a coffee cup. The original video release had cut out the entire sequence, but it has now been restored for the Arrow and Kino Lorber releases.

GORGO gives a surprise "hello" to a couple of fishermen

Once Ez does his best to restore his mother's withered husk of a corpse, he sets out on finding some company to satisfy his loneliness. Soon he goes looking for love in all the wrong places, and this is where **DERANGED** gets a bit wonky. Ez reconnects with an old friend of his mother, and we're forced to watch an awkward and poorly scripted seduction scene with a naïve Ez trying to come to terms with the advances of an obese older woman. It really doesn't fit within the rest of the narrative, and temporarily throws the film off its course.

What does work ghoulishly well is Ez's interest in local barmaid Mary (Micki Moore), who he slyly pursues. The scene where Mary finally gets to met the cadaverous "family" is truly chilling, with Ez dressed up in his unique stylish necro-fashions.

Before you can say "A box full of noses," deer season begins and Ezra goes back on the prowl again. After shooting and stalking a pretty young storekeeper, he heads back to the homestead with his "game", and the film ends with the police and neighbors finding Ez's "trophy" hung in the barn, and a gibbering Ezra Cobb covered in gore in the kitchen.

As stated earlier, it's a damn shame that **DE-RANGED** wound up being overlooked by critics in the light of the **TEXAS CHAIN SAW** hysteria (truth be known, **TTCSM** is my all-time favorite). **DERANGED** is a bona fide Halloween classic that is a must-see for true-crime hounds, and anyone looking for a true creepy throwback to 1970s horror cinema.

Since the release of the film, there have been several attempts to tell the tale of Ed Gein, and as each one has been reviewed, every write-up always comes back to **DERANGED**, and the skin-crawling performance of Roberts Blossom.

If old Eddie boy were still around, he'd undoubtedly give the film two thumbs up, two lips, a nose, and a full nipple belt…and you can't go wrong with that.

1974, CANADA/USA. D: JEFF GILLEN, ALAN ORMSBY
AVAILABLE FROM KINO LORBER

GORGO

Reviewed by Chris Nersinger

GORGO (1961) tells of a prehistoric creature that rises from the sea off the coast of Ireland right after a volcanic eruption, and of his plight at the hands of humans, his capture, and his loneliness. Will he be part of the carnival life? Is that what his future holds for him—to be gawked at? Or will he be liberated? Sean (Vincent Winter), a young orphan boy who feels Gorgo's pain and understands about be-

ing alone and parentless, tries pointing out to the adults—especially Captain Joe Ryan (the wonderful Bill Travers of **GEORDIE** [a.k.a. **WEE GEORDIE**, 1955] fame—that it might be making a mistake capturing Gorgo and taking him from the sea. **GORGO** asks the question: Do we have the right to capture and try to control nature? You decide. I, for one, usually expect consequences to arise, and in this case London and all its major tourist and historical attractions will understand when Mommy comes a-calling. Because there is no greater wrath than that of an angry, 200-foot-plus, pissed-off parent seeking out her kidnapped child. Big Ben and Piccadilly Circus don't stand a chance.

This story is also about one of the seven Deadly Sins—Greed. Thanks to Captain Ryan wanting more and more money, he goes from wanting to get paid for disposing of Gorgo to capturing him and displaying him at as permanent sideshow attraction in London. Travers' character, even from the very beginning of the film, is constantly in pursuit of the almighty dollar or in this case the British Pound… but at what cost? How many lives lost, how many buildings will be reduced to rubble before he hopefully sees the error of his ways? So if you have not guessed by now, this is not your typical giant monster movie. But is a highly entertaining bit of fantasy with a message. Kids of all ages will enjoy this.

Outside of movie magic, Gorgo is actually a suit. The suit itself was fitted with special mechanical apertures which enabled the ears to move independently of the mouth and tail. Combined at the same time with the performer inside, this gave the creature more believability and warmth. And while you are watching the film, really take in the sets and miniature work. Painstaking detail was given to the sets and nothing is more evident than when the Momma Gorgo is hulking through the streets of London, causing havoc for the military and toppling the likes of Big Ben. There has been no greater destruction of a city since Godzilla graced the screen in 1954.

Aside from the marvelous special effects, **GORGO** boasts a really wonderful score from Angelo Francesco Lavagnino, who by the 1970s had composed the soundtracks to approximately 300 films, including spaghetti westerns, sword and sandal to sci-fi with titles like **The Lost Continent** (1968), **THE WILD, WILD PLANET** (*I criminali della galassia*, 1966) and **MISSION BLOODY MARY** (*Agente 077 missione Bloody Mary*, 1965). Pay close attention to the music and one might here harps, xylophones, and an accordion, which, if you have the opportunity to pick up the *More Monsterous Movie Music* CD (includes the soundtrack to **GORGO** and 1953's **THE BEAST FROM 20,000**

FATHOMS), you'll discover in the liner notes is the unofficial instrument of the sea.

"Like Nothing You've Ever Seen Before!" is the tagline from **GORGO**, which might as well be describing the very Blu-ray release itself. Thanks to VCI, **GORGO** is stuffed and crammed with an amazing amount of extras. Everything from a digital version of the Charlton comic book from the 1960s to an isolated music score/sound effects audio track to a making-of documentary, *Ninth Wonder of the World: The Making of Gorgo*. The documentary features film historian Ted Newsom, Bob Burns (an avid collector of movie memorabilia and props), and features voiceover from the director himself: Eugène Lourié (also known for his work as art director for several classic films prior, including **THE BEAST FROM 20,000 FATHOMS**, and after that for an Oscar nomination for his visual effects work on 1968's **KRAKATOA: EAST OF JAVA**). *Ninth Wonder* was directed by Daniel Griffith, is narrated by Randall Turnball (perfect for this: smooth and enthusiastic), and produced by Ballyhoo Motion Pictures. The fact that it is so well-conceived, brimming with loads of trivia and such an incredible tale of how this classic slice of monster filmdom came together that I have watched it approximate 10 times in less than a week. Not only that, the documentary is exceptional to the point of meriting a release of its own. It does what every good piece of journalism does, it informs and stimulates the viewer/listener to want to learn more, ask questions.

The sound is crystal-clear due to the Westrex equipment used during the originally recording/filming process, and the restoration that was done for the Blu-ray release delivers a pristine picture. **GORGO** has never looked better, and like the tagline states, "Like Nothing You've Eever Seen Before".

For me, **GORGO** is a piece of nostalgia, bringing me back to long winter days spent with my buddies guzzling A&W Root Beer and Dutch Snyder pretzels. After the movie was over we went out into the snow to act out scenes from the movie, always

wondering what we would do if we found a baby dinosaur. A penny for your thoughts?

I'll say that **GORGO** is one of the best "Giant Monster" films of all time. I hope you seek this treasure out. So as we fade out and it's nearly sunset, if we squint as we look off towards the ocean, maybe— just maybe—we might be able to catch a glimpse of Gorgo and Mom wading back into the sea, and we may even hear an accordion playing in the distance…

1961, UK. D: EUGÈNE LOURIÉ
AVAILABLE FROM VCI ENTERTAINMENT

LEATHERFACE

Reviewed by Tim Merrill

In the annals of rock and roll, the Ramones busted out from the streets of New York in 1974 and kicked in our ears with something new, raw, and electrify-

A young woman has an unfortunate roadside encounter with Jedediah Sawyer, the boy who would one day become **LEATHERFACE**

ing. Throughout the years that followed, countless bands covered the Ramones, and while playing the songs well enough, none could duplicate the lightning in a bottle that the band possessed. Sure, you could play the Ramones' "Chainsaw", but not like they did.

The same year, somewhere in rural Texas, a young filmmaker would unknowingly create one of the most potently seminal horror films in history, **THE TEXAS CHAIN SAW MASSACRE** (1974). With a single blow, Tobe Hooper took the hammer to all of us innocent lambs, and hung us out to dry with his original vision of backwoods hell in Texas.

After giving up his fascination with power tools with his darkly humorous sequel in 1986, it seemed like every other year that someone new willingly looked to step up to the challenge, and pick up the saw in an attempt to bring back the buzz. If it wasn't an additional sequel to be made, it was a "prequel" that took us back to the origins of the Sawyer family and the hulking behemoth only known as Leatherface.

What wound up happening was a redneck Rashomon effect that basically gave us a number of variations of the same story. Some focused on the hapless teens, destined for headcheese, while others brought additional members to the family. Every film that followed had their own unique aspects that

were better or worse than the others, but none have been able to serve up the same gut and the gristle of Hooper's original canon. Sure, you can swing a saw, but not like that.

And here we sit in 2017, with French directors Alexandre Bustillo and Julien Maury ready to unleash their spin on the origin of the infamous Texas cannibal killer. Having made a name for themselves with the 2007 gut-punch **INSIDE** (*À l'intérieur*), many were anticipating a tight yet ripping visceral experience with their latest film, **LEATHERFACE** (2017).

Right from the get-go it has to be said that it would be a complete disservice to the film to weigh it pound-for-pound against the original seminal classic. It's a race that this dog just couldn't win, but that doesn't mean it's an abject failure. Everyone who steps up to the Sawyer chili pot is going to add their own special "herbs and spices" to make it lip-smacking good, and while some might not even want to lick the spoon, many go back for second helpings.

Before throwing on your apron and sitting down to **LEATHERFACE**, one should realize the film isn't necessarily what you may anticipate. While it is a *Chainsaw* film in theory, the directors also give us a story that veers away from the Sawyer homestead, and puts us in the midst of a classic country chase

Lili Taylor plays Verna Sawyer, a murderous matriarch who will do anything for her saw-centric family

piece by way of Terrence Mallick's **BADLANDS** (1973) and Milos Forman's **ONE FLEW OVER THE CUCKOO'S NEST** (1975).

After the "accidental" death of his daughter at the hands of the Sawyer clan, Texas Ranger Hal Hartman (Stephen Dorff) goes after matriarch Verna Sawyer (Lili Taylor) right where it hurts. Her children are taken away by the state and put into a protective institution for violent youth. The inmates are all subject to an assortment of controversial methods of treatment, including numerous bouts of electro-shock therapy. Several years later, as mama Sawyer comes looking for her kin, a riot occurs, and the boys break out and go on the lam with a kidnapped nurse in tow.

The majority of the running time focuses on the dogged pursuit of the escaped inmates by Ranger Hartman, and this is a large part of the film's problem. While there's nothing wrong with trying to put fresh teeth on an old saw, the focus needs to be on the saw, not on the drive to the hardware store to buy it. By the time the chase has finally run its course and the film steers itself back to the homestead, it's already the third act, and unfortunately too little and too late.

LEATHERFACE feels like a country-fried **NATURAL BORN KILLERS** (1994), only peppered with light elements connecting it to the titular character and his cannibal clan. To be fair, Bustillo and Maury throw a number of bones for the hardcore fans to gnaw on, as characters tied to the original film do show up throughout. They definitely know the source material, and try to weave it into their interpretation. The problem is that the characters only feel familiar in name alone, as there's no depth to any of them. While time is taken to clearly show how an act of revenge gives birth to Leatherface, there's no real exposition given to why the rest of the family were tweaked to begin with. You wonder what pushed the young cook, and Nubbins the hitchhiker (Dejan Angelov) to pursue a path of cannibal cuisine, but it's all left to speculation.

As a means to draw you into the film, Bustillo and Maury pull out an old-school McGuffin as to the possible identity of Leatherface; while it's a unique approach, the swerve is as clear as a summer sky in Texas. It would have served the film more to have focused on the character himself as opposed to setting up the guessing game that exposed him.

In terms of visuals, the Americana is portrayed well enough for a film shot in Bulgaria, as the wide-open fields and sun-baked roads are well on display. The one thing that most gore hounds want to know when it comes down to a new chainsaw film is whether or not it delivers the goods in terms of bringing the carnage. While there are a few money shots in the film that display a vengeful comeuppance to those deserving few, it isn't as extreme as you would expect it to be, all things considered. You would expect two veteran directors from the horror genre to go whole-hog on the *Chainsaw* franchise, but despite a few specific moments of over-the-top gore, the film relies more on quick edits and flash-shots. A large portion of the violence in **LEATHERFACE** doesn't even come from a chainsaw, which is surprising.

With Tobe Hooper receiving acknowledgment as "Executive Producer" in the opening credits, one is left to wonder if Tobe did get to see the finished product before his sad untimely demise. With just two films, Hooper created a rawhide tapestry of terror, and many have willingly tried to sew their own patch into the mix with varying results.

Bustillo and Maury should be commended for trying to carve out something new and unique with the series, but it boils down to a tale of two movies. While we are presented with a well-shot, hard-boiled country outlaw chase, there are just too many other elements (including an unnecessary three-way) that have nothing to do with the family nor the outcome of Leatherface himself.

Chainsaw fans are a discerning lot, and while they are open to interpretation, there's got to be a number of elements that have to be there.

As everybody knows, "The saw is family," and the family needs to be represented…not just in name alone. While there are plenty of Easter eggs contained within, which is appreciated, it also just feels like lip service to the fans.

The other essential factor is that you have to bring something substantial to the mix. If you're planning on attending a proper Texas BBQ, you've got to bring the prime cuts to the table. To quote *The Simpsons*, "You don't make friends with salad." While serving a stylish and unique meal, unfortunately

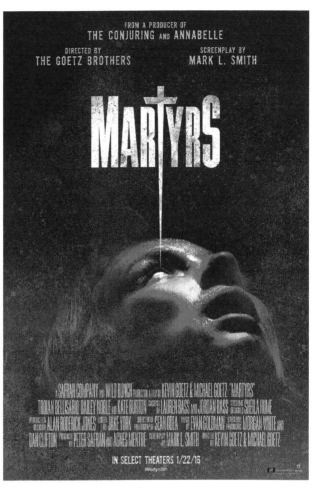

LEATHERFACE won't prove to be palatable to die-hard chainsaw brethren, and you'll be hard-pressed to find something to sink your teeth into.

2017, USA. D: ALEXANDRE BUSTILLO, JULIEN MAURY
AVAILABLE FROM LIONSGATE

MARTYRS

Reviewed by Christos Mouroukis

Two young girls (Ever Prishkulnik from **DARK AROUND THE STARS** [2013] and Elyse Cole from **DIVERGENT** [2014]) are imprisoned and brutally tortured. Fast-forward to some years later; they are now grown up and free but are still suffering the impact of the psychological and physical traumas. Lucie (now played by Troian Bellisario from **CONSENT** [2010]) is out for vengeance

The making of a martyr, in the Goetz Brothers' 2015 US remake of Pascal Laugier's 2008 French cult favorite

and she finally tracks down what appears to be the house of the doctor (Blake Robbins from **RUBBER** [2010]) that kept them locked-up there as kids and performed them terrible experiments on them. She kills him and his entire family (Romy Rosemont from **THE AVENGERS** [2012], Taylor John Smith from **A HAUNTED HOUSE 2** [2014], and Lexi DiBenedetto from **FALL DOWN DEAD** [2007]) with a shotgun, and straight after she invites Anna (now played by Bailey Noble from **THE WAITING** [2016]) to see the results as well, but the latter is not so sure about the whole thing, because as several therapists have said over the years that the whole thing may be just in their heads. In one of the first twists in the admittedly excellent screenplay, we learn that despite what hallucinations Lucie may have, this was indeed the evil doctor, and this is proven by the high-tech and well-designed chamber that he secretly kept in his basement. However, as soon as the two girls call the police, an evil elite and fundamentalist religious organization led by Eleanor (Kate Burton from **BIG TROUBLE IN LITTLE CHINA** [1986]) becomes aware of their presence…and a hide-and-seek game begins.

I have seen **MARTYRS** (2008), the original film in which this was based on, twice, the first time at home and the second time in a theatre, and both times I understood nothing. It simply seemed too complicated for me, especially for a story and a subgenre that is usually supposed to be simplistic. However, I understand its importance in the landscape of the previous decade's extreme French cinema. Its writer and director, Pascal Laugier (also known for **THE TALL MAN** [2012]), was in negotiations for an American remake as soon as the first one proved to be a sensation, and a profitable one at that. **THE LAST EXORCISM** (2010) director Daniel Stamm was briefly attached to the project but this plan was never materialized, because following his agent's advice he didn't sign to make another low-budget film. It was finally penned by Mark L. Smith (**THE REVENANT** [2015]), who went on record to say that he wanted to make a lighter movie in comparison to the original. My comment is that, for one thing you can hardly top it, and for another, U.S. writers always have to say things about character development and such stuff in order to put together financing for their projects, even when it comes to such films; it has just become part of the nonsensical Hollywood pitch. It was finally helmed by the Kevin Goetz and Michael Goetz duo (**SCENIC ROUTE** [2013]), and was soon premiered at Cannes Film Festival in 2015. It was also screened at the Los Angeles Screamfest Horror Film Festival 2015. It may over-explain things sometimes (as it is to be expected, as I believe the producers were targeting a wider audience than the niche first film), but I don't understand why everybody hated it so much. I watched it with an open mind and I was left quite satisfied and entertained, and many points which I didn't manage to figure out from the first film made more sense here. It also made a good impression to my friends with whom I watched it, and hadn't previously seen the original. Give it a try… you might like it.

2015, USA. D: KEVIN GOETZ, MICHAEL GOETZ
AVAILABLE FROM ANCHOR BAY

MURDER COLLECTION V.1

Reviewed by Christos Mouroukis

Back in 1994, when the Internet was in its infancy, a mysterious figure that went by the online name of Balan created a website entitled *Murder*, on which

thing, the narration segments come off as a bit stylish and original.

The video segments vary, and you will see: a Russian heavy metal fan and possible Satanist (Damien A. Maruscak) getting killed by his father (Daniel V. Klein) because he was making too much noise, an armed robbery, a cuckold (Jason Schneeberger) killing his wife (Lexi Jade) and taking her heart out, an abduction, a disgusting paedophile (Tom Smith) getting deservedly killed by one of his victims, a gang killing a man, a man killed in front of a cash machine, an autopsy performed by a rightfully pissed-off Japanese doctor (Dorian K. Arnold), a gang of rednecks luring a nerd into the forest and then killing him, the garrotting of another man, and lastly (and definitely the strongest), the kidnapping of a white girl by three black men that demand ransom and keep torturing and raping her until she dies.

The problem with some of these segments is that the performances are not always believable and the camera is

he presented a series of videos of real death. The website was soon shut down, but Balan was never found and therefore remained on the loose.

Fast-forward to the present day (i.e. 2009), and Balan is back with a new set of videos, which are presented in this collection along with his cynical commentary that often talks naïvely about death in the media, but at the same it also asks the most important question when it comes to movies like this: why are we watching them? But this is a film review, and it is my turn (as a member of the audience and a reviewer) to ask, why do you make them?

The answer would be really simple, as we are all curious to see how life ends, and obviously **FACES OF DEATH** (1978) was a huge inspiration for the present feature, but unfortunately the distorted narration comes across more like the recent (and lesser) straight-to-video shockumentaries that emerged from cheap U.S. distribution companies. Still, there is a lot of artistry here in the editing, and if any-

not always justified, even in the found footage sense (therefore they downgrade the believability of the feature as a whole). However, it is obvious that co-director Fred Vogel studied real death videos to—ahem—death, and he clearly does his best to emulate them here. The end result may be as depressing as hell, or as death itself, but it is an exercise that no real fan of extreme cinema should miss. Yes, this is a must-see.

It may not be as effective as the same director's *August Underground* trilogy (2001-2007) which I also review in the present issue[4], and I definitely don't know what the purpose of such art is, but let me assure you that this is definitely just that: art.

I think that I would have liked some subtitles in the segments during which people speak in Japanese and Russian, but this is a minor fault.

---

4 See pp. 120-123.

Fred Vogel (who also executive produced) co-wrote this with Jerami Cruise (the film's executive producer, special make-up effects designer, co-director and creator, who also appears in front of the camera in not one but two roles), Don Moore (who also appears in front of the camera in two roles), and Shelby Lyn Vogel (the film's producer and co-director, *also* appearing in two roles). It was co-produced by Robert Lucas (camera operator of the same year's **HIS NAME WAS JASON: 30 YEARS OF FRIDAY THE 13TH** [2009]) and associate produced by Aziza (also appearing in front of the camera).

2009, USA. D: JERAMI CRUISE, FRED VOGEL, SHELBY LYN VOGEL
AVAILABLE FROM TOE TAG PICTURES

NEVER SLEEP AGAIN: THE ELM STREET LEGACY

Reviewed by Christos Mouroukis

It is indeed weird putting together a review for a documentary on film. Such documentaries are pretty much a critique other than a presentation, and as such it may be not above criticism, yet it is awkward criticizing the critic. Or even worse, it reminds me of how movie forums' kids love tearing apart more professional movie commentators.

As you already probably know—if you don't live under a rock—this film is about the *Nightmare on Elm Street* franchise's original run, offering a lot of movie clips and "making of" footage, along with plenty of talking heads, assembling for a healthy amount of mostly historical background, and since it plays everything in chronological order and is divided accordingly in relevant chapters (giving equal amount of time to each entry), I did the same in this review.

The documentary's first fault is the failure to mention how much **A NIGHTMARE ON ELM STREET** (1984) owes to Dario Argento's style (think of **SUSPIRIA** [1977] next time you watch it). As expected, Johnny Depp does not appear for a new onscreen interview, but does get included through archive footage.

The greatest achievement is the totally hilarious segment on **A NIGHTMARE ON ELM STREET PART 2: FREDDY'S REVENGE** (1985) and its rampant homoerotic subtext (which I must add, I didn't notice when I first watched the film as a kid), although it is a pity that director Jack Sholder is downplayed (I mean, come on guys, the dude had previously masterfully directed **ALONE IN THE DARK** [1982] which is only trivially and briefly mentioned).

Next up is the **A NIGHTMARE ON ELM STREET 3: DREAM WARRIORS** (1987) segment, which is the Christian entry into the franchise, and has a lot of interesting stories about it, including Patricia Arquette's acting, Stacey Alden's nude scene, and Dokken's theme song and music video. By this point it is very clear that the *Saw* franchise (2004-2010) has stolen one idea too many

from Freddy Krueger, but no mention of this is made anywhere in the documentary.

Then we get the **A NIGHTMARE ON ELM STREET 4: THE DREAM MASTER** (1988) segment, and the best thing about it is the interviews with special effects legends John Carl Buechler and Howard Berger.

Even the *Freddy's Nightmares* (1988–1990) TV show get a brief segment, only to remind me that one of these days I have to sit down and watch that series.

The idea (and to an extension, its execution, too) of the **A NIGHTMARE ON ELM STREET: THE DREAM CHILD** (1989) segment is so silly that I'd rather say nothing about it.

One of the most interesting things I learned was that Peter Jackson had co-written a screenplay for **FREDDY'S DEAD: THE FINAL NIGHTMARE** (1991), and from what I heard about it I'd prefer it if they had ran with it, instead of the one they used, the only merit of which was Alice Cooper playing Freddy's dad. I was also expecting a Yaphet Kotto interview, but it wasn't meant to be.

My favourite film in the series is **NEW NIGHTMARE** (1994), which of course paved the way for the enormous success of **SCREAM** (1996), and the relation is analyzed.

As far as I remember, **FREDDY VS. JASON** (2003) was an entertaining and enjoyable experience, but a bit forgettable. As expected, Kane Hodder's absence is discussed.

Overall, this was a great idea, to make a retrospective out of these films, but it is so by-the-numbers-made (it is really no different from any DVD "bonus material", and it started as one), that it surprises me that it won awards left and right, which may be because of its length (240 minutes!), but people sometimes mistake quantity for quality. Its main problem, though, is the standard Hollywood interviews. In such "behind-the-scenes" interviews—especially when they are about horror films, and *especially* when the talking head is an actor or an actress—it appears that the subject doesn't speak so much with an audience of fans in mind, but rather a committee of studio executives, and tries to say the right things in order to get hired again. It's a shame that this plague is avoided only by a handful of legends, such as Robert Englund, Wes Craven, and Heather Langenkamp.

2010, USA. D: DANIEL FARRANDS, ANDREW KASCH
AVAILABLE FROM IMAGE ENTERTAINMENT

OUT OF THE DARK
(*Wui wan ye*)

Reviewed by Jeff Goodhartz

Director Jeffrey Lau was by this point in his career known as something of a specialist in the *mo lei tau* ("*Chinese nonsense*")-style comedies that Hong Kong audiences ate up in droves. Having directed such noisy over-the-top genre pics as **THE HAUNTED COP SHOP** (*Meng gui chai guang*, 1987) and **MORTUARY BLUES** (*Shi gia zhong di*, 1999), he also found even greater success directing mega-star Steven Chow in his comedic debut,

In Jeffrey Lau's **OUT OF THE DARK**, Stephen Chow plays Leon, an escaped mental patient who dresses like a Luc Besson character and fancies himself a ghostbuster

ALL FOR THE WINNER (*Dou sing*, 1990) as well as the two-part Monkey King adaptation, **A CHINESE ODYSSEY** (*Sai yau gei*, 1995).[5] All were big hits locally and it would seem a natural that Lau would combine the two by positing the ubiquitous Chow into one of his silly scare-fests. The result is either the best or worst of both worlds, depending on who you ask and, more tellingly, on which side of the Pacific they dwell.

The film opens (and pretty much stays) at an apartment complex where a group of slovenly security guards are dealing with tenants tossing things out of windows. Among the latter is Qun (the wonderfully zany Karen Mok), a lovelorn lass who is dealing with her current (and presumed umpteenth) breakup. Wandering the hallway, Qun stumbles upon a Mrs. Li (Suk-Mui Tam), who is praying to her recently deceased mother-in-law. Of course, being the kind of movie this is, the deceased returns as a ghost and threatens Li for having killed her. Old lady Li's method of doing so is by possessing her young grandson (how nice) and sending the kid after the parents with a knife. Fortunately, this bit of nastiness is stopped (at least for the moment) by Leon (Steven Chow), an escaped mental patient who dresses like his titular namesake of Luc Besson's **LÉON** (a.k.a. **THE PROFESSIONAL**, 1994) and fancies himself a ghost-buster. Assisting him in this is his trusty plant that can detect ghosts (every insane ghost-buster should have one). Leon's reward is being dragged back to the mental institution by the men in white. Smitten, Qun dons a Natalie Portman/Mathilda outfit and attempts to find

5 The latter consisting of the two 1995 feature films **A CHINESE ODYSSEY PART ONE: PANDORA'S BOX** (*Sai yau gei: Yut gwong bou haap*) and **A CHINESE ODYSSEY PART TWO: CINDERELLA** (*Sai yau gei: Sin leui kei yun*), originally released less than a month apart.

out about our would-be bio-exorcist. Proving it's difficult to keep an angry spirit down, old lady Li returns, possessing *both* of her siblings. Armed with knives, they go after the security guards. Leon reappears (his keepers are as incompetent as the security guards) and through a series of missteps, accidentally sends both Lis off the roof of the complex to their apparent deaths, despite Leon's repeated (and initially successful) attempts at resurrecting the female who angrily keeps killing herself over and over. A particularly hilarious running gag during this segment involves a wounded tenant who can't seem to avoid further bloody injuries at the hands of our "heroes". The security team brings Leon onboard to teach and train the squad (makes sense). His techniques in ghost-spotting are among Chow's best-ever bits. Mrs. Li's spirit returns and begins knocking off the members of the security team in rapid Freddy Kruger-like succession, only for Leon to point out that they are all illusions created in an attempt to scare everyone to death. This initially works, but doesn't prevent the late *Mr.* Li (Chi Fai Chow) from coming after them, chainsaw in hand. The finale manages to be equal parts harrowing and hysterical as our protagonists try everything from a banana peel to origami birds to flying head gear in an attempt to both escape and rid themselves of the Li curse.

When **OUT OF THE DARK** (*Wui wan ye*) premiered in Hong Kong in 1995, it bombed. The locals simply did not want to see their beloved Steven Chow in such a dark and unforgiving film; one which doesn't really offer up anyone for them to cheer for. Case in point: two of the security guards casually contemplate whether they should rape a female tenant now or after they have fun with a prostitute. *And these are two of the protagonists!* Chow himself plays a part far removed from his loveable upstart who ultimately sees the error of his ways. That kind of familiar character is one the locals have seen countless times before during the decade and apparently wanted to continue seeing nothing but. Here, his insane ghost-buster offers zero warmth, and that combined with some genuine bloody scares kept people away in droves. Unsurprisingly, it is for these very reasons that the film eventually found its cult following in the West, where most do not necessarily require Chow's normal brand, and gleefully go along with the nasty shenanigans on display. I personally would have loved to have seen Chow play this sort of part more often, as after watching it again for this review, I've come to realize it's one of my favorites of his. Of course anytime you have the multi-talented Karen Mok in one of these things, you know you will be in for a good time. Of all of Chow's female costars, only Mok can match her male lead in mirth and sheer over-the-top wackiness. Perhaps her most highly regarded role in this vein is as Turkey, the crazed street vendor opposite Chow in **THE GOD OF COOKERY** (*Sik san*, 1996). Here she provides the perfect foil as a love-struck borderline stalker who is nearly as nuts as her would-be soul mate. Their scenes together may lack charm (deliberately so, as there is nothing else in this picture that could be considered remotely charming), but their chemistry is undeniable, and it is clear Chow enjoys a female costar who can tackle this kind of role with such reckless abandon.

OUT OF THE DARK is terrific fun that can be enjoyed by fans of Jeffrey Lau's loud horror comedies specifically, as well as enthusiasts of *Evil Dead*-style entertainment in general. And if you are not a fan of Steven Chow (there are a number of such people), give this one a go. It and his character are just different enough that it may convert you…well, for one flick, at any rate.

1995, HONG KONG D: JEFFREY LAU
AVAILABLE FROM SHAW BROTHERS/ IVL

SANTA CLAUS

Reviewed by Steve Fenton

KGM's theatrical trailer ballyhoo really piles on the overstatement: *"It's like living a storybook adventure beyond your wildest imagination! From the North Pole of Fantasyland comes a feature-length fable with the most enchanting characters in the whole wide world, headed by the white-whiskered fellow who's the granddaddy of them all. Now, a magic motion picture transports you to an 'over-the-rainbow' land, past the doors of Santa's towering castle and the strange, mysterious 'all-seeing eye' into a fantastic crystal laboratory filled with weird and wonderful secrets no one has ever seen before. You'll see them* all, *and you'll discover how Santa can watch* every *child on Earth, and every good or bad thing they do… Now meet Merlin, the wizard of wizards, the miracle man of the ages… Come face to face with the Devil himself, a mischievous demon determined to mess things up as*

Scan of an old '80s VHS release from the Fenton Archives

which was produced by the very same outfit (Cinematográfica Calderón S.A.) at the very same studios (Churubusco-Azteca) as **SANTA CLAUS** was—sure as shit qualifies as prime *Weng's Chop* fodder in my book!

Firstly, a bit of backstory. I'm making an educated guess by presuming that just about every '*Chop*per has heard of exploitation cinema impresario/"quick sell" artiste extraordinaire K. (for Kenneth) Gordon Murray, if not necessarily by reputation, then at least by name. Sometimes less-than-flatteringly referred to as "Cagey" (=K.G.) or occasionally regarded as "the poor man's Walt Disney", Murray virtually singlehandedly invented the kiddie movie matinee as it once existed, and this was one of "his" movies—typically low-rent, snapped-up-on-the-cheap imported foreign fare, redubbed into English for quickie bookings in the stateside marketplace—which established the canny producer-dubber-distributor (an enthusiastic follower/imitator of legendary American roadshow huckster Kroger Babb who nurtured his knack for hyperbolic commercial promotion while working for many years on the carny circuit) as a force to be reckoned with in the cutthroat biz of saturation hit-and-run theatrical bookings.[6] Since I'm kicking around the idea of writing a longer article that focuses centrally on not just KGM the man himself but also the films he produced and/or distributed too, I shan't go into any other detail than the above about him here, as our current main focus is perhaps *the* movie for which he is best-remembered in certain circles, even though he had a hand in many other memorable hunks of exploitation, Mexploitation and—yes indeed!—*sex*ploitation besides.

As for the present title under review, like Tim Paxton, who (so he told me) makes a point of re-watching it every Christmas season, quipped to me on Facebook about this movie a few days back, "It's Santa vs. Satan!" And that, in the proverbial nutshell, is precisely the gist of its outrageous plot.

Yes indeed, shortly into **SANTA CLAUS**, no less than Lucifer himself—a heard-but-never-seen entity represented solely by a booming disembodied voice heard emanating from blasts of blazing hellfire—sends a (quote) "demon of Hades" to Earth in

much as he can... Leave it to that devilish trickster to sidetrack Santa up a tree! Watch the jolly hijinks of Santa Claus as he decides to fight fire with fire... You won't want to miss the entertainment wonder of the ages, the treat of a lifetime for anyone who has ever believed there really is a Santa Claus... You'll see more wonders than you can wave a wand at, as a dazzling panorama unfolds before your startled eyes. You'll Want To Shout... About the picture that won the Golden Gate Family Film Award! Everyone...Everywhere Is Waiting For...The K. Gordon Murray Presentation SANTA CLAUS."

Not only is Yuletide fast approaching, but this here baby would also make for ideal Halloween viewing too, so what better film to straddle both seasons at once? (Or better yet, you could watch it *any* time of the year!) Besides, any seasonal kiddie flick directed by the maker of **NIGHT OF THE BLOODY APES** (*La horripilante bestia humana*, 1968)—

---

6 Thanks for much of this KGM information to "The Wonderful World of K. Gordon Murray", an article by Charles Kilgore in the seminal Washington, DC-based fanzine *Ecco* #10 (July-August 1989), and also the much-revised/expanded version of his earlier article, which was published in *Filmfax* #24 (1991) under the slightly-shortened title "The Wonder World of K. Gordon Murray" (as per an advertising slogan of KGM's).

hopes of putting paid to ol' Saint Nick (a.k.a. Father Christmas, a.k.a. Père Noël et al). But not before we've had to endure a nearly ten-minute, almost unbearably-saccharine scene of Santa accompanying groups of kids—his "elves", if you will—from various nations on his enchanted keyboard (I promise I'll refrain from making any off-color and inappropriate "Santa-playing-with-his-organ" jokes. [*Oops!*]). Trust me, if there was any section of this freakily fun flick which sorely needed some judicious (some might say *vicious*) editing, it was this one! Think of the absolute poorest, most pathetic dregs/rejects of moppet-oriented TV shows like *Tiny Talent Time*—or perhaps an all-midget version of *The Gong Show*?—as most of these "cutely" caterwaulin' post-rugrats are about as tuneless/talentless as they come. But this is neither the time nor place to be putting down defenseless children, now is it?! After all, they're such a bunch of cutesy, apple-cheeked/wide-eyed li'l munchkins, I'd feel like Scrooge (or, worse yet, The Grinch) if I made any further disparaging remarks at their expense. Come to think of it, we should *pity* the poor little dears rather than mock them! Here they all are off on some faraway wintry asteroid on Christmas Eve without their parents while being forced to labor incessantly in Santa's outdoors workshop making toys—in a virtual constant *snowstorm*, yet—and he doesn't even provide them with suitable winter clothing, let alone safe working conditions, nor even proper eye protection either (faring worst of all are the African kids, who go shoeless in the snow wearing little more than leopard-skin loincloths, FFS). Talk about contravening UN child labor laws!

But let's not bother ourselves with matters of bitter reality in such idealistically optimistic/simplistic escapist entertainment as this, shall we?! Following a crazed, "expressionistic" diabolical dance number down in Hell (sorry, *Heck*; this is family-friendly fare, after all), Mr. Pitch (gangly comic actor-dancer José Luis "Trotsky" Aguirre), a long-horned pantomime greasepaint-and-red-spandex he-devil with floppy vivid-vermilion plastic XL pre-Spock ears, ascends to Earth from the *other*, way-*deeper* Down Under to wreak havoc with Christmas via either himself personally committing or else otherwise precipitating assorted forms of public mischief from various easily-manipulable mortal earthlings (to whom he remains invisible) by implanting subliminal telepathic suggestions in their psyches' subconscious. For instance, he provokes formerly wholesome, well-behaved little boys to chuck rocks through store windows, while Santa observes disapprovingly via his wacky "futuristic" gadgetry from somewhere else in our solar system beyond the dark side of the moon (?). Strangely—*perversely*, even?—enough, his chintzy gravity-defying castle (at one point described as "a palace of crystal and candy") looks like something that might well have seen later use in **FLESH GORDON** (1974), of all things, as well as simultaneously vaguely evoking the floating space fortress of the in-some-ways-quite-Santa-like King Vultan's winged Hawkmen in the original 1936 *Flash Gordon* serial which inspired that just-cited later porno parody.

Well-cast as the title tubby, bushy-bearded fellow in the present film is the fittingly top-billed José Elías Moreno (1910-1969), a popular Mexican usual character player who later played the mad Darwinist scientist Dr. Krallman—creator of the killa gorilla-man Gomar!—in Cardona's aforesaid sleaze/splatter/wrestling classic **BLOODY APES**, as well as appearing in X number other memorable Mexi-monster/fantasy movies besides. While it's great that he got to play Santa herein, it's a shame Moreno never appeared in any Santo movies, surprisingly enough. Although, he did co-star in one of my all-time favorite Mexploitation movies, namely Alfredo B. Crevenna's wondrously wacked-out subterranean creature feature **ADVENTURE AT THE CENTER OF THE EARTH** (*Aventura al centro de la tierra*, 1964)[7], not to mention also appeared in another of my taco terror faves, Rafael Baledón's for the time sometimes gruesome lycanthropy shocker **THE SHE-WOLF** (*La loba*, 1965). While Moreno was typically cast as intellectual, authoritative, professorial sorts (as in all three of

---
7 See *Monster!* #16 (April 2015), p.6

the monster movies previously mentioned in this paragraph), the year before he appeared for director Cardona (1906-1988) as Mr. Claus, the portly, distinguished-looking actor—who later starred as no less than Mexican revolutionary hero Pancho Villa—also played the "larger-than-life" fairy tale character known as *El Ogro* ("The Ogre", natch) in another eventual K. Gordon Murray / Childhood Productions acquisition, René Cardona, Sr.'s own **TOM THUMB** (*Pulgarcito*, 1958), which co-starred **SC**'s principal juvie lead Cesáreo Quezadas in the diminutive title role. Both Moreno and Quezadas would go on to co-star as the oversized-if-amiable ogre and his wee kidlet sidekick in a sequel to said '58 film, Roberto Rodríguez's **TOM THUMB AND LITTLE RED RIDING HOOD** (*Caperucita y Pulgarcito contra los monstruos*, 1960), whose a-lot-more-famous alternate title is the way-catchier **LITTLE RED RIDING HOOD AND THE MONSTERS**, which I much prefer (for obvious reasons, me being such a long-time Mexi-monster movie maven and all!). In fact, in terms of overall wackiness and entertainment value—not to mention its oodles of crazy critters!—I'd have to say that **LRRHATM** has the present film beat hands-down, although I have a *BIG* soft spot (right smack in the center of my squudgy Velveeta brain!) for both of 'em. Both Moreno's Ogre and Santa characterizations have a lot in common, size- and personality-wise, although, as well as a distinctly

José Elías Moreno as the man, the myth, the legend, the great bringer of presents, **SANTA CLAUS**

different costume, the former has a huge, bushy red beard rather than a white one. Essentially though, the two characters are near-as-dammit to the same.

In **SANTA CLAUS**, decked-out in a pintsize red-ribboned sombrero and matching poncho, Santa's *numero uno* little helper Pedro is played by Quezadas (alias *Pulgarcito* / "Tom Thumb"), who monitors his happy-go-lucky *jefe*'s goings-on down on Earth via a powerful (quote) "cosmic telescope". This dodgy-looking painted cardboard tubing-and-tinfoil thingumabob is situated in Santa's *sanctum sanctorum*, his so-called "magic observatory". In addition, this mad lab—a zany set which would have done *Pee-wee's Playhouse* right proud—includes several other goofy gizmos that assist Mr. Claus in his work. In no particular order, there's it known as the Master Eye: an "all-seeing" long-lashed, flashing eyeball on the end of an extendable length of silver-painted vacuum-cleaner tubing that sneakily snakes out like some sort of alien anal probe to covertly spy on our world from afar; then there's the amazing Earscope: a whopping great *papier-mâché* aural appendage mounted in the center of an oscillating satellite dish that can listen-in on events happening elsewhere in the universe; and, last but by no means least, we got the Tele-Talker: a speaking control console whose central feature is a humongous set of wrinkly pink humanoid (evidently female?) lips, which pucker and pout in bizarrely seductive fashion, sometimes kinda/sorta evoking a dilating and contracting anus… or maybe it's just me (yeah, that could be it. But I digress!). Just for an added "hi-tech" touch, little battery-operated "Made in Hong Kong"-type toy robots can occasionally be seen skittering about the floor un-

derfoot like the skutters on *Red Dwarf*. There. Now that I've hopefully set the scene for this spaced-out movie, it's time to dive into it headfirst…

It being the night before Christmas and all, the people on Earth who celebrate it are in a state of excited anticipation (or something like that). Even with extra manpower on the job for the occasion, the main Mexico City post office becomes so inundated with "begging" letters from kids to Santa that the place is overrun by them. After the posties' stressed-out, grouchy boss orders the massive heap of missives dumped into a furnace for disposal, instead of getting incinerated, they magically flutter up out of the chimney (courtesy of a simple reverse-motion effect) and fly off into the night sky like a swarm of rectangular white paper bats (do excuse the bad simile!), bound for Santa's magical extraterrestrial domain. Yep, forget "airmail": this stuff goes express delivery via *space*mail, no less! (And speaking of space, the then-recently-launched-into-orbit Soviet satellite Sputnik is at one point name-dropped, for topicality's sake.)

From his home planetoid (purists will no doubt be screaming, "B-b-but, he lives at the North Pole, not in outer space!"), Santa decides it's time for his once-per-annum visit to our neck of the galaxy, but first he consults with—of all people—Merlin the Magician ([Armando "Arriolita" Arriola] known as *El mago Merlín* in native Spanish prints) for some pre-flight pointers. By means of (quote) "the golden key that opens all doors" forged for him by his hirsute in-house blacksmith, which allows him to gain entry into any locked abode on the entire planet, SC freely enters people's homes in the dead of night…

gee, nothing *at all* creepy about that, right?! Having evidently been fitted with "fat-suit" underwear to further bolster his already considerable bulk, Moreno appears suitably robust and hale-'n'-hardy in the title role, giving a holly-jolly performance filled with apple-jowled grins and plentiful belly-wobblingly hearty guffaws. However, as is so typical of this sort of morally-simplistic fable fare, the real star of the show—even with his too-loosely-attached pixie/devil ears constantly flapping in the breeze—is Mr. Pitch, who's never really very diabolical in his aims or deeds, and merely impishly mischievous at worst (well, at least up till when he attempts to commit mass-murder by arson at a building filled with sleeping people, that is!). Without his performer Aguirre's demoniacally manic performance as Pitch to give it some much-needed energy, the hoary old story would be a whole lot less than it is; by that I mean *deadly dull*, more than likely, even with all its other eye candy and window dressing (sparkly/glittery tinsel and chintz which is about on a par with cheapo dime-store Xmas decorations, and probably highly-inflammable on top of it!).

Further signs of the devil's hand at work are revealed as the demon Pitch urges a little Mexican girl named Lupita (as played by the adorably cherubic Lupita Quezadas, *Pulgarcito*'s real-life baby sis) to steal toys; although morality and goody-goodness win out, for the time being at least. Some decidedly bizarre things do go on, however. Such as when a lonely "rich kid" (awwww, poor baby!) opens a pair of upright gift-wrapped, coffin-sized boxes to find... his parents! In addition, we get a *STRANGE*, lackadaisically-choreographed dance number that causes one to ponder whether 6-year-olds in the early/mid-'60s (when this crazy flick got a *lot* of play, both theatrically and on TV) might have been experimenting with LSD long before Corman's **THE TRIP** (1967) came along. Elsewhere, the pointy-eared devil, having singled her out just because she's such an incorruptible goody-two-shoes (bless 'er!), relentlessly pesters poor poverty-level Lupita to go against the Christmas spirit by doing something—*anything!*—bad. Communicating with her in the form of a giant ragdoll, the impish Mr. Pitch tempts Lupita in her dreams (*à la* a former-day Freddy Krueger?) to commit evil acts that run contrary-wise to traditional Yuletide custom, while, using those weird spying gadgets I mentioned earlier, the voyeuristic Santa periodically monitors what's going on from his moral high horse elsewhere.

Once he gets started Earthbound on his spaceflight close to halfway into the narrative, after only narrowly avoiding a head-on collision with our moon (a miniature heavenly body which looks *exactly* like a golf ball dangling on a string), Santa glides into Earth's atmosphere and touches down on his interplanetary sleigh. This rickety conveyance is drawn by a quartet of life-size clockwork white reindeer, some of whose flimsily-affixed heads and legs seem about ready to fall off at the slightest provocation once their master winds-up the key that sets them in herky-jerky motion care of decidedly primitive "animatronics" (which also cause the—*uh*—crit-

José Luis "Trotsky" Aguirre as the freaky and menacing Mr. Pitch, tormentor of children everywhere, and avid proponent of the Naughty List

Santa makng his Christmas Eve rounds, courtesy of his team of flying clockwork reindeer

ters' psychotically wide-staring eyeballs to swivel wonkily in their sockets and snort puffs of "steam" out their nostrils). And not only that, but if he hasn't returned to his home world come sun-up, said mechanical reindeer will become reduced to dust by the rising sun's rays, and he'll be left stranded in Mexico for keeps. With that precise endgame in mind, Pitch schemes to keep his nemesis marooned down here with us for all eternity. After first relieving him of both Merlin's magical sleep-dust (i.e., a pouch of silver glitter) and his white rose of instant invisibility then "treeing" the surprisingly spry ol' duffer by siccing a watchdog named Dante (in-joke alert!) on him, Pitch heaps further indignity onto Santa's brawny sack-carrying back by hypnotizing someone to send out a call to the cops in an attempt to frame him for attempted homicide.

Will Mr. Claus succeed in making a personal housecall on every last kid on Earth before cockcrow, granting all their written requests for empty material possessions? Will Lupita ever succumb to the dastardly Mr. Pitch's pitch and turn to the dark side? Will you actually give a hoot what happens to anyone, assuming you manage to make it all the way through this love-it-or-hate-it movie to find out? It, as they say, remains to be seen! (Or not. Depending on your preference…)

Stylistically speaking (if that's not too grandiose a term to use in the current humble context), this movie resembles **SANTA CLAUS CONQUERS THE MARTIANS** (1964)—or rather, vice versa—which was very likely inspired by this earlier Cardona offering, that raked-in/racked-up major profits for KGM, playing the rounds at Saturday and Sunday kids' matinees for years to come following its initial release (well into the '70s in some regions, so I've heard). A whole battery of prime Mexploi-

tation talent worked both behind and in front of the camera on this flick (including Cardona's future director son, Cardona, Jr.), whose credits are filled with names that will be familiar to any Mexi-movie geek, and you gotta love the fact that the opening titles proudly proclaim that **SC** was shot in "MexiScope" (a format which was thankfully preserved for the 1.78:1 presentation of VCI Entertainment's Region A Blu-ray edition; although, as a rule, Mexican movies were still shot "full-frame" decades after widescreen became the norm for most other movie industries around the globe).

Even the guy who played Popoca, The Aztec Mummy (Italian-born actor Angelo di Stefani a.k.a. Ángel D'Stefani) plays a supporting part here, albeit—most unfortunately indeed!—*not* all-done-up in gnarly monster makeup and tatty wrappings. And while we're on the subject of The Aztec Mummy here, as another vitally important (at least to me!) side-note of trivia, more astute, eagle-eyed viewers of **SANTA CLAUS** may well be able to spot the battered, dismantled remnants of no less than the title tincanman's metallic exoskeleton from Rafael Portillo's famous **THE ROBOT VS. THE AZTEC MUMMY** (*La momia azteca contra el robot humano*, 1957) scattered about in the background to some scenes as incidental props at Santa's palatial spatial digs (most-visible at roughly between the 44th and 47th minutes of **SC**'s total 94+-minute runtime). Said "robotic" parts were evidently dragged out of storage from the properties department of both films' production house Cinematográfica Calderón for reuse here in the interests of generating extra "futuristic" (?!) ambience. The presence of the disassembled **TRVTAM** bot's leftovers went mostly unnoticeable—blended into the scenery, so to speak—in old fullscreen (1.33:1) video copies of **SC**, whose transfer prints were fuzzier and lowerrez, as well as cropped-off short on either side of the frame, although it can still be spotted easily enough if you happen to be looking for it. In VCI's admittedly imperfect if nevertheless landmark Blu-ray version, the bot-bits are much easier to spot by far, simply due to the improved image clarity combined with its wider aspect ratio. I'm undoubtedly far from the first viewer to have spotted this welcome and probably purely unintentional throwaway "in-joke" to the earlier Popoca movie, but—call me easy to please!—I must confess it gave me quite the cheap thrill when I initially made the surprise sighting (I don't get out as much as I used to!). Although the robot suit has been completely torn apart and reduced to little more than scrap and a number of its identifying attachments/accessories have since been stripped-off (possibly for re-use by the property master and/or FX techs on other projects?), there's no mistaking it. Sometimes, as the old saying goes, it's the little things in life that mean the most to us, and that particular discovery meant a lot to me, making my fondness for this film all the stronger. I piss on the IMDb's lowly "2.5" rating for it on their meaningless Sphincter Scale! (Incidentally, when it comes to that website, while it is without doubt generally a very worthwhile and handy resource to have at our fingertips 24/7, DON'T always believe what you read there in regards to movies' "factual" [note quotes] aspects [etc.], as I spot obvious mistakes on there all the time, especially when it comes to Mexican cinema, as well as "foreign" fare in general. For instance, they frequently give years for films from Mexico that are misleading and sometimes even outright erroneous, typically listing the years of release [sometimes even giving *re*release years as those of initial releases] rather than the actual years of production, that are by no means always one-and-the-same when it comes to Mexican productions, which were sometimes completed well in advance of their actual release dates. Hence, words to the wise!)

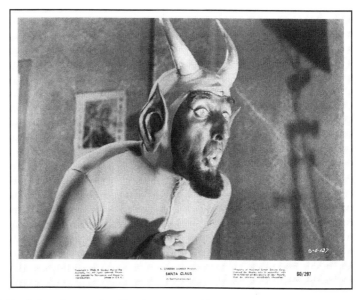

Overall, the most-fun parts of **SANTA CLAUS** for me are the scenes involving its crimson-colored villain Mr. Pitch, whether he be inciting dimple-chinned *chicos* to shanghai Santa and steal all his toys, or getting cheekily shot in the ass by a needle-sharp dart from a toy howitzer by our rotund red-clad hero; this latter while Mr. Claus is just about to place said projectile-firing plaything (non-gift-wrapped) under a family's Christmas tree for some lucky *niño*, and which prompts us to ponder just why the heck he would be giving-out such potentially dangerous prezzies to kids for? Hey Santa, you could put a darn eye out with that thing, don'tcha know!

Seriously though, when all is said and done, **SC** has an endearingly sweet simplicity and naïve idealism to it—its primary intended audience *was* the kindergartener/grade-schooler set, after all, so you shouldn't be expecting overmuch in the way of sophistication in the story or its ultimate moral message—and I'm guessing that is one of the main reasons (along with all its basic trashy/schlocky/campy qualities too, of course) why it has remained so resiliently popular and resonated favorably with so many people over the close to 60 years since it was made. It's highly doubtful that the average "too-cool" cult movie scenester would ever unabashedly admit to being sentimentally touched and moved by some of the film's sweeter moments, however.

But unless you're a completely heartless, nasty bastard, it's hard not to feel at least a slight tugging at your ol' heart-strings when teary-eyed li'l Lupita, after waking with a frightened start from a Pitch-induced bad dream, forlornly wonders aloud to her mother whether Santa doesn't like poor people, and if so, why not (cue lump in your throat here!). While at the time she was apparently no more than 4 or 5 years young, the performance by the tiny actress playing *señoritita* Lupita (which was also her own real-life first name, as you may recall) is so naturalistic that she almost doesn't seem to be acting at all, merely being her true self, reacting to all the things going on around her as she might well do in real life, and this innocently childlike (as opposed to child*ish*) simplicity and sincerity adds immeasurably to the appeal of her character. Alright, I know

I'm starting to get way too sappy here, but it is getting close to the time of year when it's okay for us to show some sappiness anyway, and I'm not quite finished yet, so bear with me...

Amidst all the surrounding kitschiness, the adult actress (i.e., the at times rather Faith Domergue-like Nora Veryán) playing the little girl's mom gives a sincerely and believably emotion-fraught performance, turning-on her own taps (i.e., tear ducts) on cue whenever her lonesome onscreen daughter prays plaintively to Heaven for Santa to bring her a dolly for an Xmas prezzy because her parents can't afford to buy her one, and she really, really wants a friend to snuggle up with. For her innate goodness and sweetness of spirit, she eventually scores a white-frillies-clad girl doll almost as big as she is, at which Madre rolls her eyes heavenwards and crosses herself in thanks (perhaps implying that, at least in her mind, the *other* White-Whiskered Big Guy In The Sky—or possibly both of them, working in cahoots?—was actually responsible for her daughter's Christmas wish coming true).

On that note... *¡¡¡Feliz Navidad, mis amigos y enemigos!!!*[8]

[Note: Special Thanks to Tim P. for sending me—and just in time for Christmas, too!—a copy of VCI's gorgeous BD, which is by far the nicest this film has ever looked on home video to date.]

1959, MEXICO. D: RENÉ CARDONA, SR.
AVAILABLE FROM V.C.I. ENTERTAINMENT

UNDERNEATH

Reviewed by Tony Strauss

Eric Linton (Blake Farris) is a quiet man who lives alone in a quiet house. At least he does now. As he starts his morning in preparation for work, it becomes apparent that the quietness might be all

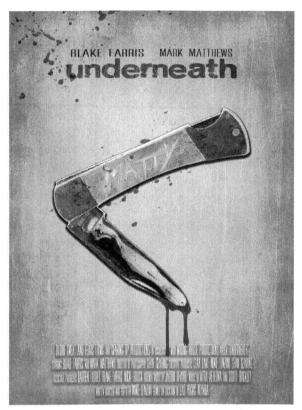

that remains of what he once was: a married man with a family. Now he lives a spartan existence in a home devoid of any familial warmth; there are now only photos of the family unit that once gave him purpose, and phone messages from his estranged spouse reminding him that divorce papers must be signed. Eric gets ready for his workday with all the passion of an automaton, brewing his single cup of coffee and immediately cleaning up to put everything back in its place. We get the sense that this semblance of structure is all he has left, and he's clinging to it as if it will eventually lead to the discovery of a new meaning in his life if he just maintains this singular track. Without hearing a word from him, we see what is clearly a damaged and empty man, just going through the motions for lack of any better options in sight.

Just as he's about ready to leave, his doorbell rings, and he opens the door to a scruffy young man named Shane (Mark D. Matthews) who claims his car has broken down and he needs to come in and use Eric's phone to call for help. Shane looks exactly like the kind of person you want to keep *out* of your house under any circumstance and at any cost: rail-thin, pale, jittery, sunken-eyed, with all the telltale indications that he's got a serious monkey on his back. Not only does Shane's alleged "break-

---

8 This review is a majorly-overhauled/revised (i.e., barely recognizable) version of one I originally put to paper the better part of three decades ago in one of my first-ever (hand-written!) Xerox 'zines, *¡Panicos!* #1 (Spring 1990). Whilst this new version bears only the scantest resemblance to its ancient progenitor, I figured I should mention it anyway.

have at least subconsciously intuited, as we the audience have, that there is something lurking just below Eric's calm surface demeanor...something that our senses warn us is dangerous. But now it's too late for them both; the gate is open, and they're both about to come face to face with what lies **UNDERNEATH** (2015)...

You've probably noticed by now that I tend to get pretty damned excited whenever encountering an indie film that delivers big on a small budget. As a cinema junkie, I've become terribly jaded by traditional, tried-and-true storytelling tropes, and constantly

down" sound iffy (there's no abandoned car in sight, and he obviously had to walk past dozens of other suburban houses before coming to Eric's door), but he's unnervingly insistent that he be let inside to use the phone. Eric—at first politely then necessarily sternly—declines, sending a none-too-happy Shane on his way before going back inside to finish getting ready.

But when Eric steps back outside to leave, guess who's outside waiting for him. That's right...and this time Shane greets him with a gun pointed at Eric's face, forcing his way into the house. Predictably, he wants any and all valuables there are to be taken, and is not the least bit withholding of invective against Eric for having not let him inside in the first place, threatening death in response to the slightest resistance.

Based on Eric's eerily calm, ice-cold compliance, however, we quickly sense something that Shane will soon wish he himself had sensed: Eric is not a man with whom one should fuck. Perhaps, had Shane not been so single-mindedly honed-in on the means to his next fix, he would

hunger for original voices or creative new takes on familiar concepts. This is why I tend to avoid most cineplex fare like it was a junkie trying to get into my house; even when mainstream product seems to offer up an interesting idea, more often than not that idea is besmirched by committee-driven decisions in an effort to make it "safe," "accessible" or "marketable".

Which brings me to the present film under review, the sophomore feature from indie filmmaker Mike Lenzini, who, you just might remember, debuted with the well-executed but poorly marketed **BEAST: A MONSTER AMONG MEN** (2013), which I reviewed in my Pollygrind festival coverage back in *Weng's Chop* #5.[9] That first film, although

---
9 See issue #5, p. 32 for the Pollygrind article (my review of **BEAST: A MONSTER AMONG MEN** can be found on p. 63).

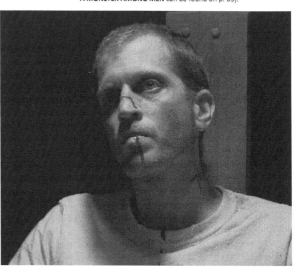

Blake Farris as Eric (top) and Mark D. Matthews as Shane (right) engage in an intensely reflective confrontation in Mike Lenzini's gripping psychological thriller, **UNDERNEATH**

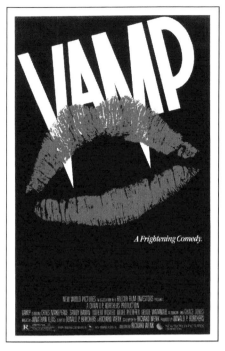

admittedly flawed in some not-uncommon-for-first-timer ways, was a standout for me at that festival, not only for its refreshingly different take on seemingly familiar ideas, but for its surprisingly depth of characterization rarely seen in underground/micro-budget films. Lenzini's second feature, thankfully, does not break the promise of things to come made by that first film—if anything, it surpasses them. Also thankfully, Lenzini has taken distribution matters into his own hands, and is retaining control of the manner and means through which this film is marketed. He's clearly learned a few things since his first film, not just on the business side but also on the storytelling/filmmaking side, and the viewer only benefits from this.

From the synopsis I gave above, you will rightly predict that this offering falls into the "home invasion wherein the invaded are scarier than the invader" subgenre, but that will most likely be where your accurate predictions end. This is no cat-and-mouse, hide-and-seek thriller about seemingly normal suburbanites with terrible secrets *à la* **DON'T BREATHE** (2016) or **THE PEOPLE UNDER THE STAIRS** (1991). No, this is a surprisingly straightforward, unsettlingly quiet thriller that confidently shines its light on the kinds of disturbing thoughts and feelings that exist in almost all of us… thoughts and feelings that are in danger of coming to the surface with just the right (or wrong) exterior stimuli. In my eyes, the most horrific things we can be presented with in scary movies come from within the darkness inside humankind, made all the more frightening when we can identify elements of that darkness within ourselves. This takes much of the safe detachment away that comforts us while watching more spectacular, over-the-top suspense fare.

Essentially a one-location, two-character presentation, **UNDERNEATH** relies heavily on atmosphere and performance, and in both categories, it delivers big. Farris portrays Eric with an incredible amount of subtlety and nuance, never once giving in to broad-stroke depiction of his seething, barely-held-together personality, and thus instilling in us a relentless uncertainty of what shape his anguish and rage will take when it's forced to come bubbling to the surface. His restrained silence can be truly terrifying to watch. Conversely, Matthews' portrayal of junkie Shane is the polar opposite of restrained, blurting out any and every negative thing that enters his drug-addled mind as he tries to negotiate his predicament. Yes, he's loud; yes, he's annoying; yes, he swears too much…but have you ever met an angry or scared junkie? Pretty spot-on, if you ask me. The dynamic between the two characters becomes all the more fascinating as layers are peeled away from both of them, and we discover more facets of their possibly equally disturbed personalities. The single location used here only adds to the foreboding, claustrophobic atmosphere closing in around us as we helplessly bear witness.

Folks looking for a thrill-a-minute, high-octane home-invasion flick will probably want to skip this one, though. Despite the fact that it clocks in at a tidy and efficient 78-minute runtime, **UNDERNEATH** is not out to thrill and excite you… this film is out to slowly press on the bruises you're trying to ignore away, and force you to stare into the mirror at your ugliest thoughts and feelings toward your fellow man. And when it's all said and done, it's still not over, because those thoughts and feelings will still be lingering with you, and those bruises will still feel fresh.

2015, USA. D: MIKE LENZINI
AVAILABLE ON VOD FROM BLUE SKY MEDIA, LLC

VAMP

Reviewed by Chris Nersinger

Taglines: *"Ever have one of those nights?", "The first kiss maybe your last"*

Arrow Films have been giving many cult classics the red-carpet treatment for quite some time, and their new Blu-ray release, **VAMP** (1986), is no exception—loaded with bonus material and extras galore. It is a campy send-up of vampires *à la* **FRIGHT NIGHT** (1985), with the role with the fangs being displayed by none other than the crazy, flamboyant soul singer, Grace Jones. And don't think for a moment that even though I mentioned campy that this film doesn't have its thrills and chills; if wasn't for the tongue-in-cheek approach and over-the-top performances from the supporting cast, this would have been a real nail-biter. As they say, not only has the curtain risen, but the moon is full and the city is awake...even the vampires are out tonight.

VAMP is nothing more than a delicious slice of sheer '80s mix of fun and horror, campy and popping with color like a '66 *Batman* episode. It's surprisingly non-cliché, with an unusual turn for Chris Makepeace as the hero Keith, and his buddy of all buddies, Robert Rusler, as AJ. Featuring New York City as the backdrop, which gives us a place where anything can happen and everything is acceptable. This is a movie that takes place in one day and a night, and I love stories like that because they seem to zip along, and because the audience does not have to keep track of the timeline it is easier to immerse themselves within the story and the characters.

Our heroes Keith and AJ are charged with the duty of securing entertainment for a frat party, and that in turn means a stripper. Along for the ride—actually he is their ride—is Gedde Watanabe (from **GUNG HO** [1986] and **SIXTEEN CANDLES** [1984]) as Duncan, who is in serious need of friends and he'll do just about anything. You know where our gang is going to wind up: none other than—you guessed it—the After Dark Club.

Now what really makes this film for me is the connection between Keith and AJ; these guys have such a great time on screen, due to the fact that Chris and Robert spent most of their time bonding before the filming even started to develop this chemistry. They each know what the other is thinking almost to the point of finishing each other's sentences. I was not only able to believe them but it brought me back to my high school/college days and the way my friends and I used to pal around and even ended up in a similar situation one night...just minus the vampires (though they might have been vamps, just not the ones with fangs), nonetheless it did not make our adventure any less exhilarating. I actually had a friend like AJ and he was the ladies' man. This friendship that Keith and AJ share is what puts this film in overdrive when, after trying to secure a dancer, AJ disappears within the club and Keith will not stop until he finds his best friend.

The real treat here is the cast of off-the-wall supporting characters and the wonderful actors that play them, including the exotic Grace Jones as Queen Katrina, a chilling vampire with a bad temper. Portrayed with very little dialog, but instead relying mostly on her body language and facial expressions (with which Grace says more than words ever could), she has such an amazing physical presence that when she is on camera you're thinking, "Please can I have more of this!" I looked up the word "vamp", which refers to a seductive woman who sexually exploits men. And in keeping with that definition, a female vampire who exerts her control over a man or men is indeed a vamp, hence the title of this film and the theme that is sprinkled throughout—if you keep your eyes on Grace Jones in the film when she is on screen she just exem-

Grace Jones as the exotic and dangerous Queen Katrina in **VAMP**

on screen you can just feel her love for Keith is genuine, and she lends a quirky-yet-smart performance which really lifts this film to another level. Another delight of this movie is Billy Drago, who is absolutely superb as Snow, the leader of a punked-out goth gang who has it in for Keith and AJ. Billy is, as always, way over the top, but this only helps add to some of the tension at times and also lends itself to some comic moments to help ease the scarier moments that take place on screen. My favorite non-lead in the film is Sandy Baron as Vic, our "Renfield" of the story (every vampire has to have one). Vic is the emcee/host at After Dark; he is completely dedicated to Queen Katrina and is a pretty smart whip at times. One of the craziest scenes to shed some light on the fact that this club is not all that it seems is when Keith walks over to Vic's podium to ask a question, and goes to grab a handful of what he thought were peanuts that Vic had just been munching on…and it turns out to be cockroaches! I actually cringe every time I watch this scene.

VAMP, just like **C.H.U.D.** (1984)[10] takes full advantage of its surroundings and incorporate them creatively into the story, with several scenes taking place

plifies this to a T. The casting could not have been more perfect, for she is every bit of her seductive, and she definitely wields her influence over the male population of her realm, in this case the After Dark Club, which is a bevy of all-female exotic dancers who just happen to be the bloodsucking type…literally. There is a scene about a quarter of the way through that shows the male audience spellbound after Katrina's performance on stage and the club just goes completely quiet for a long moment as if no one could believe what they just saw, then everyone suddenly starts applauding and throwing bills at the stage. The look on each of their faces is of awe and excitement with a little bit of spellbound thrown in for good measure.

Some of the other actors rounding out the cast include Dedee Pfeiffer as a long lost acquaintance Keith's who is very bright but spiked on love, only he doesn't know it's him. Even when Dedee is not

within the subterranean world just below the After Dark Club, including Queen Katrina's lair with its oversized tunnels within the sewer system. The lighting in the film exudes a sort of **BATMAN FOREVER** (1995) appeal with greens and purples, especially once we arrive at the club, and more so once the story moves *under* the club. But keep in mind that **VAMP** was produced a few years before even the first Tim Burton **BATMAN** (1989). Maybe Joel Schumacher's turn at the helm was slightly influenced by the present film—who knows? Richard Wenk's intuitive direction well-captures the heart of what makes a piece of celluloid a great horror film, and the ending really benefits from the sets and the sheer talent of its cast—it's a real edge-of-your-seater and very rewarding. The showdown between Chris's character and Katrina puts him in the old "Mexican standoff" situation…I can only say thank goodness bows and arrows have many applications.

10 See review on p. 127.

self-respecting vampire fan just dripping…with anticipation. Well, I say drink up and be merry!

1986, USA. D: RICHARD WENK
AVAILABLE FROM ARROW VIDEO[11]

LUCIFER VALENTINE'S VOMIT GORE TRILOGY

Reviewed by Christos Mouroukis

SLAUGHTERED VOMIT DOLLS

Okay, many reviews tried to give a synopsis of this, and you might want to check them online and in print, but for my money this is just a random selection of moving images whose only purpose is to gross you out. There is no narrative to speak of, at least not in the traditional sense (so it might be a bit difficult for regular cinema-goers to get through this), and therefore I see no value in reprinting what others made of it. After all it is a very well-documented film and you won't have trouble doing your own digging (pun intended). What I understood of it is that amidst endless scenes of rape, something is wrong with the main characters that seem to be vomiting frequently (hence the title). The focus, though, is Angela Aberdeen (Ameara LaVey), who is a stripper that also turns tricks (meaning she is a prostitute, as well).

The special effects and makeup lend an almost "modern Hammer" look. I love when Grace is about to put the bite on AJ and, after undulating her body, her fangs grow and nails extend and then her eyes roll backwards—very wild and scary! Keep your eyes peeled for scenes like this throughout.

Arrow has provided another release with lots of goodies in the form of extras—the only thing I felt was missing was an audio commentary. What we do have is a wealth of behind-the-scenes and making-of footage, with interviews and comments from the main cast and crew. This archival footage is really a treat because Chris Makepeace does not grant interviews anymore and left showbiz quite some time ago. After enjoying the film and then watching *One of Those Nights*, the retrospect documentary, it is clearly evident that this is as much a joy to behold on screen as it was to make.

Also for our viewing pleasure is a short comedy/horror musical directed by Wenk entitled *Dracula Bites the Big Apple* (1979), which is a real hoot and has to be seen to be appreciated. I'd love to hear some behind-the-scenes stories from the making of this 22-minute short, because how some of these musical numbers were shot—in places such as the top of the Empire State building—is beyond me. Obtaining permission to film there is extremely tough, even back in the day, considering the logistics alone. *Whew!* And the short is genuinely funny, to boot. Rounding out the extras are blooper reels, trailers and a gallery. This is enough to leave any

The vomit is obviously real here, and so might be the bruises on Angela's body, as this is certainly a movie about abuse. It is extremely violent, to the point that I would go as far as calling it painful to watch (in the literal sense of the word "pain"), especially due to its top-notch practical special effects that are an achievement in themselves, considering the low budget this had (a reported $100,000, but I believe it was much less).

Auteur producer/director/editor Lucifer Valentine's style (he coined the term "vomit gore") is that of a film student that went mad, and comes replete with shaky handheld camerawork, and with editing that achieves maximum effect with its obvious minimal resources. At times it doesn't even feel like a real movie; it feels more like an experience and I am saying this in an absolutely good way. But, to be honest, sometimes I caught myself wondering, what am I watching—*and why?*

---

11 The film is also available on a no-frills Blu-ray from Image Entertainment, but the far-superior Arrow edition's MSRP is only one dollar more, so you make the call. –Ed.

REGOREGITATED SACRIFICE

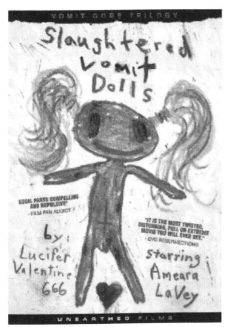

Dialogue excerpts: "I like it when you rape me", "I promise to be a perfect child of Satan"

Writer/director Lucifer Valentine and star Ameara Lavey return for this sequel which manages to top the original in just about every way—let's see how.

For starters, this comes with a "Director's disclaimer" which I found to be very responsible on the part of the filmmakers, yet very much in contrast with the rest of the images parading the screen. These include the separation (via a butcher's knife, no less) of two Siamese twins who then proceed to become incestuous lesbian lovers, and going as far as including a pregnant lady in their sexual escapades.

Things also get hardcore (in the first film pretty much everything was kept within soft-core limits, at least sexually) as we get to see pissing, drinking of piss, further vomit aplenty, squirt, rape, spit in the mouth, blowjobs, semen on the face, vagina torture that even includes a tarantula, etc. But, believe it or not, the sexual situations onscreen are not the most unsettling element here, nor are the multitude of gore moments (that include beheadings, scalping, etc.); it is in actuality the uncomfortable confessions that some of the female stars make on camera that seem unbearably believable, and made me think that I am seeing the real thing. This is also what distinguishes this film from other similar ones from the era (such as the *August Underground* trilogy[12]);

There is a lot cynicism on display here, especially in a scene where a girl's hand is cut off and then she is asked to play the guitar. But amidst all these attacks on my sensibilities, I honestly found poetry here, and I even wanted to cry in the end (and I am not joking). This is very powerful stuff indeed, and you might be unable to eat for awhile after watching it. Imagine Max Hardcore doing a soft-core version of his videos with horror elements aplenty.

12 See reviews on pp. 120-123.

Well, what do you expect from a movie called **SLAUGHTERED VOMIT DOLLS**?

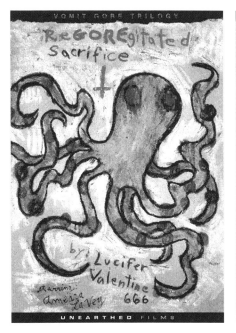

the film under review is about multi-dimensional people that seem to be genuinely troubled.

The style is pretty much the same as with the first movie, although the editing has become much fancier at this point (and dare I say—professional?), and if you thought that you've seen it all after viewing the *Guinea Pig* series, you're in for a surprise, as this surpasses the Japanese classics in terms of being gross.

SLOW TORTURE PUKE CHAMBER

If you got as far as this stage you should expect more of the shame (yes, more of the shame; and also more of the same), with the filmmakers rightly putting a title warning and two disclaimers (one from the main actress, and the other more generic) in the beginning, but be assured there is nothing responsible about the mayhem that follows.

What we have here is further puke (if anything, the title is deserved and honoured), pissing in buckets, pissing on faces, pissing in mouths, vomit in shot glasses (which of course are then drunk), masturbation of both solo nature and with the assistance of a crucifix, rape aplenty, the slaughter of a pregnant woman and the decapitation of her baby, and a probably a few more things that I didn't catch because I was looking away in disgust.

All in all, this had me thinking how far I went with my viewing habits, to the extent of giving me the awkward idea of watching a Disney movie next in order to come back to my senses. It also had me wondering what I am subjecting myself to.

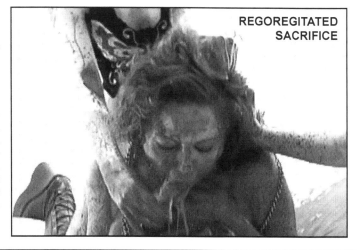

REGOREGITATED SACRIFICE

SLOW TORTURE PUKE CHAMBER

Movies are definitely like music volume, and it has stages. All your life you're watching **THE LAST HOUSE ON THE LEFT** (1972) and the like, and you think you know extreme cinema, and then you come across this, and you come to the understanding that maybe you shouldn't have pushed the volume up to 11.

The series was supposed to end with this third instalment (they were always supposed to be a trilogy), but then not too long ago director Lucifer Valentine made a fourth film, **BLACK MASS OF THE NAZI SEX WIZARD** (2015), which I have not seen as yet.

SLAUGHTERED VOMIT DOLLS: 2006, CANADA/USA. D: LUCIFER VALENTINE
REGOREGITATED SACRIFICE: 2008, CANADA. D: LUCIFER VALENTINE
SLOW TORTURE PUKE CHAMBER: 2010, CANADA. D: LUCIFER VALENTINE
AVAILABLE FROM UNEARTHED FILMS

WHAT WE BECOME
(*Sorgenfri*)

Reviewed by Jacob Gustafson

In *Weng's Chop* #9 [p. 215] I reviewed Danish horror film **WHEN ANIMALS DREAM** (*Når dyrene drømmer*, 2015). It was a unique riff on the werewolf mythology and I really enjoyed it a lot. When we think of great European horror, we don't often think about the small and statistically very happy country of Denmark. Intrigued by how much I enjoyed **WHEN ANIMALS DREAM** and other recent Scandinavian horror films, I was eager to see more. **WHAT WE BECOME** (*Sorgenfri*, 2015) is another Danish horror movie and, although writer/director Bo Mikkelsen had nothing to do with **WHEN ANIMALS DREAM**, I was excited to check it out to see if **WHEN ANIMALS DREAM** was a fluke or if perhaps Denmark was a new hot spot in horror.

WHAT WE BECOME is about a small affluent town. It's sleepy and tranquil with a tight-knit community. We are introduced to a family consisting of a mother, father, little sister and a teenage big brother. A cute girl moves into the neighborhood and the brother has the hots for her. His parents don't get along with him and the daughter is starting to grow out of childhood as well. It's your typical family. Reports pop up on the news about a strange illness going around their area, but it isn't until they are warned to stay indoors that they take notice. Soon the military comes and enforces a quarantine of the neighborhood. Each family is locked in their houses and given rations. If they try to leave they are killed. Their Internet access is cut off, as is their

power. They are completely locked in their homes and locked out of information regarding the illness. They discover soon however that the illness is deadly and very contagious. Yes. It's a zombie plague.

Now wait. Before you skip to the next review, understand that, like most horror fans, I'm really sick of zombie movies. They have been played-out for a decade and yet filmmakers still seem compelled to go to the well and make more. At this point it's very difficult to make a unique zombie flick. Just about everything that could be said *has* been said, and it's likely it was done better somewhere else. Denmark, however, has never had (to my knowledge) a zombie film, or at the very least there haven't been any high-profile films to make it into large distribution in North America. That, however, isn't enough for me. I don't need to see a zombie film from every country in the world. It isn't the country of origin that makes this film unique—it's the film itself. Stylistically, the film is lit with natural light, which gives it a very realistic feel. The score is minimal but does have some nice synthy moments. The violence, at least early on in the film, is off-camera. This makes the proceedings feel that much more eerie. I like gore as much as the next guy, but it would feel out of place in this film and would cheapen it. There are a couple of graphic scenes and the film waits until poignant moments to unleash it rather than beating the viewers head with guts. The graphic violence is there for a reason, not just to satisfy gore hounds. The acting is excellent with very natural performances from each player in the film.

As the story progresses it becomes bleaker and bleaker, with a very grim ending. The characters' situation gets worse and worse. The presentation of the zombie outbreak is realistic. The struggle for safety, food and water when all of these things are no longer an accepted reality is frightening. Each of us are not far away from being in such dire straights should our food and water supply be extinguished by a natural or unnatural disaster. The suspicion of each character that strangers or even their own family member might be a carrier of the plague mirrors our own modern-day fears that there are those among us that want to do us harm. The military in this film is not depicted as saviors but as ruthless, faceless, enforcers who think nothing of dispatching anyone that disobeys. This chilling portrayal of officialdom also mirrors a growing fear of totalitarian government actions across the globe as we see time and again the people rising up against their governments for freedom only to be squashed by similar military enforcement. Sure, this movie is yet another zombie movie, but unlike many gut-munching paint-by-numbers movies, this one taps into very current widespread fears. It is a natural, realistic, grim, and well-made film that thankfully manages to breathe a little bit of life into the very tired zombie genre. Is it completely original? No, there have been several zombie films that have used these tactics before to make similar comments. But it is well-executed, topical, and intimate.

WHAT WE BECOME is another solid entry in Denmark's horror output. I'm looking forward to what comes next from Bo Mikkelsen and from Denmark. I'll be keeping my eyes open for sure.

2015, DENMARK
AVAILABLE FROM SHOUT! FACTORY

WHAT WE BECOME

SHAITAN MADE ME DO IT
Two New Variations on The Old Theme
by Tim Paxton with Kinshuk Gaur

Since this is a mini-issue of Weng's Chop, *I was not prepared for my usual comprehensive analysis of one aspect or another of Indian films. Instead, let me focus on two of the newest Indian horror films that are currently in theatres in India (and, in the case of* **ISLAMIC EXORCIST***, also streaming in the USA).*

THE HOUSE NEXT DOOR

Unlike here in the US or much of the cinematic family worldwide, the horror genre has largely been part-and-parcel a popular part of the art form. More so in the last decade, which has seen an explosion of horror-centric 'blogs, self-published books, artwork and films the world over. There have even been some years when a supernatural thriller has topped the box offices—besting "happier" fare such as comedies and musicals. Ghost films in particular have been popular with audiences and critics in The Americas, as well as in Japanese, Chinese, European and Southeast Asian movie-houses for more than a century. Basically, horror films are a worldwide phenomenon because folks *love* to be scared.

Except, it seems, until recently in India, that is. And I'm including *all* of the Indian subcontinent's myriad domestic film industries in that sweeping statement, by the way. True, India's film audiences as a whole are a fickle bunch, more so perhaps than in any other country on the planet. It's a rare occurrence that even a phenomenally popular movie will remain a top box-office earner for more than a few consecutive months, and India is notorious for its regional prejudices, which keep many a non-Hindi film from becoming a major smash hit (the exception to that rule has been the runaway success of the Southern fantasy/period piece **BAAHUBALI 2: THE CONCLUSION** [2017, Telugu/Tamil; D: S.S. Rajamouli] which, as of this writing, is *still* running in theatres many months after its initial April 2017 release). And the horror genre has always been a thorn in the side of the majority of Indian film critics for the past 40 years since the first modern horror film was produced in India (ignoring the numerous reincarnation and romantic ghost films which have been produced there since the late 1940s).[1]

For the most part, the world outside of the subcontinent lumps any film produced in India under the generic "Bollywood" label. *That* is a misnomer of monstrous proportions! Hindi movies are readily accepted in Northern India, especially if the Hindi-speaking stars of the Bollywood movie industry happen to have nationwide popularity. So, if you have a mainstream actor from Bollywood in your movie it increases the chances of your product becoming popular in other regions of India. To reiterate what I've explained repeatedly over the past four years in my writings for *Weng's Chop* and *Monster!*, I'll say again that Bollywood is *Hindi* cinema, and its output does *not* represent the majority of films made in India as a whole. The Hindi horror scene has been floundering since Ram Gopal Varma's genre-changer **RAAT** in 1992 and the same director's **BHOOT** in 2003. But that was *ages* ago, and you would think that other filmmakers (not just RGV, a Telugu director who has had many hits in both Telugu and Hindi as well) would have followed his lead. Vikram Bhatt's *1920* (2008) and **HAUNTED 3D** (2011) came close, but too much schmaltz deadened most of the horror which might otherwise have been squeezed from their derivative source material (e.g., **THE EXORCIST** [1973], **THE ENTITY** [1982] *et al*).

So *what happened* to the Hindi horror scene over the past decade or so? You would think that with the average Indian consumer's manic theatrical and rental consumption of Western films like those from the *Conjuring* and *Paranormal Activity* series (along with the multitude of Thai and Japanese ghost films, etc.) on the rise, that some of the better Indian-made movies would have affected local filmmakers. Besides all the usual rip-offs, what *good* Hindi horror films have been made…?

Above: Dr. Krishnakanth (Actor-screenwriter Siddharth) wonders just what is up with those weird Christians who moved into **THE HOUSE NEXT DOOR**.

Previous page: Dr. Krishnakanth has a close encounter with something both terrifying and unexplainable.

Again with the Hindi clarification, and there is good reason for this. It seems that the best horror films—those with even the slightest smidgeon of originality or style—have come from Southern Cinema's Tamil and Telugu industries, made with all-region actors or Hindi casts and crews. Their horror films are *very* popular indeed, and many of them even succeeded in amassing highly respectable box-office receipts in their Hindi-dubbed versions as well. This is all well and good, with the only problem being that many of those horror films are also so-called "comedies"— and *annoying* ones at that! It's baffling to me as to the addition of stupid sound effects, musical stings, and never-ending comedic sequences to what might have otherwise been a perfectly decent ghost movie. And these movies pack 'em in at theatres!?[2]

Which is what makes Milind Rau's recent film **THE HOUSE NEXT DOOR** (2017) such a breath of fresh air. It is both a Hindi-language film and one that takes itself very, *very* seriously. So seriously in fact that it doesn't have any musical interludes other than for an extended opening credit sequence wherein we see our two main characters meet, fall in love and get married.

As it turns out, **THE HOUSE NEXT DOOR** is indeed Hindi…well, *kinda*. It *is* a Kollywood film shot simultaneously in three languages, including Tamil by its director Milind Rau (its original Tamil title being **AVAL**, which translates to "She" in English).

---

[1] Which I have covered *ad nauseam* in umpteen issues of *Monster!* and *Weng's Chop* –TP

[2] Granted, I have not seen *every* Indian horror/possession film released in the past ten years, but I have sat through roughly 50 titles, many of which I wrote about in an article on ghostly/possession films for *Weng's Chop* #10. So, I think I *may* have at least some idea what I am talking about! –TP

The Hindi-langauge poster for **THE HOUSE NEXT DOOR**. Like many Bollywood posters from Northern India everything is in English, India's second official language.

This is no doubt primarily because the Hindi-speaking audience could not relate to the actors from southern part of India. That is odd, considering the lead, Siddarth (as Doctor Krishnakanth), is a popular Tamil actor who has starred in several Hindi movies. Another familiar face is Atul Kulkarni (as Paul), a versatile actor who has starred in over 60 Hindi, Tamil, Malayalam, Telgu, Kannada, Marathi and English-language films. Apart from those two cited cast members, all the other major characters are played by actors from within the Telugu and Tamil industries. A similar incident happened with RGV's first horror film **RAAT** (1992), which was simultaneously filmed in both Telugu and Hindi, but he did so with no major (at that time) Northern stars other than Om Puri. Although **RAAT** faltered at the Hindi box office (but did well in the South), it is now considered a milestone in Indian horror from a time when the genre was fading from public appreciation. When RGV made **BHOOT** a decade later, he cast some very recognizable and influential Hindi-language stars, such as Ajay Devgn, Rekha, and Urmila Matondkar, and it was both a critically-acclaimed and financial hit in many markets. Director Rau succeeds in this genre where veterans of Indian horror like Vikram Bhatt and RGV have stumbled over

It was also filmed in Telugu and released as **GRUHAM** ("Home"). This practice of shooting films in numerous languages rather than just dubbing the actors (which is often the case anyways with post-production, something that was a constant for Italian cinema from the '60s to the '80s/'90s) can pay off artistically.[3] However, the Hindi version of the movie has fared very poorly at the box office.

[3] A good example would be trying to locate the blockbuster film BAAHUBALI on DVD or BD in its original Telugu, because for me at least, listening to the Hindi-dubbed version is annoying as hell. As it turns out, there is now a good chance that most blockbuster Tamil- or Telugu-language films may never be released to a physical medium except as Hindi-dubbed product. Seems that, while the consumption of a film like BAAHUBALI on DVD or BD is high in the North (with an English subtitle option), Southern distributors are now opting to release many of their films directly through YouTube or other online streaming services. I was finally able to see BAAHUBALI in its "native tongue" of Telugu (it was simultaneously released in Tamil and Malayalam as well) by purchasing a steaming version of it on a YT channel. No other option was available to me other than a pricey German DVD or various sketchy (and badly "redubbed" Telugu copies) via the numerous torrent fan sites. And bear in mind that most of said streaming options *do not* include English subtitles. However, I was lucky enough to have that option when I bought my YT copy of BAAHUBALI. –TP

the past decade. It boggles the mind that, since **THE HOUSE NEXT DOOR** was released in November of 2017, it has been flopping majorly at Hindi box offices, despite the positive reviews it has generated.

The film opens with what looks like footage from an old Chinese film from pre-Independence India (*circa* 1934), wherein a mother comforts her daughter near the well of the family homestead. This somewhat confusing sequence will eventually make itself deadly clear as **THE HOUSE NEXT DOOR**'s plot gradually unfolds. However, it is now "the present", and we see a happily married couple enjoying their life together in a beautiful house located in the picturesque location of the Himalayas. Their scenes are frank and sexy, playful and schmaltzy, complete with stolen kisses and so forth (but then they are legally married, after all!). This setup is not that unusual for mainstream Indian cinema, and it's a good way to let the audiences know that major *shit* is about to hit the fan for the people you've come to care for. Krishnakanth (Siddharth)—a.k.a. "Krish" for short for most of the film—is a well-respected "deep brain stimulation" neurosurgeon, while Lakshmi (Andrea Jeremiah) is his lovely wife. They are greatly enjoying their happy marriage until a new family moves into the house next door to theirs…

Krish's and Lakshmi's new neighbors are the D'Costa family: the patriarch Paul (Atul Kulkarni) and his wife, who are accompanied by his two daughters: the 20-something Jenny (Anisha Angelina Victor) and her preteen half-sister Sarah (Khushu Hajare), as well as Paul's father-in-law. After an exchange of cordialities, Krish and Lakshmi are invited to a housewarming party at the D'Costa residence. Jenny is impressed by the studly brain surgeon, and immediately warms to the man, awkwardly flirting with him on two occasions. Amidst all this, the young woman experiences several odd moments within the house, and the party ends when she, in what seems to be some sort of trance or seizure, jumps into an open well behind the home. Krish witnesses the incident and saves her.

Later on, additional weird, inexplicable things happen to Jenny, and Paul, fearing his daughter has some mental disorder, seeks help from Dr. Krish for her medical treatment. Krish is unable to discover any reason for Jenny's unusual behavior, so consults with his long-time psychiatrist friend Dr. Prasad (veteran Telugu actor Suresh, who starred in Kodi Ramakrishna's 1995 "angry goddess" classic **AMMORU**[4]). After a diagnostic session with Jenny, Dr. Prasad visits the D'Costa home to see what (if anything) there might help him to understand his patient's bizarre behavior. After further analysis, he concludes that Jenny is feeling lonely and depressed due to the death of her mother (her father Paul thereafter remarried), and moving into a new home has increased her sense of isolation/alienation. This, combined with Jenny's mistrust of God (the family are Pentecostal Christians), her infatuation with the Devil and fascination for horror movies, attraction towards gothic culture, and the usage of drugs…well, she was *bound* to go nuts! Dr. Prasad's conclusion? Jenny believes she is being haunted by an unknown entity. In hopes it will work like a placebo on her psyche, the head-shrinker plans to perform a "false" exorcism with the help of the D'Costas' priest Father Joshua (popular Kannada theater, film, television and media personality Prakash Belawadi), in a bid to convince Jenny that whatever devil or evil spirit within her has been cast out.

Okay, now the action really gets going…

The D'Costa family agrees to go along with Dr. Prasad's scheme, and a phony Christian exorcism is performed, but following what seems to be a success, all hell breaks loose! Jenny proves to indeed be possessed by an evil spirit, and in classic "**EXORCIST**" fashion, begins to stab herself in the crotch with a cross while snarling bestially and hurling curses at her tormentors (both Christian and Hindi alike). In typical demoniac fury, Jenny then clobbers everyone in the room who attempts to subdue her, ultimately putting the family holy man into a coma before she herself passes out.

As the film progresses and still more horrible supernatural things occur, it becomes evident that the house *is* haunted…if *not* by your traditional Indian-type ghosts. After the death of the D'Costa's superstitious maid in a very grisly manner (i.e., wound-up in a bed sheet with a huge nail driven into her skull!), Jenny's grandfather calls for further aid in the guise of a local Hindi *tantrik* whose mystical ju-ju bag of powers includes a form of psychom-

Siddharth and Andrea Jeremiah star in **THE HOUSE NEXT DOOR**, which was filmed (not dubbed) in three languages, something not that uncommon for Indian cinema. This is promo art for the Tamil version known as **AVAL**.

---

4 See *Weng's Chop* #4, p. 131.

etry: the ability to feel/sense something beyond the physical realm after handling an object and receiving emanations from it. He discovers that there are not just one but fully *three* (3!) ghosts in the house, and they are *not* Indian in origin, but rather—and here's a nifty twist, just for a change of pace!—from China.

Terror mounts as one of this trio of powerful entities—the ghost of an evil man who sacrificed his only daughter so that his wife would bear him a boy child—is hell-bent on repeating the horrendous crime from 90 years previously…by possessing Krish and killing Jenny's sister so that Lakshmi (who's only just learned she's pregnant) will have a boy (possibly for the purpose of reincarnation?). Can the ghost be stopped in time before completing its grisly task…?[5]

That's it for plot, as spoilers will ruin it for potential viewers!

Cinematography by Shreyaas Krishna is excellent, as is Lawrence Kishore's editing, both of which are complemented by Devesh Patel's visual effects, which are both subtle and (for once in an Indian film) actually *believable*. Girishh Gopalakrishnan's sparsely-used background score lacks any of the usual garish sound effects thanks to tasteful sound designers Vishnu Govind, Sree Shankar and Vijay Rathinam, who understand that simple *silence* is every bit as scary—if not more so—as any assortment of loud squeals, random screams, and other ridiculous noises that are so oft-utilized by more seasoned directors like Vikham Bhatt. The end result? An overall atmosphere that succeeds where many of the recent Hindi horror films have failed, giving credence to the film's overall spookiness and increasing its spine-tingling abilities considerably.

Online promo poster for the Tamil edition of **THE HOUSE NEXT DOOR**. Despite the nod to **THE RING** in poster design, the film isn't too much of a rip-off of anything specific.

THE HOUSE NEXT DOOR seemed to be doomed right from the outset, getting the proverbial shaft from the paying public like some of the other better Hindi horror movies from the past two years or so. Pavan Kirpalani's 2016 Hindi psychological thriller **PHOBIA** opened with plentiful critical praise, but for whatever reason did poorly at ticket wickets. While it wasn't an actual horror film *per se* (nor supernaturally-themed in any way, either), Kirpalani managed to put together an intriguing product that had horrific elements without resorting to any blatantly-inauthentic material lifted virtually verbatim from another source.[6]

---

5 If this film makes it to Netflix in the West—and I'm sure it will—you'll have ample chance to find out. *–TP*

6 Although there has been comparison of the film to that of Ram Gopal Varma's superior 1999 psycho-thriller **KAUN**, which featured a lone heroine and her antsy battle against an unknown intruder.

And now for something (not so) completely different: Despite the ballyhoo that **ISLAMIC EXORCIST** is something new, the film trots out the usual tropes associated with the genre. In the top photo, a concerned mother named Aeshya (Kavita Radheshyam) wonders what has possessed her moody daughter, and how the evil *djinn* has taken control of Aeshya (above).

Tinu Suresh Desai's **1920: LONDON**, the third instalment in Vikram Bhatt's 1920 series, was *clearly* a "real" horror film. In addition to a few chilling moments, this 2016 Hindi production had the makings of a powerful possession story; however, the soppy romantic angle of the script and the blatant **EXORCIST** rips (William Friedkin's 1973 film *still* infects new Indian films—*unbelievable!* But then, it also influences many a non-Indian film too, come to think of it, so perhaps it's not really that surprising after all). Had there been more care taken in making **1920: LONDON** an entirely original concept, then it might well have been *great.* Instead, it failed to impress anyone.

Being ardent horror movie fans, after each twist and turn we are forced to recall the inspirations of various sequences within **THE HOUSE NEXT DOOR**. Over the course of the film's 137 minutes, there are more than a few obvious nods to **THE EXORCIST, THE EXORCISM OF EMILY ROSE** (2005), *The Conjuring* series (2013-present),

DARK WATER (*Honogurai mizu no soko kara*, 2002)[7]; and **RINGU** (1998) / **THE RING** (2002). But still, the writer and director have done a fair job of binding the various elements together. This sort of thing happens all the time in India's film industries, but so far I haven't used the word plagiarism. Why? In this case because, while it's obvious from where the sequences were lifted, they are herein rendered with enough freshness and style that the derivativeness of the source material(s) isn't so glaringly obvious as it so often is in other, less-creative emulators.

In summation, **THE HOUSE NEXT DOOR** is a slickly-polished horror movie, and a damn *good* one at that, despite some of its moments that were inspired by other movies. Most Western horror film fans are aware of India's rather odd fascination with unofficial remakes and/or creative theft from popular cult horror movies. The Ramsays were guilty of it in their era (for example, their 1993 film **MAHAKAAL**[8] was a blatant rip-off of the first **A NIGHTMARE ON ELM STREET** entry). Then there's RGV and Vikram Bhatt in the modern era, too. But what makes Milind Rau's film stand above much of the competition is its execution. Indian viewers have always been fond of horror movies, but have by no means always been catered to appropriately. This is one of the few Indian movies of its type that achieves its objective without pandering to its audience with unnecessary, unfunny comedy.

Kudos to the director for sticking to his genre. For once.

But, even so, this movie is still *TANKING* big-time!

2017, INDIA (HINDI). D: MILIND RAU
NOW IN THEATRES

7 Remade in the US in 2005.

8 See *Monster!* Digest #2, p. 37.

Online promotional art for **ISLAMIC EXORCIST** (which was filmed in Hindi and English), which, like many Indian posters and teasers, features some inane taglines.

ISLAMIC EXORCIST

THE HOUSE NEXT DOOR is a prime example of what can go right with an Indian horror film, while **ISLAMIC EXORCIST** (2017) is the absolute *antithesis*.

India, like the USA and elsewhere, is made up of many different peoples and their various religions. Granted, the majority of the subcontinent's populace is Hindu (85%), Muslim (10%) and Christian (2%), with the remainder of faiths being Sikhism, Buddhism, Jainism, Zoroastrianism, along with a smattering of tribal religions, as well as Judaism. The majority of Indian films dealing with possession (of a type that is more spiritual than all-out demonic) typically fall into the Christian "category" when it comes to exorcism; or else a combination of Christianity and Hindu practices. It is exceedingly rare for an Islamic-style exorcism to come into play when some angry spirit or monster is running rampant. Images of the Koran were used to help thwart the vampire Neola in **BANDH DARWAZA** (1990, Ds: Shyam Ramsay and Tulsi Ramsay) and also helped put the *kibosh* on the creature in Mohan Bhakri's 1991 **ROOHANI TAAQAT**. But a full-on Islamic exorcism in Indian cinema? There are no others that I know of, which may be why taglines on the present film's posters shriek *"India's first Muslim Exorcism!"*, *"Based on Actual Events!"* (etc.). Indian filmmakers so *love* to boast!

Islamic horror films are *not* a new thing in world cinema. Turkey beat India to the punch with a 1974 film called film **SEYTAN** (D: Metin Erksan), which was a nearly frame-by-frame rip-off of Friedkin's **THE EXORCIST**; whereas India's equivalent **JADU TONA** (Hindi, 1977, D: Ravikant Nagaich) was a lot looser in its blatant plagiarism, and includes a Hindi exorcism via a Hanuman priest and the use of religious magic. In more recent times, Turkish director Hasan Karacadağ's **D@BBE** (2006) and **SEMUM** (2008) were low-budget explorations into Turkish demonology and Islamic religious mythology (involving djinn, etc.) and exorcisms.

All that aside, I guess what we have here is probably the first ever Indian/*Islamic* **EXORCIST** rip-off. So, in that case, I suppose it *is* a genre-changer of sorts. Well, um…*kinda*.

As the narrative gets started, we meet Natasha, whose brother has recently become possessed, and she is visiting a woman named Aeshya (Kavita Radheshyam), hoping to find out what happened to Aeshya's adopted daughter Anna. According to police reports, Anna was murdered by Aeshya's husband Sameer, who evidently killed the little girl because she was possessed by a djinn.

The backstory: Sameer is a hard-working police detective and Aeshya is his devoted stay-at-home wife. However, their formerly happy home life begins to go sour when Aeshya has a miscarriage while carrying their first child. The grieving parents turn to adoption as an alternative and bring home a cute 8-year-old named Anna, to raise as their own daughter. Unfortunately for all concerned, it turns out that "their" new child is indeed possessed by a djinn, and she begins to exhibit all the usual "**EXORCIST**"-style kinds of personality changes as she curses her adoptive parents, beats-up her foster aunt, and so forth.

Following several horrific incidents, at her wits' end, Aeshya consults a local holy man for help. His suggestion? "*Kill her!* Finish off the evil child!" It is Sameer, however, who kills little Anna instead (after he finds the creepy kid spying on him while he is on the phone with her foster mother Aeshya).

But wait…suddenly there's a twist!

[*ATTENTION: SPOILER ALERT!*] The demonically-possessed Anna doesn't actually exist, you see, and Natasha is in reality a psychiatrist hired by Sameer to help cure his mentally ill wife. Natasha decides the only way to deal with the woman's "changing personality disorder" (gobbling raw chicken, swearing and cussing, making rude faces with her tongue waggling, etc.), is to bring an Iman with her into the crazy woman's home. The Islamic priest confronts Aeshya with prayer beads and plastic bottle of holy water in hand. Let the "exorcism" commence!

Lead actress Kavita Radheshyam has had a modest career in the low-budget Hindi thriller and horror genres, and she rather reminds me of actress/director Revathi (from Ram Gopal Varma's **RAAT**)… albeit without her acting chops! Radheshyam has also been the darling of **ISLAMIC EXORCIST**'s director Faisai Saif, who previously featured her in his action spoof **MAIN HOON RAJINIKANTH** (2015), as well as his next scheduled film project, another horror ghost/possession film called **SHRAAP 3D** (Tamil/Hindi). Never a good sign, that film has been languishing in post-production purgatory for the past year, and may (or may *not!*) see the light of day sometime in mid-2018. Recently, Radheshyam has been embroiled in a scandal involving a sala-

According to pre- and post-Islamic lore eons old, *djinn* come in all shapes and sizes, from the graveyard inhabiting *ghul* (where we get our word ghoul) to the all-powerful Iblis who is associated with The Devil in Islamic culture. This *djinn* is called a *shaitan*, which is the go-to trigger word for most Islamists if and when bad things happen in their lives. Hence the alternate title of this online add for **ISLAMIC EXORCIST; SHEITAAN** being another word for a certain species of *djinn*.

cious 2016 semi-nude photo shoot to protest animal cruelty in India, and then spouting anti-LGBT remarks ("*Aren't #LGBT Against Nature? Whatever Is Against Nature, Shouldn't Live*") after the 2016 Orlando, FL nightclub shooting. Priceless!

Faisai Saif's filmmaking career only began fairly recently, and his output thus far has left me wondering about what his target audience might be. His efforts are clearly *not* arthouse projects created to make one pause and ponder about various aspects of the human condition. Nor are they mainstream horror films like **THE HOUSE NEXT DOOR**, either. Nope! They are mildly brash, anti-establishment, low-budget productions. He seems to want to "shock" his viewers with outrageous themes, cuss-word-filled/hackneyed scripts and hyperactive acting. His micro-budget productions recall the insanity of prime Kanti Shah movies from the early 2000s, but without any of their reckless, surreal zeal (and no Sapna!). I see potential in his work, and despite what I've so far said about **ISLAMIC EXORCIST**, it isn't as bad as it sounds. Granted, there are scenes in the film made in bad taste which I find questionable. For example, the film straddles religious bigotry when, in one key scene, Aeshay visits a local holy man. The *baba* listens to her story of a mismatched marriage (she is Sunni and married a Shia), and declares: "Shia Muslims are considered as kings of Voodoo and Black Magic." But then again, Saif wants to "shock" his audience, a demographic which seems to be mainly Muslims and the curious (like me).

The film is simply-shot on what appears to be HD video with little to no post-production special effects. In fact, that every (possible) paranormal incident is represented with a minimal amount of camera tricks is greatly appreciated. The horror of the possession is basically depicted via garish makeup (i.e., the usual "hollow" eyes and cracked/scarred skin of the afflicted individual) and overzealous, histrionic acting. I can't fault the director there. The main problems are the script and certain of what appear to be unrehearsed sequences with the actors delivering their lines in a halting, unsure manner. Of course, this could just be Saif's style, since it seems to be prevalent in at least two other films he's directed. In a way, **ISLAMIC EXORCIST** is very much in line with many of the zilch-budget horror films made in the past half-century, ever since they began to flood the drive-in market, then the VHS shelves, and are now streaming here in the States. This is gonzo filmmaking, Indian-style, very much in the same manner as Kanti Shah. For that reason, I am interested in seeing how far the director will take his vision in future.

2017, INDIA (HINDI). D: FAISAI SAIF
NOW IN THEATRES AND STREAMING ON AMAZON PRIME IN THE USA

Shit Done Hit the Fan: The Violent Shit Collection

By Brian Harris

Schnaas, Buttgereit, Ittenbach, Rose, Bethmann. If you're familiar with the names, you've likely seen a few examples of what most hardcore horror/cult cinema fans would deem one of the most entertaining horror sub-sub-genres: German splatter. It's really like nothing you've seen before--outside of perhaps the Japanese *Guinea Pig* series. If you're a new or casual horror fan and you're not familiar with German splatter cinema, you may be in for a gruesome treat.

Or, not.

Whether you end up enjoying German splatter will likely be determined by your ability to sit through epically bad acting, comparably bad—though hilarious—subs and sometimes dubs, threadbare stories that only exist to set up one gory setpiece after another and, of course, copious amounts of gore. And when I say gore, what I really mean is startling amounts of red, meaty carnage, ocular and genital mutilations galore and seemingly unending amputations. The kind of material that will have you wondering just how some of these films managed to get made on such meager budgets, and how they ever saw the light of day considering the relatively uptight eras they were released in. Pioneering, legendary low-budget stuff.

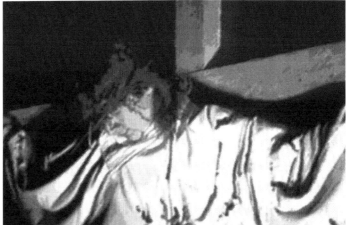

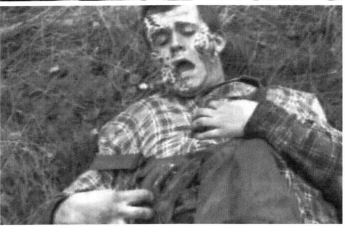

Unfortunately, not all legends are what they're cracked up to be. German splatter films are what most would consider "hit or miss", leaning more toward "miss" much of the time. Then again, if you're under no illusions that there will be a good story or acting, you may find yourself sufficiently entertained. Some films go so balls-deep into gore effects that it's hard not to smile. For me, **VIOLENT SHIT** (1989) is just such a film.

After conversing with a demonic entity while locked in a cellar, young Karl Berger (writer-director Andreas Schnaas, credited as "K. The Butcher Shitter")[1] brutally murders his abusive mother. 20

---

[1] "K. The Butcher Shitter"'s name is revealed to be Karl Berger in **VIOLENT SHIT II** (1992).

years later, he escapes police custody during a transport and stumbles off into a forest. Now free to roam the countryside, K. The Butcher Shitter slaughters everything in his path.

VIOLENT SHIT makes no sense whatsoever. It is exactly what the title describes. There can be no accusations of false advertising here. There's really no denying it, so it makes no sense to further stress the point. If you're expecting anything more than a psycho running around a forest dispatching victims, you're expecting too much.

Schnaas plays the shambling Karl effectively enough and his motivations are fairly clear—even if his hideous boils and odd behavior are not: basically, murdering and mutilating every living thing. Viewers are "treated" to one shocking sequence after another, all leading up to…well, a rather baffling finale. You'll have questions, guaranteed. There's no commentary so we can't be sure what Schnaas was going for here, but most of the folks that will enjoy this film simply won't care. One almost gets the feeling he was attempting to add some symbolism and artistic flare, almost arthouse-like, in a few instances but it's really all for naught. Pearls before slaughtered swine.

So, what is a teen to do after he's made a notorious, and not-so-good, slasher film with no story but tons of offensive violence and gore? A trip to Disneyland? Seek the calming embrace of a fine young lass? Nope. *Make another film!*

Not content to let **VIOLENT SHIT** slip into obscurity, Schnaas returned to the dry well a few years later and hauled up, **VIOLENT SHIT II** (a.k.a. **VIOLENT SHIT 2: MOTHER HOLD MY HAND**, 1992). That's right, Karl The Butcher is back…sort of.

Twenty years after Karl's murderous rampage, his son Karl Jr. (Schnaas) picks up the mantle, encouraged by his adoptive mother (Anke Prothmann), and begins his own reign of horror.

The first thing you'll notice about **VS2** is there's a plot, though the story is super thin. Schnaas didn't have a very good handle on writing, and it was only made worse by the amateur directing. However, he

clearly attempted to make a sequel that was more than just kill after kill. That's to be commended.

Noticeably influenced by Miner's **FRIDAY THE 13TH PART 2** (1981)[2], Buttgereit's **NEKROMANTIK 2** (1991) and American and HK martial arts films, Schnaas mixes in some action and incest into the goblet of gore and the resulting concoction is equal parts entertaining and head-slappingly bad.

Is **VS2** better than **VS**? In some ways, yes. **VS2** illustrates Schnaas' growth as a filmmaker and desire to offer more than just scenes of mutilation. He wanted to give **VS2**'s graphic violence some context this time, and to varying degrees he succeeded. To some he may have lost a bit of his edginess, but I think it shows more maturity.

2 See coverage of the entire *F13* franchise in issue #10, p. 71.

Naturally, the gore is still front-and-center, but Schnaas doesn't waste time having Karl Jr. hack his way from person to person, like his father. No, this time he drops his antagonist into group after group, allowing him to rack up a larger body count using sharp objects and a handgun. It felt like Schnaas was going for a Zodiac Killer/Jason Voorhees thing with Karl Jr., with a little Sloth (from **THE GOONIES** [1985]) thrown in for good measure...but again, no commentary. Was Karl Jr. mentally handicapped? Was all of his speaking actually internal dialogue? Fill in the blanks yourself, I guess.

One particularly gruesome scene I found myself chuckling through had Karl Jr. slicing the top of a young woman's head off, cramming a bowl under the neck, stomping on her chest and filling the bowl with blood. Once finished, he tops it with her head and presents it to his "mother". Though it's all executed in a rather tongue-in-cheek manner, with the dopey-sounding Karl Jr. insulting his victims as he feeds them their own excrement and staples their vaginas closed, it's still quite disturbing.

VS2, I thought, was a step up. The framing device featuring an investigative journalist talking to an informer from the Dept. of Justice is useless, but the film actually holds a small finale surprise for viewers, and there's always Karl Jr.'s doinky-doinky-doinky-diddly-doinky-doinky-doinky, light-hearted insults to keep us occupied. It works, barely. **VS** is raw, ambitious, and vicious. **VS2** is more refined, attempts to engage the audience instead of solely disturbing it, and even offers some brief comedic relief. Karl Jr.'s cheesy '80s training montage was cinephile gold.

If **VS2** was Schnaas lobbing a few curveballs at viewers by incorporating different influences into his filmmaking though, **VIOLENT SHIT III: IN-FANTRY OF DOOM** (a.k.a. **VS3: INFANTRY OF DOOM**, 1999) is him throwing the whole damn genre-film kitchen sink right out the second-story window. Subtlety? Restraint? Continuity? Nowhere to be found in this third installment.

Karl Jr. is back, as is...*his father*? Okay. The duo has somehow claimed an island for themselves and they've staffed it with a private army of loyal, mask-wearing psychopaths.

As if a cult of killers weren't enough, their resident mad scientist is working feverishly on a formula that reanimates the dead!

When a small handful of guys get stranded on the island, they find themselves in the twisted clutches of Karls Senior and Junior. Forced to participate in a deadly game of cat and mouse, the survivors will need to join forces with cult defectors if they're to survive.

VIOLENT SHIT III: INFANTRY OF DOOM, released in 2002 by E.I. Entertainment—home of all those awful Misty Mundae flicks—under the title **ZOMBIE DOOM**, is...a movie. Need more? It's a nutty movie. Like the previous two films, you will have questions. For instance, how in hell is Karl The Butcher Sr. back from the dead? Why does Karl Jr. not resemble **VS2**'s Karl Jr.? When did Karl Jr. develop the ability to speak? And if Karl could always speak, and his dialogue in **VS2** wasn't actually inner monologue, why doesn't he still speak like a buffoon? What's with the magic? Wait, ninjas? Man.

Honestly, **VS3** is entertaining, in its own way. It still feels very amateurish, despite being Schnaas' fifth film. But unlike **VS**, and to some degree **VS2**, there's a sound plot here, and it's heavy on the genre influences. Though it may not find much appeal

with horror-lite viewers, it's already found a place in the hearts of cult cinema fans, as it combines fun stuff like **THE MOST DANGEROUS GAME** (1932), **DAY OF THE DEAD** (1985), **ANTHROPOPHAGOUS** (1980), *Mad Max*-style post-apocalyptic films and chop-socky genre fare. It's quite bizarre and busy as hell. Gore, psychos, zombies and ninjas—what's *not* to love, right?

I have to say, one of my favorite things about **VS3** is the occasional documentary-style film inserts. It actually gives the film a gritty, Mondo/exploitation cinema vibe. Very **CANNIBAL HOLOCAUST** (1980), if you will. Naturally, there are some continuity issues between the video and film footage, it appears as though the inserts were shot at a later date and inserted to pad things out, and perhaps add some style to the production. One example of the differences in footage was Karl Jr.'s changing facial hair. What can you do? Still, pretty cool.

Minor Spoiler Ahead

So, with both Karls unceremoniously dispatched in **VS3**'s bonkers finale, one would assume the door has finally been closed on the concept, but no… unfortunately Schnaas isn't finished with Karl The Butcher Shitter just yet. Like most of the great slasher icons, he simply will not die. Much to the detriment of this low-budget series.

Enter lowest point: **VIOLENT SHIT 4.0: KARL THE BUTCHER VS AXE** (2010).

11 years after **VS3**, Schnaas returns, this time with filmmaker/Hip Hop rapper Timo Rose (**BARRICADE** [2007]) riding shotgun, to resurrect Karl The Butcher Sr. for what probably sounded far better on paper.

This time, good old Karl (Sr.) is sent by the devil himself to the land of the living—with mask returned and powers restored—to kill the current "Butcher", a metal-masked, axe-swinging badass that goes by the name of… Axe. Why the devil would want to stop a killer from sending him more souls is beyond me, but return Karl does, and he immediately sets out in search of his formidable foe.

Meanwhile, we're introduced a handful of gangs, all seeking to control the few remaining precious resources the wasteland offers. The only thing standing in their way is one another, Axe and his sister Vendetta, and the recently-returned-from-hell, Karl The Butcher. Alliances must be forged and all-out war will be required in order to determined who will rule the world.

When Karl and Axe finally come face-to-face, sparks will fly (literally), heads will roll and the gangs will finally meet their match.

VS4 is a groan-inducing train wreck of a film. Unlike the other installments, this production actually suffers quite a bit from its poor writing and low budget. If they were purposely trying to target the Troma and E.I. Entertainment crowds with over-the-top bad, so be it. Purposely making a bad movie doesn't make that movie bulletproof, though. I'm betting *Violent Shit* fans are wondering what in the hell Schnaas and Rose were thinking with this one.

Exteriors seem to be shot in a junkyard, or industrial park, and interiors all feel like they were shot in the same garage, or factory. They simply slapped different banners on the walls in some shots, and sheets in others.

The gangs, instead of being intimidating crews of genuine baddies, come off more like the drunken denizens of a late-night tavern. While I understand that the budget may not have allowed for 20 or 30 extras per gang, three or four guys just doesn't cut

many reused with masks and helmets—lining up to have Karl, Axe or Vendetta take them out. There is a major "twist" to be had but most will see it coming. I mean, come on, folks, Schnaas and Rose do their best to beat you over the head with Axe and Vendetta's "mysterious" parentage. You'd have to be blind not to figure it all out. Astute viewers will probably enjoy spotting the homages to **MORTAL KOMBAT** (1995), **RIKI-OH: THE STORY OF RICKY** (1991) and more. So, I guess there's that.

it. Props where props are due, though: they did a fine job with wardrobe, the actors actually made for passable post-nukers.

The effects, while gold in some instances, disappoint with the overuse of cheap, spraying jugular gags—often shot from behind the victims, so throat applications weren't needed. This series was built on insane gore, and **VS4** comes nowhere near any of the films in the creative blood 'n' guts department.

The acting…well, it's low-budget so you can't fault the production for that. However, some of the actors went above and beyond the call of bad, specifically Eileen Daly (**RAZOR BLADE SMILE**, 1998) as Queen Scara, and her hissing cohorts. Whether it was scripted or improv, it's the job of the director to pull performances back before they chew, and ultimately destroy, scenes. That simply didn't happen here and it was hard to watch. Even harder still, watching Daly's character guzzle, gulp and belch "cum wine", a rather tasteless idea that really served no purpose. Truth be told, all of the so-called comedy in this film is poorly timed, dysfunctional drivel. None of it is actually funny, like the lame **HALLOWEEN** j(1978) oke in the beginning of the film or the idiotic way Karl walks. Still, Daly—no stranger to low-budget films, tacky comedy or nudity—shines as one of the best things in this film. I must admit, she also has amazing breasts for a (now) 54-year-old woman.

Speaking of nudity, there is some, so exploitation cinema fans can breathe easy. Nothing major, mind you, just a few full- and partial- sequences. Don't bother locking the door and grabbing the tissues, though: they're brief and bereft of any erotic charm, like a dated Euro strip club. They bored my pants *on*.

The finale really was a chore to get through. It's pretty much just gang member after gang member—

At the end of the day, **VIOLENT SHIT 4.0: KARL THE BUTCHER VS AXE**, in my opinion, is a failure. Not much worked and just the thought of me having to sit through it again makes me want to take a nap. I'd normally recommend skipping a film like this, but if you've purchased the box set—which I'd recommend to gore film completists—you may as well check it out.

Lastly, on the film front, this special "shit-ition" features Schnaas's "between **VS** and **VS2**" zombie film, **ZOMBIE '90: EXTREME PESTILENCE** (1991). This production is classic, early Schnaas, meaning the writing is atrocious. The film goes absolutely nowhere, but just meanders back and forth between armed zombies attacking, hacking, and eating people and two doctors on the trail of absolutely nothing. The dubbing, obviously intended to be outrageous, felt improvised and for a while is pretty funny…until it stops being fun and gets aggravating. By that time, you'll know you're watching a hot mess. The worst part is, the film never rights itself, it just keeps getting harder and harder to watch. I actually found myself wishing I was back watching **VIOLENT SHIT 4.0: KARL THE BUTCHER VS AXE** again. No exaggeration, that's how inept it was. Chalk it up to Schnaas being young and inexperienced. It's cool that Synapse included **ZOMBIE '90: EXTREME PESTILENCE** in this set, especially for Schnaas fans with godlike trash tolerance, but for casual viewers it may take all they have not to skip through this.

On the extras front, the pickin's are slim. We get footage from a theatrical premier, a teaser, trailer and behind-the-scenes segment, all for **VS4**. There are zero extras for *Violent Shit* entries 1-3.

The behind-the-scenes featurette is just that. Nothing revelatory, just some action and FX sequence set-ups and general on-set clowning. It's not in-depth, and I really don't feel all that disappointed about it. I suppose if the film had been better, maybe.

The film premiere footage was interesting, to say the least. I won't knock Schnaas or Rose's hustle, but it looked like only about 20 people showed up to the premiere, which sorta bummed me out. Maybe there were more, who knows. In any case, it wasn't flattering. The true purpose of the extra seems to of been to promote Rose's Hip Hop career by featuring his rap act with actress Magdalena Kalley—she played Vendetta in the movie. Once again, nothing wrong with that. If it works for folks that enjoy **VS4**, cool. I'm not sure the majority of the viewers that will be enjoying these films will be Hip Hop heads, but you never know.

I think something noticeably missing from this set is the presence of Andreas Schnaas. I'm not privy to any insider info regarding these films, so I can't verify this, but I got the impression there was some kind of issue/fallout with producer/cinematographer Steve Aquilina that may have precluded Schnaas' involvement. Once again, just a feeling. Usually that's the case when the films that put a filmmaker on the map are released with the help of a producer, without the filmmaker's involvement. I could be wrong. It would have been cool to get some commentary on these films, though.

I think another thing I would have liked to have seen was a short documentary on German splatter, spotlighting some of the notable films and filmmakers and how the scene developed. Nothing. You can't fault a product for not providing the extras you feel it should have, but it would have been nice. I can't imagine newer generations of horror fans will have any idea how significant **VIOLENT SHIT** was to the splatter film community.

So, shot on-the-cheap with primitive equipment, these films aren't gems of clarity. Audio-visual aficionados that demand top-notch quality won't find it here. Outside of improved colors, this is a "you get what you get" collection. It would have been a waste of time and resources to release these films to Blu-ray. As I'm not acquainted with previous releases of these films, and I don't do a ton of fretting over aspect ratios, black crush and so on, I cannot offer any real technical opinion here. These films didn't look great—**VS4** was better, of course—on my 52" inch Samsung, but they didn't look bad either. If you're all about HD and super-clean trans-

fers, these films will probably drive you crazy, but it's no fault of Synapse.

Synapse Film offers a fair-priced collection of splatter films here, and if you're a completist I have no doubt you'll grab these. Those of you that have never seen these films and have no specific interest in SOV German splatter films, I'm not sure I can honestly recommend you purchase. Perhaps seek out a friend that owns this set, grab some refreshments, and check them out first.

VIOLENT SHIT
1989, GERMANY. D: ANDREAS SCHNAAS
AVAILABLE FROM SYNAPSE FILMS

VIOLENT SHIT II
1992, GERMANY. D: ANDREAS SCHNAAS
AVAILABLE FROM SYNAPSE FILMS

VIOLENT SHIT III
1999, GERMANY. D: ANDREAS SCHNAAS
AVAILABLE FROM SYNAPSE FILMS

VIOLENT SHIT 4
2010, GERMANY. D: ANDREAS SCHNAAS, TIMO ROSE
AVAILABLE FROM SYNAPSE FILMS

ZOMBIE '90: EXTREME PESTILENCE
1991, GERMANY. D: ANDREAS SCHNAAS
AVAILABLE FROM SYNAPSE FILMS

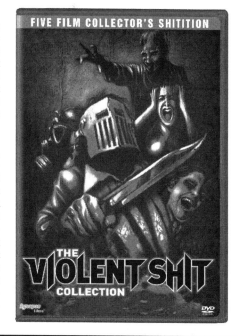

ABOUT THE CONTRIBUTORS…

Stephen R. Bissette – a pioneer graduate of the Joe Kubert School, currently teaches at the Center for Cartoon Studies and is renowned for *Swamp Thing*, *Taboo* (launching *From Hell* and *Lost Girls*), *"1963"*, *Tyrant*, co-creating John Constantine, and creating the world's second "24-Hour Comic" (invented by Scott McCloud for Bissette). He writes, illustrates, and has co-authored many books; his latest includes *Teen Angels & New Mutants* (2011), the short story "Copper" in *The New Dead* (2010), and he illustrated *The Vermont Monster Guide* (2009). His latest ebooks are *Bryan Talbot: Dreams & Dystopias*, the *Best of Blur* duo, *Wonders! Millennial Marvel Movies* and *Horrors! Cults, Crimes, & Creepers*, and his brand-new print book, *Cryptid Cinema*, which is now available through Amazon.

Joe Deagnon – has worked in the entertainment industry since 1989. A classically-trained animator from Sheridan College, he has worked in every facet of the industry, eventually honing his storytelling skills as an editor. He has authored two comic series, *Paranoid Tales of Neurosis*, dubbed "A Mad Magazine for the 90s" by drive-in movie critic Joe Bob Briggs and *Chicken Outfit*, which has been called "Fantastic! An excellent book that should be in everyone's collection. Essential." by the *Comix Press*. He has contributed to *Exclaim*, *Weng's Chop*, *Strange Kids Club* and *Film Threat* magazines. He is currently self-employed and works on a number varied and eclectic web and print publishing ventures.

Steve Fenton – prefers to remain as much of a mystery to others as he is to himself.

Jeff Goodhartz – is a self-righteous and self-serving man of the people who has been watching and writing about Asian Cinema for far too long. His current 'blog is *Films from the Far Reaches* (as he's never above a shameless plug). He's quite shameless.

Jacob Gustafson – (a.k.a. "Uncouth") holds a BA in Film from CSU Monterey Bay. He regularly contributes to *Paracinema.net*, fanzines *Fang of Joy* and *Lunchmeat*, and maintains his own site, toxicgraveyard.com. He is the co-host on the *Good Movies for Bad People* podcast. He also hosts a weekly "bad" movie night in his town. He believes the only *truly* bad films are the boring ones.

Brian Harris – has written for *Ultra Violent* magazine, *Exploitation Retrospect*, *Serial Killer* magazine, *Gorezone* magazine (UK) and *Hacker's Source* magazine. He's written nine books, four of which are still available, five are out-of-print. Brian has also run several websites including Joe Horror, Wildside Cinema, CineKult and Box Set Beatdown.

John Harrison – John Harrison is a freelance writer based in Melbourne, Australia. A regular contributor to *Monster!*, Harrison has written about Charles Manson for *Crime Factory* magazine, as well as in his own 2011 Headpress book *Hip Pocket Sleaze*. In 2004, he curated a season of Manson cinema for the Melbourne Underground Film Festival, and has written a chapter on vintage Manson-inspired pulp paperbacks for the upcoming book *Beat Girls, Love Tribes, and Real Cool Cats: Pulp Fiction and Youth Culture 1950-1980*, which is due to be published by Verse Chorus Press in May, 2016.

Michael Hauss – lives in Cincinnati, Ohio with his daughter and their two cats, Rotten Ralph and Fatty Boo-Boo. He has had articles published in various 'zines, and has been an exploitation film fanatic since his youth growing up in the frozen northeastern part of Ohio. He is a one-time member of the Gary Coleman fan club.

Karl Kaefer – "worked" at a drive-in, where his mind was warped by watching too many Italian Eurotrash and HG Lewis films. He graduated to the grindhouse theaters of NYC, where he would spend afternoons watching Kung fu & Blaxploitation flicks. He still finds the strange and bizarre much more comfortable than the bland and boring. Karl co-writes a blog with Ms. Vicki Love, and no matter what she says, the 1970s were the best decade in film.

Tim Merrill – When he isn't busy with his day gig as a lifeguard tending the lake of fire, Tim can usually be found pouring through the vaults, looking for the next AIP or Shaw Brothers eyegasm. He has written for *Asian Cult Cinema*, *Asian Eye* and the *Korean Herald*. Tim is proud to have had the opportunity to throw in on the bad ass greatness known only as *Weng's Chop*. He lives with his Peke protector Boo (a.k.a. Boocifer, Boozila), the mighty devil dog herself.

Christos Mouroukis – was born in Italy and has an MA in Feature Film from Goldsmiths University of London. He has directed award-winning and internationally broadcasted short films and music videos. He writes about genre movies in Greek (for horrorant.com) and in English (for *Weng's Chop* and *Monster!*). He lives in Athens with his wife Faye, and their cats Arte and Franco.

Chris Nersinger – was born the same year that **DR. NO** (1962) premiered. His first movie, viewed at age 3, was **MONSTER ON THE CAMPUS** (1958), which led to a series of recurring nightmares with a floating hand…and was hooked on monster movies and *Famous Monsters* from that moment on. By age 8 he had his own movie theater and ran it successfully for several summers in his garage thanks to an 8mm sound projector and good old Castle and Blackhawk films. He appeared as an extra in **FEAR NO EVIL** (1981), and always knew marketing and promotions would play a very important role in his film-loving life. He's worked in promotions for Time Warner and Regal Entertainment (**QUANTUM OF SOLACE** [2008] was his 2nd promo job!), and knows there's nothing wrong with reading comic books and watching cartoons well into your 50s. He loves writing and claims that's what keeps his brain all squishy and nimble-like.

Adam Parker-Edmondston – is a huge pop culture fan, especially monster movies and VHS. He writes for numerous websites including *Attack from Planet B*, *Cult Collective* and *Grizzly Bomb*, as well as regularly contributing to *WC*'s sister publication, *Monster!* Digest.

Tim Paxton – has been publishing stuff about monsters since 1978, and currently lives to write about fantastic cinema from India. He is even considering publishing a book on the subject. What a knucklehead.

Mark Reynolds – is a New York City-based computer animator and VFX artist whose work can be seen in the upcoming Troma feature, **RETURN TO RETURN TO NUKE 'EM HIGH AKA VOL. 2** (2017). He is also the editor of the occult review, *Scroll of Thoth*.

Steven Ronquillo – is a pretentious know-it-all who looks down on his fellow film fans and refuses to reveal his faves to them unless it makes him look good.

Tony Strauss – has been writing about cinema in print and online for over two decades. His existence as that rarest and most annoying of creatures—an artsy-fartsy movie snob who also loves trash cinema (yes, it's possible)—often leaves him as the odd man out in both intellectual and low-brow film discussions. Most movies that people describe as "boring" or "confusing" enthrall him, while the kinds of movies that are described as "non-stop action" usually bore him to tears. He has a BFA in Film, but don't hold that against him.

Weng's Chop is published as often as humanly possible, with lofty ambitions of a quarterly schedule. ©2017 WK Books. All rights reserved. No part of this publication may be reproduced, distributed or transmitted in any form or by any means, including photocopying, recording, or any other electronic or methods, without prior written permission of the publisher, except in the case of brief quotations embodied in critical reviews and certain other noncommercial uses permitted by copyright law. For permission requests, write to the publisher, addressed "Attention: Permissions Coordinator", at the address below.

4301 Sioux Lane #1
McHenry, IL 60050
USA
wengschop@comcast.net

VOLUME 5 · ISSUE 2
NUMBER 10.5 · DECEMBER 2017

Weng's Chop includes photos, drawings, and illustrations included for the purpose of criticism and documentation. All pictures copyrighted by respective authors, production companies, and/or copyright holders.

Made in the USA
Middletown, DE
13 July 2018